Scottish Antiques

Sir Alasdair T. Munro, Bt.

Schiffer Publishing Ltd

4880 Lower Valley Road, Atglen, PA 19310 USA

Library of Congress Cataloging-in-Publication Data:

Munro, Alasdair T.
Scottish antiques/by Sir Alasdair T. Munro, Bt.
p. cm.
ISBN 0-7643-1916-7
1. Antiques—Scotland. I. Title.
NK934 .M86 2003
745.1'09411'075—dc21
2003013611

Designed by John P. Cheek
Cover design by Bruce Waters
Type set inLydian Csv BT/Aldine 721 BT

ISBN: 0-7643-1916-7
Printed in China
1 2 3 4

Published by Schiffer Publishing Ltd.
4880 Lower Valley Road
Atglen, PA 19310
Phone: (610) 593-1777; Fax: (610) 593-2002
E-mail: Schifferbk@aol.com
Please visit our web site catalog at
www.schifferbooks.com
We are always looking for people to write books on new and related subjects. If you have an idea for a book, please contact us at the above address.

This book may be purchased from the publisher. Include $3.95 for shipping. Please try your bookstore first.
You may write for a free catalog.

In Europe, Schiffer books are distributed by
Bushwood Books
6 Marksbury Ave. Kew Gardens
Surrey TW9 4JF England
Phone: 44 (0)20 8392-8585; Fax: 44 (0)20 8392-9876
E-mail: Bushwd@aol.com
Free postage in the UK. Europe: air mail at cost.
Please try your bookstore first.

Contents

Acknowledgments

Every author depends in huge measure on the help, encouragement and forbearance of a multitude of people. Knowing full well that I will inevitably forget one or more, I will now attempt to recognize them and thank them for their help.

First, of course, my family, to whom this book is dedicated. My wife, Maggie, has endured with stoic patience numerous bouts of author's anguish during the time it has taken to birth this book, sometimes more stoically than others. Second, my faithful Black Labrador Fergus, who has been deprived of numerous walks and tummy-rubs over the last few years, while I slaved away at the i-Mac™.

I would have been unable to absorb the background for this book without the help of a number of Scottish relatives, both present and past, including my late father, Sir Torquil Munro, two favourite aunts, the late Carmen Munro and Morna Walker-Munro, and Lionel Walker-Munro.

Numerous people and organizations have contributed to the book directly and indirectly; I will not attempt to delineate their specific contributions, but merely to name and thank them: Cassie Bell, Claude Lucbernet, Brooke Cunningham, Eric Galloway, Noel Gibson, Hugh Davidson, Norma Spencer, James Forman, Bill Bradley, David Tractenberg, Thomas Keith, Dover Publications, Ginny Dawes, Thomas Callan, Kaja Veilleux, June and Tony Snow, Phillips Auctioneers, Katherine Grosfils, Colonial Williamsburg Foundation, John Hyman, Dorothy Wood, The Scotch Whisky Association, and XYZ. If you're not named directly, please consider yourself duly thanked under XYZ.

Finally, I would be amiss not to thank my patient editors, Doug Congdon-Martin, and Nancy Schiffer, and publisher, Peter Schiffer, the latter particularly for his forbearance during my recent illness which resulted in several missed deadlines.

Introduction

What This Book Is About And What It Is Not

"What it isn't" is perhaps easier to deal with, initially, than the former. It is *not* about furniture, and here's why. I detest lifting things that are too heavy for their own good, so many years ago, when my wife and I first "slid" into the antiques business, we adopted a very simple credo. In order to qualify for our attention (and funds), an article has to fulfill three criteria:

1. It has to be Scottish.
2. It has to be antique (admittedly, defined somewhat broadly).
3. I have to be able to lift it with my left hand (I'm right-handed); otherwise, we pass it by.

Accordingly, I attempt in this book to examine those things that fit our criteria. Come to think of it, there's a fourth (and highly important) criteria: we both have to like a piece before we study and buy it. Therefore, you'll find some things not addressed in this book, one has to draw the line somewhere.

So, we hope to give you an overview of small Scottish antiques and articles unique to Scotland, as well as a look at the odd book or two, plus things that popped up as we pottered along through the book-writing process.

One or Two Other Bits and Pieces

After you have read a few pages (and I hope you're at least interested enough to do that, you will run across the odd phrase or two which may strike you as a bit daft, but just take it in stride. You are, after all, reading a book on Scottish antiques, so the language used to describe them should be in the *lingua franca*, or should I say *lingua Scotia*?

I have always felt that knowledge is usually easier to absorb if it is not too heavy-handed. No one ever said a book on antiques has to be boring, or imposing, or stuffy. Having said that, some of the ones I've read have tended to be just that, as though any "lightness" in the writing style would take away from the authenticity of the subject. In any event, we hope you find this one to be "un-stuffy." We have tried to keep it light, interesting, and informative.

Finally, I think it only appropriate, if you are going to enjoy a book on Scottish antiques, that you have an appreciation for the country; it's people, it's geography, it's history and thereby, perhaps, to understand better how its antiques took the shape and form they did.

With great creativity, the first chapter is simply entitled "Auld Scotia." Here we have attempted to boil down a thousand plus years of time into a few pages. It provides an overview of Scotland's turbulent history, and a very abbreviated, broad (and selective) summary of various social, economic and political trends that influenced the times and the items in the succeeding chapters.

Those of you who are familiar with Scotland, it's people, and it's history, feel free to skim; those who aren't, read on.

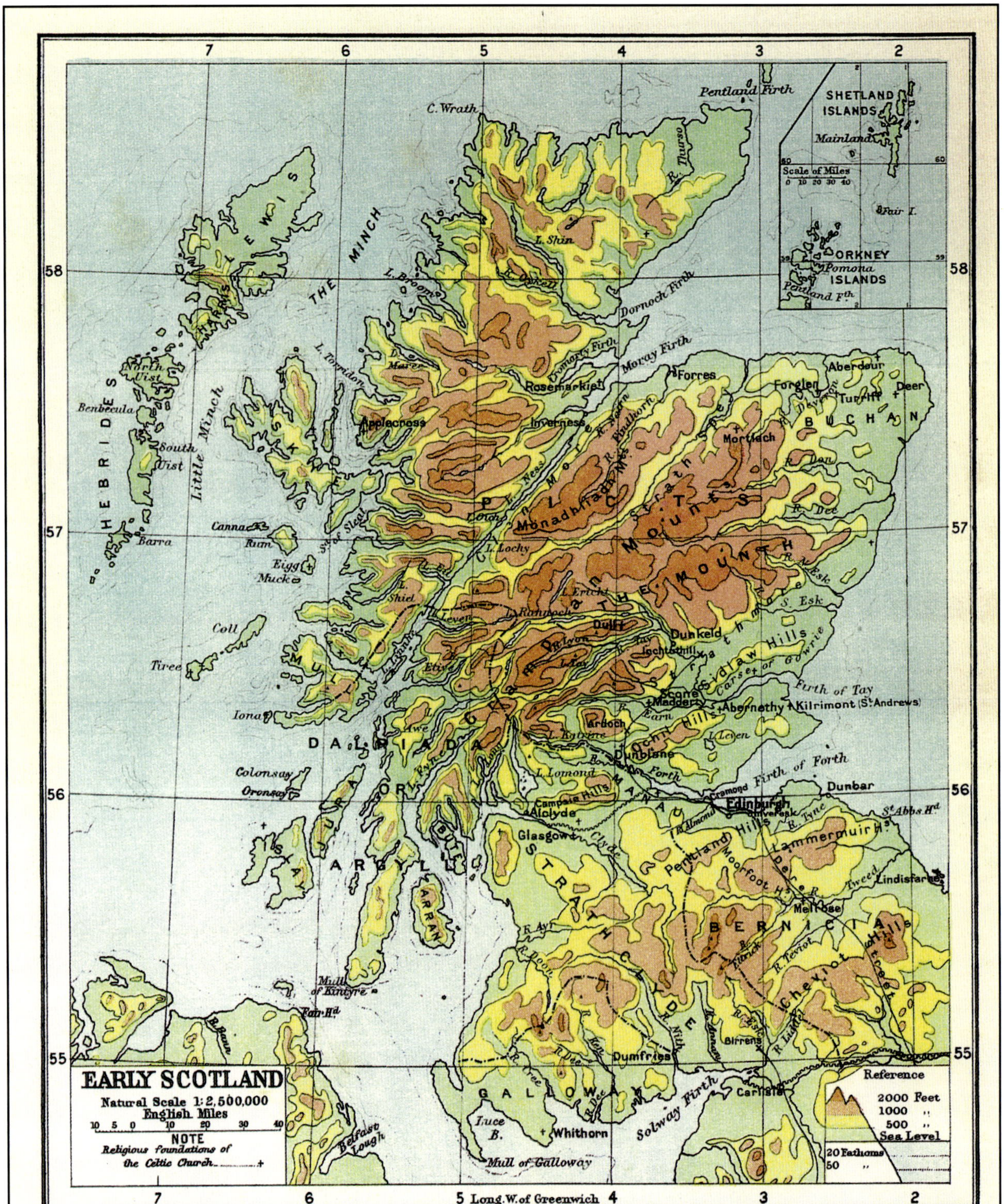

Early map of Scotland showing the principal mountain ranges and other geographic characteristics.

Chapter One

Auld Scotia

A Thousand Years of History, 1000-1999

A Quick Geography Lesson

Scotland, as many of you already know, is the small area sitting on top of England. If you travel by road from the southernmost part of Scotland, the border with England, near Carlisle, to the northernmost at John o'Groats, you'll travel some 400 miles. Across the widest part of Scotland, east to west, you'll only go about 200 miles. The country is surrounded on three sides by the ocean; the Atlantic to the west and north, the North Sea to the east and north.

Think of Scotland as being divided into four quarters from northeast to southwest. The upper quarter is generally mountainous, and is bordered on the south by the Glenmore rift, almost creating an island of the northern quarter. The next quarter contains the Grampian mountains and somewhat more arable land. The third quarter contains Scotland's bread-basket, highly arable land, plus coal and iron deposits, and hence the location of the larger population centres. The lower quarter, above the border with England, is generally higher uplands and more suitable for sheep and cattle than crops.

The prevailing winds generally are westerly, off the Atlantic, and thus provide considerable moisture (more than necessary, according to many a drenched visitor.). Heavy snows are the winter fare in the north and on the hills, considerable ice, rain, and wind at lower elevations. The weather is extremely changeable, caused in large part because there is nowhere in Scotland that is more than about 80 miles from the ocean. Summer temperatures are quite temperate; a day over 85 degrees gets front-page mention. Not often realized by non-geographers, is the fact that Scotland is at virtually the same latitude as Canada's Hudson's Bay. That being so, you ask, why isn't Scotland frozen solid? It's because of the Gulf Stream; after sweeping up the east coast of the United States and across the Atlantic, it runs up Scotland's west coast. In fact, in the sheltered bays on the west coast, palm trees, and other semi-tropical vegetation grow quite well as long as they are sheltered from the north winds and gales off the Atlantic.

Another advantage of Scotland's high latitude is that summer daylight stretches well into the evening. I have read a newspaper outside by natural light as late as 10PM. The off-set, however, is that it gets dark at 4PM in the winter.

While Scotland's mountains do not achieve the heights found in the Rockies or the Alps, there are some 294 peaks over 3,000 feet, called "Munro's," after Sir Hugh Munro, 4th Baronet of Lindertis, who mapped them all between 1890 and 1900. I happen to know this since he was my grandfather.

The First Third of the Millennium

Scotland, as we will shortly see, was a land that has been in a virtual state of conflict and war since the start of time. Before the 12th century, Scotland was a country of ancient pagan beliefs, including the power of witches, the existence of fairies, superstitions, the use of healing charms and the like. The Romans had arrived in the first century AD, and attempted to subdue the native peoples. Despite their vaunted legions, they were unsuccessful, and withdrew behind the safety of "Hadrian's Wall." Christianity arrived in Scotland with the followers of St. Ninian and St. Columba in the 6th century. Later, in the 9th century, the relics of St. Andrew (later Scotland's Patron Saint), were brought to Scotland's east coast. The familiar Scottish flag, the saltire, or the Cross of Saint Andrew, was attributed to a vision of a white cross cloud formation against a blue sky seen by St Andrew. Perhaps the attribution is erroneous, since similar legends date back to 312 AD in which the Roman Emperor Constantine won the battle of Milvain Bridge.

Seventh century Pictish memorial stone, depicting warriors, animals, hunters and the moon. Many of these same themes are seen today in jewellery, arts and crafts, and other arts. *Courtesy of Dover Publications*

There is no doubt that Scotland's people are of a well-mixed origin, including the Gaels from Ireland (c.500), the Angles in the eastern areas of Scotland, the Picts in the highlands, as well as the Norse who invaded the western islands in the 8th century. In 843, Kenneth MacAlpin succeeded to the Scottish throne, and the Picts were submerged by the Gaels, leaving little to mark their passage, save a few stone carvings. MacAlpin was followed by a succession of Scottish kings, all attempting to consolidate their power and protect themselves from their enemies, both from within and outside. Erin (Ireland) was the predominant country in the area, with a well-developed centralized society. Erin's influence on Alba (Scotland) was considerable, particularly in manner, appearance and language.

In the highlands, the name of the game was survival agriculture. To exist, you farmed—some cereals and some cattle. Despite this basic existence, with most houses being little more than turf huts, clothes were still of importance in the highlands, but there is no evidence of checks or tartans or kilts being worn at this early stage. In the 9th and 10th centuries, there was considerable development of small articles with a high degree of artistic accomplishment—caskets, illuminated manuscripts, tombstones and the like. The inter-lace design, descended from the Norsemen, flourished on tombstones, brooches and other articles. Virtually the same design appears on 19th and 20th century antiques and jewellery.

Gradually, the highlands and the lowlands of Scotland started to draw apart. A contemporary chronicler, Fordun, in 1384 made the distinction in this way:

> The manners and customs of the Scots vary with the diversity of their speech. For two languages are spoken amongst them, the Scottish and the Teutonic; the latter, which is the language of those who occupy the seaboard and the plains, while the race of Scottish speech inhabits the highlands and outlying islands. The people of the coast are of domestic and civilised habits, trusty, patient and urbane, The highlanders and the people of the islands, on the other hand, are a savage and untamed nation, rude and independent, given to rapine, ease-loving, of a docile and warm disposition, comely in person but unsightly in dress, hostile to the English people and language, and owing to diversity of speech, even to their own nation, and exceedingly cruel. They are, however, faithful and obedient to their king and country and easily made to submit to law if properly governed.[1]

The contrast between the highlands and lowlands continued. The lowlands started to benefit from commerce and industry, transport and communications, utilization of natural resources, all resulting in more wealth and improved living. On the other hand, such growth in the highlands was constrained by the physical barriers of the terrain. Further, very little of the vast areas of land were suitable for cultivation, and the climate, to say the very least, was detrimental to agriculture.

In the highlands, then, the feudal system emerged, by necessity, as the predominant social force. The basic concept was that, in return for occupation of land, there was an obligation to the superior of administrative and military service. Thus was born the beginnings of what we today know as clans. Clan leadership started to be determined to a large degree by the principle of *primogeniture*, the eldest son succeeding the father both as to title and possessions, with the younger children subordinate to the elder, a principle which continues in Scotland today.

The modern version of the sky formation of a white cloud cross against a blue sky. Now called the *Saltire*, it is proudly flown as Scotland's national flag.

Even in these early days, foreign influences were at work. The English from the south, the merchant traders from Germany and northern Italy were bringing new, more sophisticated goods into the lowlands. Anglo-Norman families were amassing great wealth in the form of land. Trading centres were cropping up, patterned along the lines of the European "burghs", frequently centred around a castle with a military garrison, a useful tool in propagating the English language, and controlling the "savage heart" of the Scots.

Previous to this southern influence, the native Gael wore no body armour and his principal weapons were bows and arrows. Learning the hard way by a series of military setbacks, the Gaels started to wear chain mail and padded coats.

Old traditional craftsmanship was evident in the 12th and 13th centuries. Caskets were proud family possessions (made of whalebone, strapped with bronze and carved with inter-lace decoration), and were frequently illustrated on gravestones of the period. The church was active and many Norman and English churches were built.

The Scots, surrounded by the sea, had traditionally used skin covering on their modest vessels. Now, they adopted the Norse-style of ship-building of clinker-built galleys, which they called *birlinn*. These proved their value, particularly in the road-less stretches of Scotland's west and islands. Frequently, images of these "Viking ships" are found on jewellery produced even today.

During the second half of the 13th century, Scotland continued to be in turmoil. Edward, King of England, brought his armies north to Scotland and subdued his own appointed "king", John Balliol. It would appear that Scotland was now in the hands of the English, but not for long. On the scene appears William Wallace, Scotland's hero, who defeated Edward's armies at the Battle of Stirling Bridge; only to be defeated at the battle of Falkirk by Edward in 1298. Once again, another Scot rose to the occasion. Robert Bruce had himself crowned at Scone, and embarked on his "War of Independence" to drive the English out of Scotland, which he finally succeeded in doing at the Battle of Bannockburn, in 1314.

In the 14th century, a series of Scottish kings ruled, continually fighting off the English attempts to re-conquer Scotland. But they did not succeed. Once more, Scotland reverted to English control. In the mid 14th century, Scotland suffered along with the rest of the world with "Black Death" disease, losing a vast number of people. Another series of Scottish kings and/or Guardians came along one after the other. In general, they were somewhat inept, and Scotland continued to be a land torn by local disputes between clans and noblemen. This culminated in the Battle of Harlaw near Aberdeen, not between the English and the Scots, but between the Highlanders and the Lowlanders. The Highlanders, under the command of the Lord of The Isles, Donald, met the Lowlanders, under the command of the Earl of Mar. Basically, the conflict ended in a draw.

The Second Third of the Millennium

Finally, at the start of the 15th century, a somewhat more consolidating force came on the scene, the dynasty started by King James I. As a boy, he had been imprisoned by the English for many years until the Scots paid the ransom demanded for the return of their king. He in turn was murdered by his nobles, and succeeded by his son, James II ; and so to James III and James IV. James IV came to the throne just at the time of the start of what we refer to as the Middle Ages, and with it came such "shaping events" as the invention of the printing press, the age of discovery, Columbus, de Gama and Cabot, the invention of gunpowder, and the end of the feudal system under the Scottish kings where a strong central control had made it "work." Nevertheless, feudalism persisted in some of the remoter highlands and islands well into the 18th century. At the conclusion of the 15th century, the rule of the Lord of the Isles, who had controlled the Scottish highlands for over 150 years came to an end, and Scotland was finally under one king.

Whereas in Europe a "dress sense" had developed, the fighting men of the highlands generally went barelegged with a Plaid (*breachen*) to cover the body, linen shirts, generally yellow in colour, and no hats (the flat bonnet didn't appear until the 17th century). The bagpipe, which had been previously widely used in Asia and Europe, came to replace the harp and human voice as the highlander's "war-music", and fueled the spirit of the highlanders as they developed their much-feared battle-tactic of a wild downhill charge with waving swords.

At the start of the 16th century, a series of events occurred which dramatically shaped Scotland. First was the marriage of King James IV to Margaret Tudor, daughter of Henry VII of England. (A hundred years later, their grandson, James VI was to become King of England, Scotland and Ireland; ever after, the three countries were to be ruled by a sole sovereign). James IV was killed in yet another battle with the English at Flodden, and was suceeded by his son, James V. The Reformation came to Scotland early in his reign, and James was determined that Scotland (strongly allied to France), should remain a Catholic country. He married a Frenchwoman who became the mother of Mary Queen of Scots. Mary came to the throne at the tender age of seven days, following her father's death. And her reign was not a calm one—anything but. The nobles were joisting for power, and Henry, king of England continued to raid the borders. Both England and Scotland turned to Protestantism, but the tug-of-war between England (and Protestantism) and France (Catholicism) heightened. Henry tried to get the infant Mary to be married to his son. Mary of Lorraine (Mary's mother), had herself declared Regent, and the little Mary was married to Francis, the Dauphin, heir to the French throne. Eventually, after Francis' death, Mary returned to Scotland in 1561 as Queen at the age of eighteen, .a Catholic, and also Queen of France.

Now, it really gets complicated (with overtones of a virtual soap-opera). Mary married Lord Darnley, but soon tired of him, and started to favour David Riccio, an Italian musician. Riccio was murdered by Darnley and his allies. Mary then proceeded to give birth to a son (James VI of Scotland, and later James I of England), who was baptized a Catholic. Meanwhile, Mary had taken a fancy to James, Earl of Bothwell. And, perhaps you guessed it, Bothwell, using the newly discovered gunpowder, blew up Darnley. Shortly thereafter, Mary married Bothwell. Eventually, right on the verge of a civil war in Scotland, between Protestantism and Catholicism, Mary was imprisoned in Loch Leven Castle and persuaded to give up the crown in favour of her son, one year old James, with the Protestant Earl of Moray appointed Regent. About a year later, Mary escaped from Leven. After a battle between the Regent's forces and her own nobles and men, she was defeated and placed herself under the protection of Queen Elizabeth of England, never to return to Scotland again.

Portrait of Mary Stuart in her youth.

The young King James was represented by a series of Regents, all of whom were killed by ambitious enemies. Then, in 1587, Mary Queen of Scots, after being held prisoner by Queen Elizabeth for eighteen years, was executed. After another decade and a half of warfare, internecine battles and pulling and tugging between the two religions, Queen Elizabeth died, and James, at the age of thirty-eight was chosen as her successor to the

Mary, Queen of Scots.

English throne. He ruled Scotland from England, (visiting Scotland only once), through a Privy Council, all of whose members he appointed. He established the Scottish religion of Episcopacy, and suppressed Presbyterianism. By one means or another, he established peace in the highlands and islands. Justices of Peace were introduced into Scotland, and manufacturing started to make its impact. For the first time, glass, soap and leather were made in Scotland. Edinburgh became important, housing the Privy Council, law courts and a university. Other universities were established at St. Andrew's, Glasgow, and Aberdeen. The Union of Crowns in 1611, formalizing the union of England and Scotland was a mixed blessing. Scotland lost its independence, the court (and it's economic benefits) was removed to London and Scotland came to be ruled from London by kings who knew little of the land they governed. At this time, firearms were too expensive for the average highlander, and bows and arrows continued to be the weapons of choice. The massive cross-hilted claymore was gradually being replaced by the basket-hilt sword, a lighter sword of Continental design.

Eight years after Charles I succeeded his dead father, he came to Scotland to be crowned King of the Scots. To say that he was not well liked would be an understatement. He confiscated land from Catholic nobles, and tried to force his form of Episcopacy on a population that favoured Presbyterianism. The people rebelled, and the Covenantors, as they became known, forced the king to allow their religion to be that of the Scottish nation, and formed an army to make sure that the king followed through. This army eventually marched on England and joined the English Parliament in their effort to overthrow the King. However, not all was quiet in Scotland. The powerful Marquis of Montrose, an ally of King Charles, rallied the Highlanders and battled the Covenanters, plundering the countryside as he went. Montrose and his followers were finally defeated, and the "rebellion within a rebellion" put down. Meanwhile, in England, Oliver Cromwell and the "independents" rose up, seized the king and executed him.

Mary, Queen of Scots in front of Edinburgh's Hollyrood Palace. Here pictured in an extremely fine miniature on ivory, probably executed in first half of 19th c. Signed, but illegible. 2" x 3.5", $950. *Photo by William B. Bradley*

Oliver Cromwell

The Scots promptly crowned Charles I's son, King Charles II, but he also was no match for Cromwell, and ended up in exile on the Continent. Now the Scots were in total disarray—their armies defeated, the populace torn into religious fragments, and the king was gone. They were at Cromwell's mercy and he determined to do what no English king had been able to do, subdue Scotland. And so he did, and established himself as the Protector over England and Scotland. Cromwell finally died in 1658 and his son, Richard, took over; only to be thrown over in favour of Charles II once more. Only in this way were the Scots freed from the English usurpers, as they saw them to be.

Great jubilation greeted Charles II's return to the throne of his father and grand-father, a true Scottish line. But, the wishes of the general populace were once more ignored. All that the Covenantors had fought for were thrown out. Once more, Episcopacy was the religion of the land, and Charles II ruled from London, never visiting Scotland in his 15 years on the throne. This was a miserable time for the Scottish people, with constant fighting between the opposing religious factions, the Covenantors and the Royalists.

Finally Charles II died and was succeeded by his brother, James VII, a Catholic. Many of the Covenantors were rounded up, had one ear chopped off and were shipped to America as slaves. His tyrannical rule pleased no one, and in 1688, William and Mary of Orange (Protestants; she the daughter of James), were invited to take over the throne of England, and eventually Scotland; James was exiled to France, after his army was defeated. The Revolution put an end to the "House of Stewart" after 300 years in Scotland. But, given the innate rebelliousness of the Highlander, William and Mary were not destined to be left in peace to rule. The Highlanders rebelled, winning a famous battle at Killiecrankie in Perthshire in 1689. They in turn were defeated at Dunkeld, Parliament established Presbyterianism as the religion of Scotland, and The Church of Scotland remains so to this day. Sadly for Scotland, however, peace was still not to come soon.

One of the most infamous parts of Scotland's turbulent history was about to take place. William decreed that all Scottish chiefs must take an oath of allegiance to him or forfeit all their lands. All chiefs did, save Alexander Macdonald of Glencoe. A troop of soldiers, commanded by members of Clan Campbell (sworn enemies of the Macdonald's), came to Glencoe to enforce the taking of the oath. Following the unwritten rule of the highlands, they were taken in by the Macdonalds, fed and provided shelter. Early in the morning, the Campbells killed Macdonald and his wife and 38 of their clansmen, plus some other clansmen, including Munro's. This perfidy became known as The Massacre of Glencoe.

One final perceived insult to Scotland was the Darien Expedition. William Paterson, a brilliant Scot and founder of the Bank of England, put together a scheme to colonize the isthmus of Darien (Panama), perceiving that worldwide trade could be conducted from there, including to the growing areas of the American colonies. The ill-conceived scheme failed and the Scots blamed it on King William and the English merchants who didn't want any Scottish competition on "their" turf. The 17th century ended with the English and Scots about as bitterly divided as ever.

The infamous Pass of Glencoe, the location of a still-remembered event in Scotland's distant past.

The Third Third of The Millennium

Scotland, at the start of the 18th century, bore little resemblance to the country-side of today. Crops were largely grown on the hillsides, since the valleys were mostly lochs and/or un-drained wetlands. The hillsides were bare of trees. The few towns and villages, other than the major cities, still had stone houses, with turf roofs, and the people scratched out an existence. The constant fighting over the preceding 300+ years had allowed very little in the way of business/economic growth of the kind we accept for granted today—craftsmen still had to join a craft (i.e. guild). To manufacture something required a patent (i.e. "permission"), from the Crown. There was great belief in witchcraft. Every community had its resident witch. The last execution for witchcraft in Scotland occurred in 1727. One positive event did occur in the early 18th century: carrying weapons was outlawed, unless licensed, contributing greatly to the public peace.

After William's death in 1702, he was succeeded by Queen Anne, daughter of the exiled James VII . The last Scottish Parliament met in Edinburgh in 1706, and passed the Treaty of Union, by which England and Scotland became one country, Great Britain, with a single Parliament in London, equal rights to "the colonies" by both English and Scots, separate law courts and laws for each country (as before), one flag (the "union jack"), the same coinage, etc., etc. Even after the Treaty went into effect in 1707, many of the Scots continued to oppose it. The use of English tax-collectors, a tax on malt, the base of the common man's ale, and other perceived snubs by the English rankled the Scots, who were encouraged in their opposition by the Jacobites, friends of the exiled King James.

Under the Treaty, Sophia of Hanover, James VI's granddaughter was to succeed Queen Anne. She died a short time before Anne, so her son, George, became King George I. He had plusses and minuses. The plusses were that he was a Stewart descendant and a Protestant. The minuses were that he spoke no English, indeed he never learned, and the Scots knew little about him. As soon as he was made King in 1714, the plotting of the Jacobites intensified to restore James or his son, the Pretender. The rebellion was started at Braemar, where the standard was raised to James VIII in 1715. The rebel forces at first managed to do rather well, taking Perth and other strategic places. Emboldened, they marched on England and were decisively defeated at Preston. Later, at the battle of Sherrifmuir, the rebels suffered a further defeat, thus ending the 'Fifteen, and the early hopes of the Jacobites.

To forestall another rebellion, a certain English General Wade was sent to Scotland to confiscate all arms. The canny Scots, however, saved the good "stuff" and only turned in the old and useless weapons. General Wade did do one tremendously good deed for Scotland. He built a network of 250 miles of roads across Scotland, connecting all the main forts and cities, a previously road-less territory. In 1739, the famous "Black Watch" regiment was first raised, as a sort of police force to keep law and order, after to become a Regiment of the Line and one of the Empire's most famous and feared fighting forces.

George II succeeded his father in 1727, and was to reign for some 33 years. Now one of the most famous of all Scottish names appears on the scene, known variously as Prince Charles Edward Stewart, the Young Pretender, but perhaps best latterly, as "Bonnie Prince Charlie." At age 25, he determined to reclaim the Scottish throne. He had hoped for help from the French, the land of his father's exile, which was not forthcom-

Prince Charles Edward Stewart, or more familiarly called Bonnie Prince Charlie, in an early portrait.

ing. Undaunted, with only seven companions, he landed on Scotland's west coast at Arisaig, and started raising up the Highlanders to his cause. He was handsome, persuasive, and a hero in the making. First joined by the Camerons and the Macdonalds, he raised his standard at Glenfinnan, the start of the 'Forty-Five rebellion. He decisively annihilated the English forces under General Cope at Prestonpans, near Edinburgh. He had expected as a result to be welcomed by the lowlanders as their saviour. But, it wasn't to be. Once again the old split between the highlanders and the lowlanders emerged. The lowlanders feared if the Bonnie Prince won out, it meant a return to Catholicism, and they regarded the Prince's highlanders as mere savages.

Hoping to find a more friendly reception in the north of England, Charles took his army south, taking Carlisle, and continuing on to Derby, in the heartland of England, and within striking distance of London. But, he never found the support among the people that he had to have to overthrow the king. He was forced to turn back at Derby, and it seemed as if the "spirit" was gone. Instead of the handsome Prince marching at the head of his army as he did on his way south, on the way back northward he was gloomy, depressed, and the last to leave camp in the morning. Safely back in Scotland, the Prince beat back an English force at Falkirk, then further retreating northward to Inverness, and the more sure safety of the highlands. Five miles from Inverness, the stand was taken at Culloden Muir. Outnumbered almost two to one, Charles' men traded gun and cannon fire with General Cumberland's well-trained English troops, finally making their famous highlander's charge with pistol, claymore and dirk against the English line. But Cumberland had cleverly lined up his troops in a three line deep formation. The second and third lines poured a merciless hail of fire on the hapless highlanders and they were cut down virtually to a man. Charles fled the field, spent five months in hiding in the highlands and western islands, with the help of his highlanders and devoted followers such as Flora Macdonald. Ultimately, he made his way to exile in France and Italy, ending his days in virtual poverty and dissolute living, a sad end to a man with such promise.

In the mid-eighteenth century, the commercial life of Scotland slowly started to awaken. The production and export of linen provided jobs and in-coming money. Highland cattle exports to England rose dramatically. But the star was the trade with America, linen out and tobacco back, making many a rich man in the Glasgow area. Agriculture also started to develop. Fields were fenced in with stone walls, crops of potatoes, cabbages and turnips were being grown, and timber planted. Cities started to grow both in size and wealth.

After 1745 and Culloden, the Scottish countryside enjoyed a relatively peaceful existence, no more Scot vs. Scot. To curb the Scottish national spirit, under the Disarming Act of 1746, weapons were prohibited, the wearing of the kilt outlawed, but finally repealed in 1782. The warlike highlanders gave up their centuries old habit of raiding their neighbours in the lowlands, stealing their cattle, and the occasional woman. Being the best fighting men on the face of the earth, many found employment in Highland regiments in the British armies or as mercenaries around the world. Their clan chiefs took to cattle-raising and sheep-raising, dispossessing many highlanders from their land and forcing them to emigrate to Canada and other parts of the Empire, including America. This sad chapter in Scotland's history became known as the "Clearances." Nevertheless, life went on. A new road-building program was commenced in Scotland, and the great Caledonian canal constructed, all further enhancing the growth of trade.

In the last half of the 18th century and on into the 19th, the Age of Machinery, or The Industrial Revolution, arrived and much progress was made on many fronts. Agriculture was further improved with the iron plow and the threshing machine, manufacturing of woolen cloth, carpets and other articles provided jobs not heretofore available. Scotland was blessed with rich deposits of coal and iron, ultimately resulting in the invention of the steam engine by James Watt, and John Macadam's road surface invention of the same name. People started to move from country to town for employment, cities grew; by the mid-19th century Glasgow was second only to London in size in Great Britain. And, Scots contributed greatly with their other inventions and skills (bridge-building, the steam-boat, ship-building on the Clyde, machinery for manufacturing, the "factory system") and scientific discoveries too many to delineate. Perhaps one of the more familiar (and popular) exports of Scotland was whisky (spelled without the "e"). *Usquaebach*, (Gaelic for whisky) provided considerable income to the Highlands starting in the latter half of the 19th century.

The latter half of the 18th century also was highlighted by the growth of the British Empire. Enabled by the voyages of discovery, the British forces, and in particular the navy, grew into one of the most formidable forces ever seen in the world to that date. India, Canada, North America, vast portions of Africa, the Caribbean became British territory as a result of victories over both Spain and France. Explorations into the Pacific were laying the groundwork for future colonies. Needless to say, Scotsmen were in the forefront of this effort. Among them was the author's forbearer, Sir Thomas Munro.

Major-General Sir Thomas Munro, Bt, K.C.B., 1st Baronet of Lindertis (1761-1827). Governor of Madras, India, 1820-27. One of many of Scotland's sons who built and staffed the Empire. Original painting by Martin Shee, now in the National Portrait Gallery, London.

George III succeeded his father in 1760. His government was corrupt, and he was an intriguer and an obstinate man. In his government's view the colonies were there to serve him, not their people. We know well the results of the Stamp Act and other repressive acts, resulting in the loss of the valuable American colonies.

One of the more important change to impact Scotland was the growth of transportation and communications. The railroad and the telegraph started to truly open up Scotland. This was important for a number of reasons. First, the ability to easily transport goods produced in Scotland to England and overseas was paramount to the continued growth of the manufacturing industries of Scotland. Secondly, it provided a means to allow visitors to come to Scotland. One of the first to do so was George IV in 1822, who arrived in Edinburgh fully outfitted in Highland dress, kilt and all. Unfortunately, he somewhat ruined the overall effect by wearing pink tights under the kilt. Mercifully, being dissolute and having few redeeming qualities, he only reigned for ten years and was succeeded by his brother, William IV. He also had a short reign, and was succeeded by his niece Victoria at the tender age of 18 in 1837. Here begins one of the more beneficial periods in Scotland's turbulent history, the Victorian era, and one to which much of Scotland's antiques owe their genesis.

Queen Victoria on the morning of her accession, June 20, 1837.

It would be incorrect to close out the period of the last half of the 18th and first half of the 19th centuries without recognizing the achievements and contributions of Scotland's people in an intellectual sense. Foremost among them were Robert Burns and Sir Walter Scott. Burns (1759-1796) only lived a scant 37 years but became known as Scotland's poet laureate because of his ability to capture the "essence" of the common man in his songs and verse. Sir Walter Scott (1771-1832) in the "age of romanticism" did so much in his novels to provide to his readers an image of Scotland that "lived", and one that attracted them. This also was a period of the resurrection of some of the old music of Scotland, the growth and increasing popularity of both Highland and Country dancing, as well as the use of the bagpipe and kilted attire as both a symbol and imagery of Scotland. There is considerable dispute as to whether or not tartan is, in fact, an ancient mode of dress, or a product of the fertile imagination of certain Victorians. At the start of Chapter Three on Tartan Ware, there is a review of this contentious matter.

We should also recognize Scotland's role in the spread of higher education in the 18th and 19th centuries. Because of the calibre of Scottish teachers and philospohers, Scotland's universities were at the "cutting-edge." In fact, it was common for sons of both continental and English families to attend Scottish, rather than home, universities.

Charming colour lithograph of Queen Victoria's beloved Balmoral Castle in the Scottish Highlands. *Photo by William B. Bradley*

Previously we have alluded to the prowess of the Scots as fighting men. Nowhere in their history was this more evident than in this period. The Black Watch regiment was one of Great Britain's premier fighting forces in the American War of Independence. They, and other Scottish regiments, were in the forefront of all of the 18th and 19th century conflicts, Napoleonic wars (Waterloo), the Crimean war, and the Boer war. But at this time, the zenith of The Empire, Scotland's people were also playing a highly important role in a less antagonistic sense. It was said at the time, that wherever you went in the world, the Scots were there, and running things. The King, Queen, or prime minister would be advised by a Scot, the banker would be a Scot, also the doctor, the minister, the engineer. This, indirectly, brought much wealth to many Scottish families.

It did not take Queen Victoria long to discover Scotland. Two years after marrying Albert in 1840, she made her first visit to Scotland and was enthralled by the people and their friendliness, the scenery and the soft air of the highlands. They acquired an estate near Ballater in the Deeside in 1848, and rebuilt the relatively small house to accommodate their family, which ultimately consisted of nine children. The family spent every autumn at Balmoral until Albert's early death from typhoid fever in 1861. Their greatest enjoyment was to travel by pony or cart around the highlands, pick-nicking along the way, faithfully attended by the *ghillie* (servant), John Brown.

The easy railroad journey from London to Scotland caused a tourist "rush" by the English to emulate the holidays of their Queen. "Things Scottish" became the height of fashion. Every aristocrat or man of means aspired to have his shooting lodge in the highlands. Deer stalking and grouse shooting were the sports in favour, and the kilt and it's accoutrements were suddenly fashionable, if not a downright "must". Scottish portrait artists and landscape artists achieved fame during this period, and kilt-makers were literally overwhelmed with orders. The Queen's happiness in Scotland was marred once again by the death of John Brown in 1883; he had been her constant companion since Albert's death. Nevertheless, she returned to Balmoral two and sometimes three times a year until her death in 1901, after the longest reign of a British monarch in history.

Her Majesty, Victoria, Queen and Empress, in the late 19th century.

As the 20th century dawned, the world map reflected, in red, the massiveness of the British Empire. Victoria's reign could perhaps best be described as "useful", despite the many wars that occurred during her reign (the Crimean, Indian wars, three wars with China, and the Boer War at the end of her reign), all marked up to the "cost of empire." But the most profound change was the development of self-government both in Great Britain and in the colonies, with a complete democracy, nearly universal suffrage and full control of the government by the majority of the population. Victoria's eldest son, The Prince of Wales, became King Edward VII; only to die after nine years on the throne. His son became King George V. He had been trained in the Royal Navy, which was to serve him in good stead in the near future. Great Britain depended on the freedom of the seas to trade with the world, and so a strong navy was a firm policy of the country. German imperialism threatened the world, and the Great War of 1914-1918 was the result. Without citing specific statistics, there was scarcely a family in Scotland who had not lost a member or relative in this "war to end all wars". Great Britain and her allies prevailed of course, and the world came "back to normal" in 1919 after 5 years of turmoil.

Next followed a period of peace for Great Britain lasting until World War II, but not without other travails. The Great Depression, felt around the world, made a severe impact on Scottish industry. Labour strife was prevalent, but was conducted in a generally passive fashion. Ultimately, in the mid 1930s, Scottish industry recovered and in particular, the shipbuilding on the Clyde brought new jobs and economic prosperity to the area. King George VI succeeded his father in 1936, and saw the nation through the destructive and dangerous period of World War II. Nazi air attacks on the British mainland devastated large parts of her manufacturing base and city centers at the costs of thousands of lives. Scotland was not as hard hit as England, but damaged nevertheless. Once again, Scotland's contribution to the successful conclusion of the war in 1945 was her manufacturing strength and the fighting men she provided the allied forces. And again, the loss of Scottish blood was more than considerable.

An early steel engraving of Glamis Castle in the county of Angus, in Scotland's verdant and beautiful vale of Strathmore, roughly 80 miles due north of Edinburgh. When the engraving was made, Glamis was spelled with two "m"s and was in the county of Forfarshire.

Finally, the hostilities over, life gradually returned to normal. Cities needed rebuilding, manufacturing had to be re-energized and up-dated, new roads built, and despite the "hiccup" of the Korean War in the early 1950s, Scotland prospered. A combination of factors created an economic climate most favourable to industry. A well-educated and stable work-force, government stability, a relatively benign climate, natural resources for affordable construction and low cost utilities, research capabilities in Scotland's universities, all attracted businesses of every type. Of particular note, starting in the 1970s was the influx of "high-techs", to the point where a stretch in Scotland between Edinburgh and Glasgow became known as "Silicon Glen."

Considerable relief was afforded to Highland crofters, tenant farmers, in the 20th century. They were given security of tenure, compensation for improvements, and their heir allowed to succeed. The forestry industry was developed (an excellent use for non-arable land), water-powered electricity generation was fostered, and oil and gas reserves in the North Sea were discovered and developed. Also, the charms of Scotland were re-discovered, as in Victorian times, as a tourist destination. All the necessities of tourism had to be provided, all to Scotland's economic benefit. Queen Elizabeth II had succeeded her father in 1953, and having grown up in Scotland at the family home, Glamis, she became almost as rabid an exponent of "Things Scottish" as her great-great grandmother, Queen Victoria. In fact, Balmoral has seen more of Queen Elizabeth and her family than the "original" owner. It is ironic that Queen Elizabeth was to preside over the "dis-memberment" of The British Empire, formed during the reign of her ancestor, Queen Victoria. Self-determination throughout the Empire resulted in complete separation (e.g. India), or a "looser" separation (e.g. Canada and Australia)

Finally, as the 20th century drew to a close and a new millennium was starting, the British Government embarked on a process they called "Devolution." The process had been somewhat of a "work in progress" since the Union in 1707, in varying degrees of strength and enthusiasm. The Scottish Nationalist Party had for many years advocated that Scotland should separate from England, that Scottish money in the forms of taxes was being siphoned off and used to support the social activities in English cities at Scotland's expense. At one point, they even advocated that Scotland should have it's own army, navy and air force. This degree of militancy was not generally supported by the population;

however the party was a small, but growing, political entity. So the British Parliament voted to establish a Parliament in Scotland, it's first in almost 300 years. This Parliament, domiciled in Edinburgh, would deal with contract law, the environment, health and welfare, local planning, education, property and land law and local taxes. The "old" Parliament in London would still be in place, with some Scottish representation and would deal with international matters, foreign policy and British matters as in the past. And meet the Scottish Parliament did, on May 2nd 1999, with 129 elected representatives. (Similar devolutions of varying degrees took place in Wales and Northern Ireland). And less you think that this brought an end to the monarchy, far from it. Witness the out-pouring of affection on the occasion of The Queen Mother's one-hundredth birthday in 2000. And, the Jubilee celebration for Queen Elizabeth II in 2002 further demonstrated the British people's feelings towards the monarchy (the British popular media notwithstanding).

The character of the Scottish people is a factor often remarked upon by foreign visitors. If you ask a visitor to Scotland what he remembers most, it is usually the friendliness of the people rather than the scenery, history or other factors. The trait of "cheapness" so often ascribed to the Scots is more of a music-hall myth than a reality. True, Scots are frugal and "canny", but not cheap. They still, today, have a tremendous work ethic, even though plagued with perhaps more than their share of the world's drug problems. Perhaps their one major failing is their fondness for a "wee" drink (or two). They have, time and time again, proved their loyalty "for King and Country" throughout history. And that loyalty remains to this day.

And so, our geography, social, and history lessons are concluded, and we hope it provides a framework and perhaps a better appreciation of the chapters to come.

[1]Grant, I. and Cheape, Hugh. *Periods in Highland History*, New York, Barnes and Noble, 2000, pg 34.

Bibliography

Brown, P. Hume. *A Short History of Scotland*, Edinburgh, Oliver and Boyd, 1924.

Cheyney, Edward P. *A Short History of England*, New Edition, Boston, Ginn and Company, 1932.

Duff, David. *Queen Victoria's Highland Journals*, London, Lomond Books, 1994.

Grant, I. and Hugh Cheape. *Periods in Highland History*, New York, Barnes and Noble, 2000.

Herman, Arthur. *How the Scots Invented the Modern World*, New York, Three Rivers Press, 2001.

Kermack, W. R. *Historical Geography of Scotland*, Second Edition, Edinburgh and London, W and A. K. Johnston, Ltd, 1926.

Millar, Delia. *Queen Victoria's Life in The Scottish Highlands*, London, Philip Wilson Publishers, Ltd, 1986.

Millar, Delia. *The Highlanders of Scotland, (The complete watercolours commissioned by Queen Victoria from Kenneth MacLeay of her Scottish retainers and clansmen)*, London, Haggerston Press, 1986.

Prebble, John. *John Prebble's Scotland*, London, Pimlico, 2000.

Chapter Two

Mauchline Ware

A Uniquely Victorian Collectible

Early steel engraving of Mauchline street scene, Gavin Hamilton's house.

Origins and Overview

The town of Mauchline is a typical small Scottish town , located about 11 miles from the town of Ayr, on the west coast, and about 30 miles south of Glasgow. Starting early in the nineteenth century, Mauchline (pronounced "Moch'lin" or "Mawk-lin," but never "Mosh-line") was the scene of what, by mid-century, became a thriving industry in the production of wooden souvenir articles. These articles, beautifully crafted and generally utilitarian in nature, were exported all over the world, to be sold by local newsagents/gift shops and the like. The Mauchline firm of William and Andrew Smith was the largest producer; smaller firms in nearby towns also produced similar items, but all became know as "Mauchline Ware." The term *treen*, or *treenware*, generically covers a multitude of small wooden objects, of which Mauchline Ware is but one.

Another town, however, figures prominently in the development of these collectibles. Alyth, in Perthshire, was the home of an invalid inventor by the name of John Sandy. He invented the "secret hinge" or "hidden hinge" snuff box. For those of you who are unfamiliar with snuff, it's a powder of ground tobacco stalks, and is used by inhaling it into the nostrils. By alternating the "knuckles" of the hinge from the box lid and the back of the box, and then pinning them with a metal rod passed horizontally through the knuckles, Sandy provided a virtually air-tight closure, vital to the freshness of the snuff. The tiny metal rod was disguised by wooden plugs at the ends. The wood used was generally sycamore, called "plane" wood by the Scots, which was easy to work, close-grained and with few knots and sap. One way or another, the "secret hinge" didn't stay a secret for long, and found it's way to the west coast, where it was used in snuff boxes manufactured by a multitude of producers, the largest being W. & A. Smith. The early snuff boxes were hand-decorated in coloured paints or by pen and ink drawings, finished with numerous coats of varnish (very necessary for protection, since many boxes were kept in the pocket, along with coins, keys and whatever).

Small, early Mauchline snuff-box, with remnants of original foil lining. Note air-tight over-hanging lip on lid, and Sandy's "secret" hinge design. *Photo by William B. Bradley*

Unfortunately, in the second quarter of the century, the "snuff habit" was just about to nose-dive (pun intended) since the medical fraternity had started to recognize the dangers of the habit to a long-term "snuffer". It was essential that the Smith's and other manufacturers diversify their line. And diversify they did. The first new items were tea-caddies, valuable tea also requiring air-protection. By the middle of the century, the firm had developed a line of souvenir items that numbered well into the hundreds of different articles, many in different styles, and ultimately in different finishes.

In Chapter One, reference was made to the growth of international trading by Scotland in the mid 1800s. Here is a perfect example of that trend. The Smith's built their quite considerable business in this fashion. The basic product was produced in Mauchline to very exacting standards, beautifully crafted and executed. It was often decorated with a transfer scene (later, with photographs) of a particular locale. Smith's agents sold the article to newsagents and other vendors in the locale of the scene, where they were sold as souvenirs. Travellers of the day would buy them to take home as a "memory" piece, or as a gift for a friend or relative. Mauchline Ware articles were exported and sold all over the world, first, of course in Scotland and England, but also in France, Belgium, Spain and elsewhere in Europe. And, Smith's selling agents didn't stop there, Mauchline Ware articles are found with scenes of locations in Australia, South Africa, Canada, and most notably the United States. (Over 1000 US scenes have been identified; with more being found constantly). It's amusing to contemplate a nineteenth century Scottish visitor to Australia buying a piece of Mauchline Ware with an "Aussie" scene and taking it home as a present for "Grannie" in Glasgow, not realizing that it started life only some 30 miles down the road.

The Product Range and Finishes

The product range is huge, Andrew Smith once observing that the firm was making almost anything that you could conceive as being possible to make from wood, from stamp boxes to tea trays. A partial list of products illustrates:

Sewing-related– such as etuis, needle-cases, knitting-yarn balls, crochet hook and bodkin containers, scissors cases, darning mushrooms, thimble containers, tape measures, knitting needle containers, containers dispensing thread, ribbon, etc. (many with the manufacturer's labels inside or on top of the lid), pin/ needle cases and pin cushions

Selection of Mauchline Ware, Front row, left to right: Barrel-shaped sewing kit, with tartan paper applied to top & bottom; rare combination. $325. Vertical bodkin, transfer of "Absecon Lighthouse, Atlantic City", $185. Retractable tape-measure, transfer of "Mohonk Lake, NY", $165. Small sewing egg, with rare "Colorado" transfer, $165. Round tape casket, with coloured fern decoration, $165. Sewing egg, with transfer of "Pier, Old Orchard, Me.", $165. Folding needlecase, transfer of "Burns' Monument." $185.
Back row, left to right: Rectangular pin cushion, storage drawer under, two "Inverness" scenes, $165. Pincushion in bellows format, "Glasgow" transfer, $225. Retractable tape-measure, "Portland, Me." transfer, $225. Round string-holder with floral decoration, $165. *Photo by William B. Bradley*

Tobacco-related– snuff boxes, match boxes (also called match safes and vestas), cigar and cheroot cases, wall-hanging match containers

Card/game-related– card boxes, bezique or whist scorers, trumps indicators, cribbage boards, game counters, checkerboards and backgammon boards, dice cups.

Four snuff-boxes, all with integral hinge. Largest (front left) has early pen & ink drawing of hunting dog, 3.5" x 2", $450. Rear left, colour transfer of hunter, 2.5" x 1.5", $285. (Next are two examples of typical dry Victorian humour!); Right rear, two donkeys in field with caption "When shall we three meet again?", $285. Right front, colour transfer of rooster covering hen, "Gratis", 1.25" x 1.25", $285. *Photo by William B. Bradley*

Desk/book-related– rulers, stamp boxes, book-marks, page-turners, paper-knives, pen trays, straight pens, pen-nib/stamp boxes, desk portfolios, picture frames, "rocker" blotters, inkwells, thermometers, book covers, pencil cases

Selection of Mauchline Ware, Front, left to right: Rocker blotter, transfers of "Melrose Abbey and Abbottsford", 4.25" x 4.25", $165. Round ruler. Pull-off ends with original pencil and eraser, 7", $275. Book-mark, colour transfer of robin & "Happy Xmas", 5", $125.
Rear, left to right: Desk-box for stamps, pen-nibs, etc, in form of butler's knife-tray, with two transfer scenes of "Exeter", 5" x 2.5", $295. Desk portfolio with English holiday beach scenes at corners, 6" x 9", $125. Desk calendar with cards for day, month, year complete. Transfer of "Margate", 3.5" x 4", $295. Hinged-lid box, with colour transfer of Queen Victoria, "Jubilee Year, 1837-1887". 5.25" x 4". $185. *Photo by William B. Bradley*

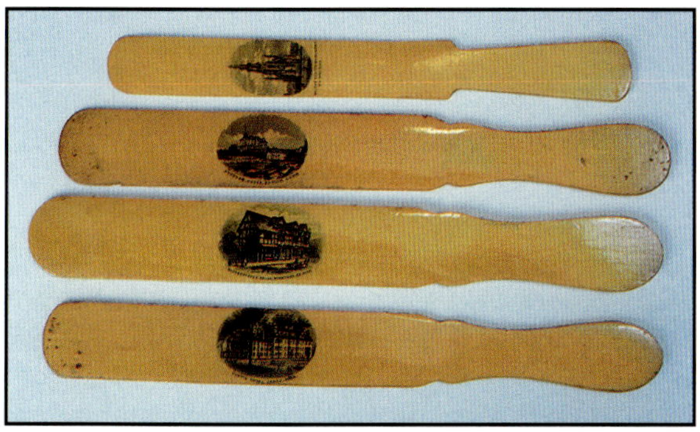

Four page turners. Top to bottom: Transfer of "Sir Walter Scott's Monument, Edinburgh", 9.25", $85, Transfer of "Edgecomb House, Groton, Conn.", 10.75", $105. Transfer of "Shakespeare's house, Stratford-on-Avon", 11", $115. Transfer of "Curtis House, Lenox, Mass." 10.75" $85. *Photo by William B. Bradley*

Four Mauchline Ware stamp boxes. Front, left: single-stamp box with pinned-lid and transfer of "Dryburgh Abbey", 1.5" x 1.5", $225. Front, right: hinged-lid, double-stamp box with transfer "Steamboat Landing, Nantucket", 3.5" x 1.25", $225. Left rear: hinged-lid double-stamp box, "The End of Yankee Land, Provincetown, Mass.", 3.25" x 1.25", $225. Right rear: Sliding-top stamp box, "Burns' Cottage, Alloway", 3.25" x 2.25", $225. *Photo by William B. Bradley*

Fashion-related– bracelets, earrings, brooches, parasol handles, poesy-holders, glove stretchers, cuffs, ring trees, powder boxes, rouge pots, other cosmetic containers, clothes brushes, hair brushes, handbags, knitting bags, coin purses, cuff-links, spectacle cases, jewellery boxes

Child-related– popguns, money boxes (banks), toy windmills, whistles, skipping rope handles

Novelty items– cradles, puzzle boxes (usually money boxes or match safes). wheel barrows, boat-shaped boxes, saucepan-shaped boxes

Domestic items– napkin rings, spill vases, egg cups, egg cruets with egg cups, egg-timers (both wall-hanging and free-standing), candle holders, tea caddies

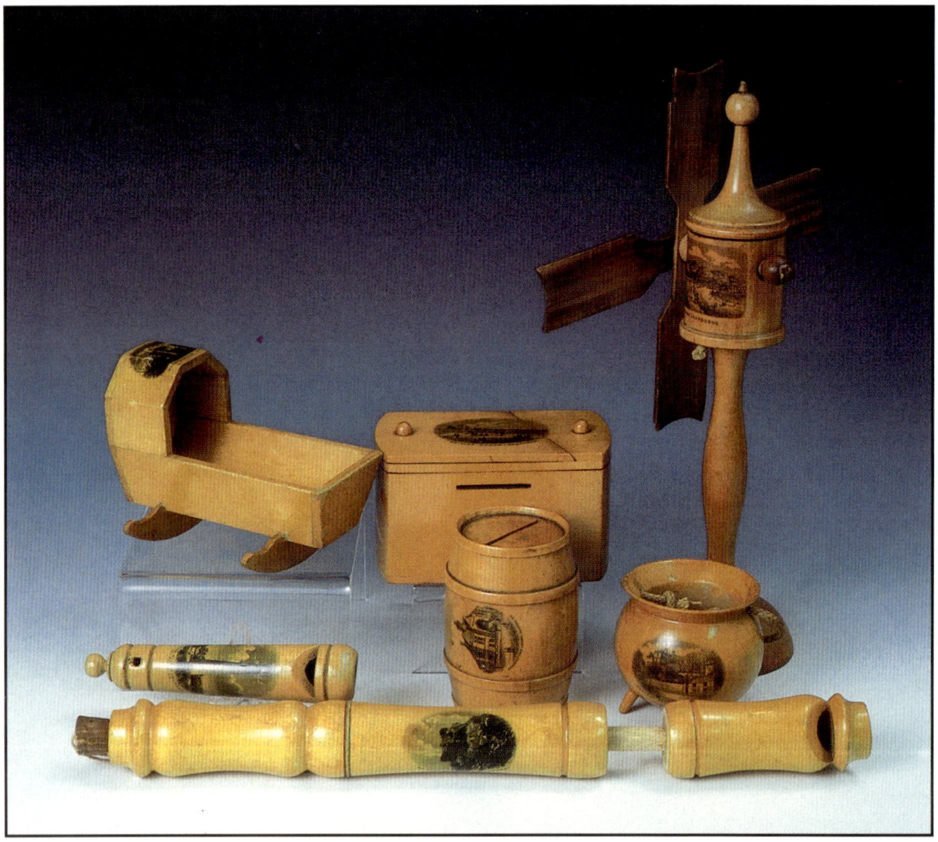

Children's and novelty items. Front: children's pop-gun and whistle, transfer of "Douglas" (Isle of Wight), 11", $285. Middle: child's whistle, transfer of "Bunker Hill Monument, 221 Ft. High", 4.75", $185. Child's barrel-shape money-box, with transfer of "Richard's Free Library, Newport, N.H", 3.25" h., $165. Pin-holder in form of cooking cauldron, with transfer of Scottish castle, 2.5" h., $105. Back: hair-pin holder in shape of baby-cradle, transfer of castle, 4.5" x 3.5", $195. Child's rectangular money-box, with "puzzle-opening", and transfer of "Southend", 4" x 2.5", $365. Child's "whirligig" toy. Pull cord downward and windmill turns. Transfer of "Llandudno" (Wales), 11", $425. *Photo by William B. Bradley*

A Mauchline Ware mixture. Front: bedside watch-holder with glass viewing window. Transfer of "Eastbourne". 3.5" x 4", $285. Egg-timer, with top transfer of "High School, Norway, Me." 3.25" h., $185. Pair of glove-stretchers, with transfer of "Burns' Monument", 7", $185. Back: standing picture frame, with transfers of four Perthshire (Scotland) scenes, 4.5" x 5.75", $195. Egg-cup, with transfer of "St. Andrews", 4" h., $165. Cedar Ware scent container and original cut-glass container inside. Transfers of Lake District scenes. 2.5" h., $235. *Photo by William B. Bradley*

Bell-shaped thread-holder, with patent mark and transfer of "New Suspension Bridge", unusual brown markings, 4.5" h., $185. Match safe or "vesta" with flip-ends, both for access. Transfer of "Carlisle Cathedral". 2" x 1", $165. "Go-to-bed" match safe. Top half of cylinder lifts off to access matches; striker on bottom; match placed in ivory finial at top to light your way up stairs to"go to bed." Transfer of "Wallace Monument, Abbey Craig." 3.5" h., $185. *Photo by William B. Bradley*

Child's barrel-shaped money-box, transfer of "Richard's Free Library, Newport, N.H." 3.25" h., $165. Obelisk-shaped thermometer, with ivory scale, and transfer of "Summit of Mt. Washington", 7", $365. Novelty hatchet in Cedar Ware, with colour transfer of Home of Washington, West Front", 7.25", $95.

These scenes ranged from holiday locales, The Isle of Wight and other English and Scottish sea-side resorts being favourites, .along with Atlantic City and Niagara Falls in America, to pictures of famous people ("Rabbie" Burns, Sir Walter Scott, Queen Victoria, General Robert E. Lee), and famous buildings (Alloway Kirk, Abbotsford, Bank of England, as well as Mount Vernon, The US Treasury Building, The White House, US Capitol, etc). Other views included special events (the 1886 International Exhibition in Edinburgh, The 1893 World's Columbian Exhibition in Chicago, Queen Victoria's Golden Jubilee of 1887). Obviously, being a Scottish product, a large number of Mauchline Ware pieces relate to Robert Burns and to Sir Walter Scott, two of Scotland's more famous sons of the 18th and 19th centuries.

Very rare and unusual full-length transfer of "General Lee," on lid of memento box, 5" x 2", $365.

The "plain vanilla" Mauchline Ware items uniformly have a most attractive "honey" patina, emanating both from the wood itself and the varnish finishes (multiple coats of oil copal varnish were used to protect the wood from damage). The earliest pieces were hand-painted or decorated with pen and ink drawings. By the early 1850s, black transfers of scenes were used to decorate the object. Depending on the size, the object could have a single or multiple transfer scenes.

After the invention of the photographic process, Mauchline Ware began to show up with photographic scenes in lieu of transfers. Many of these were done at the Caledonian Box Works in Lanark, started by Archibald Brown in 1866. Most of the photographic scenes found on Mauchline Ware date to the period between the late 1860s and the very early 1900s.

Other Finishes

Another finish used on Mauchline Ware was called Fern Ware. Manufactured in lesser quantities than it's predecessor, it was produced in one of several different ways. One was to print the fern pattern on paper and glue the paper to the object. A second was to lay the fern itself on the object and stipple on a dark brown paint; then, by lifting and discarding the fern, the pattern remained in relief form. These articles had a non-souvenir appeal, solely for their beauty, although sometimes they would be further adorned with a transfer or photo. Some full sized furniture (tables, chests, etc) were made in Fern Ware also. Generally, Fern Ware dates from about the 1870s.

Large rectangular double card box in coloured Fern Ware, with card-fan on lid. 6" x 4.5". $375.

Lady's face-fan in coloured Fern Ware, with turned handle. Face-fans were used by ladies to protect their complexions from the heat coming from a fireplace in the days before central heating. 16" x 7" oval on fan. $575.

Close-up of fan detail

Superb book with tooled leather spine and Fern Ware board covers. *The Poetical Works of Thompson, Falconer & Blair,* published in London, 1871 by T. Nelson & Sons. 445 gold-edged pages. 5" x 7". $425. *Photo by William B. Bradley*

Two more examples of Fern Ware. A small pivoting pocket aid and memoir, with legend "Souvenir of Dawlish" Devon, 2.25" x 3.5", $265, and lift-off lid powder box, 3.5" h., $185. *Photo by William B. Bradley*

Other finishes employed in the manufacturing of Mauchline Ware included transfers of coloured ferns and seaweed, and a quite wide range of objects in black lacquer. The latter finish appears to date from the 1880s and is found both with transfer and photo applications as well as fern/floral decoration. Further finishes include chequer ware, geometric ware and cedar ware (the latter generally from the Lake District of northern England).

One of the more popular finishes of Mauchline Ware is Tartan Ware. Because of it's importance (and just because I like it), the entire next chapter is devoted to it alone, so rather than repeat myself, be patient until you get to Chapter Three, and feast your eyes.

Left: large knife-box-configured calling-card box, with combination of floral/fern transfer and black transfer of "Kirkby Lonsdale," 4.5" x 3.5", $275. Round hanging string-holder in unusual floral design. 3.5" dia., $285.

Two pieces of Black Lacquer Ware. Left: spill vase with floral cartouche and transfer of "Shakespeare's House, Stratford-on-Avon", 6" h., $225. Right: hinged-lid souvenir memento box with floral decoration and transfer of "Penrhyn Quarries," 4.5" x 3", $205. *Photo by William B. Bradley*

Black Lacquer hinged-lid memento box. Large colour transfer on lid. On front of box is game, with brass spinner to select an answer to question "What is Your Fortune, My Pretty Maid?" Delightful Victorian memento. 9" x 5", $425.

Black lacquer hinged-lid memento box, with same fortune game as above. On lid is colour transfer of two children, and "Present from Brighton." 4" x 2", $325.

Pair of small black lacquer trinket boxes with colour transfers to lids. Transfers depict young boys dressed as a hunter and a dancer. Each measures 2.5" x 1.25" x 1". $325.

Black lacquer lift-off lid card box, with floral transfer-decorated lid, and ace of heart card. 4.5" x 3.25" x 1.5". $185.

Final Thoughts on Mauchline Ware

Prices in this chapter (and throughout the book) are quoted in US$. As with any antique, price depends on many factors including rarity and, most importantly, condition (the latter being a very subjective evaluation). Price quotes are therefore based on articles at the higher end of the "generally acceptable" range.

Prices of Mauchline Ware have escalated (as have those of the majority of collectibles) over the last few years, but not to the extent of Tartan Ware (see chapter Three). I would estimate that Mauchline Ware prices have, in general, doubled in the last ten years. However, as collectibles go, Mauchline Ware is still "affordable". Napkin rings can still be found for $20-30, simple boxes for $85-125; naturally, rarer items or scenes can be pricey. Objects with scenes in the New York Catskill Mountains, for example, seem to run 3-4 times more than the same object with a different scene. Obviously, there are a few people "chasing" the Catskills. Some collectors have decided to "specialize" their collections, egg-cups, sewing items, banks, match safes and so on. It helps sometimes to create a focus by specializing and not trying to generalize. One rule is paramount, however, always go for the quality item. You're far better off to have fewer pieces of superior quality, than a large number of pieces in marginal condition.

Quite often I am asked by collectors about the "care and feeding" of Mauchline Ware. The usual answer is "as little as possible". As is the case in most antiques, unless an item is in "distress", you're better to leave it alone, and not to try too many artificial enhancements. Having said that, here are a couple of little things you can do. If, for example, you buy something that is obviously "grimy" (finger-grease, good old dirt or whatever), and the varnish cover is still intact (protecting the transfer or photo), try washing with a mild solution of Murphy's Oil Soap™, then thoroughly rinsing with clean water to remove any soap residue, dry with a clean cloth and allow to further air-dry. In extreme cases of grime, I have, on occasions, used a small amount of car cleaner (the kind used to remove oxidized paint). Again, followed up by clear water rinse, and air-dry. Once the exterior grime is removed, I apply a little Butcher's Wax™ and buff to a shine. A caution, however, always proceed incrementally, try a little soap and observe the results, if more is needed, add it. If not, stop now. Just don't get "carried away with the program". Some "purists" would prefer to leave the article in "as found" condition. If you're one of them, be my guest and ignore the proceeding advice.

One of the "fun" parts about collecting Mauchline Ware is the "mystery" factor. What I mean is this.

While the vast majority of Mauchline Ware, in all it's variations, was produced in the second half of the 19th century, production continued in steadily decreasing volumes up to 1933. By then, because of the diminished demand for it's product, the W. & A. Smith factory had only a small fraction of the 400 employees that it had in its 1850-1880 heyday. It was then that disaster struck. A fire consumed the factory, known locally as "the box works", and it burned to the ground. With it went all the records of almost a hundred years of manufacturing. To this day, no one knows with certainty the number of pieces produced, the full variation in form and product, the different transfer or photo scenes used (and on what objects). Ironically, the site of the "box works" is now that of the Mauchline Fire Department.

So, therein lies the mystery and the fun. You'll never know if "you've found it all". New scenes turn up constantly as collectors "winkle" them out of their hiding places.

I've seen Mauchline Ware articles that I would swear had been kept in a drawer since they were produced 150 years ago, and had never seen the light of day. Some Mauchline Ware collectors have been at it a lot longer than we have, and they tell me that they are constantly running into things they didn't know existed. So it's not too late to "join in". Maybe, just maybe, you'll be lucky enough to find "the last piece". But, you will never know for sure if it *is* the real last piece.

But you don't have to search alone; there's a great organization willing to help. In 1986, a British group got together and started The Mauchline Ware Collector's Club. For a very modest annual membership fee, they publish a semi-annual newsletter of excellent quality; most interesting articles about the field, with colour pictures, prices, sources and so on. Further, they organize a MWCC Weekend Convention about every 18 months. These, held at various locales throughout Great Britain (usually wherein there is a Mauchline "connection") feature guest speakers, trips to museums or other sites of Mauchline interest, an auction, member's displays of Mauchline Ware, etc. Contact the Mauchline Ware Collectors Club, PO Box 158, Leeds, LS16 5WZ England, UK.

Website: www.mauchlineclub.org

E-mail: enquiries@mauchlineclub.org

There is a most active branch on the western side of the "pond," with some 200 plus members throughout the United States.

Bibliography

Baker, John, *Mauchline Ware*, Shire Album 140, Princes Risborough, England, Shire Publications, Ltd, 1985.

Pinto, Edward H., *Treen, or Small Woodware Throughout the Ages*. London, B. T. Batsford, 1949.

Pinto, Edward H. and Eva R., *Tunbridge and Scottish Souvenir Woodware*, London, G. Bell and Sons, 1970.

The Journal of The Mauchline Ware Collectors Club, Romsey, England, Mauchline Ware Collectors Club, 1986-2003.

Tractenberg, David and Thomas Keith, *Mauchline Ware — A Collector's Guide*, Suffolk, England, Antique Collector's Club, 2002.

Chapter Three

Tartan Ware

Tartan: Ancient Gael Garb or Victorian Myth?

In the first chapter on Scotland's history, we made brief note of the controversy over Scottish tartans. There are two opposing views. The first is that the true origin of tartan is lost in the mists of time, but that it was the ancient "dress" of Scotland, and that the various clans had their own colours and setts (patterns), which came down through countless generations. The second view (and one perhaps somewhat more supportable on a factual basis) is that tartans were the probable result of a desire for a national "costume" and a symbol of a proud race of people, based upon some evidence that the Scots made extensive use of coloured/checked fabric for cloaks/ plaids/shawls/ which were the traditional clothing for both men and women. The colours involved were mostly natural dyes, red, green and brown, found in the countryside.

Prior to the 16th century there is no evidence that tartans (as we know them today) existed, and particularly no evidence of distinctive tartans for each clan. In the next two centuries, however, we start to see the evolving picture of Highland dress, and with it the tartan. Noblemen in the late 17th and 18th centuries are painted as wearing an early form of kilt, a belted plaid in checked patterns (often black and red). As we noted in Chapter One, tartans were outlawed after the 'Forty-five, and not allowed again until the law was repealed in 1782. Only then did tartans start to reappear.

The Highland Society, formed in London in 1778, gave considerable impetus to the "tartan movement". In an effort to preserve some of the old traditions of music and dress, they started to collect samples of tartans from clan chiefs. Now, for the first time there was a repository of the tartans used in the middle of the 18th century. And, as we saw in Chapter One, George IV in his 1822 visit to Edinburgh gave the Royal imprimatur to tartans, (closely followed by Queen Victoria's further imprimatur, Balmoral and "all that"). The demand for tartan was so heavy that the looms couldn't keep up. In his excellent book *Tartan*, Hugh Cheape examined the records of one of the leading producers of tartans in the early 1800s and concludes:

> Names of tartans and clan associations had origins that were probably in most cases more commercial than historical... Aristocratic patronage always provided a touchstone of authenticity and the Highland nobility and gentry were keen to provide what they regarded with confidence as the correct answer. Thus they colluded in the commercial process.[1]

In the 1840-1860 period, a series of books attempted to "legitimize" the history and the association of clans and tartan. The first of these, *Vestiarium Scoticum*, was published in 1842, followed by *The Costume of the Clans*, in 1845, written by two brothers who claimed to be grandsons of Bonnie Prince Charlie. They traced the origins of tartans back to medieval times and 16th century manuscripts. Known as the Sobieski Stuarts, they

A truly magnificent Scot!! In the "Ogilvie" tartan as depicted by painter Robert R. McIan in 1845 publication *The Clans of The Scottish Highlands*. Original hand-coloured print together with text on the clan,10"x 14", $325.

were soundly denounced as frauds by no less an authority than Sir Walter Scott. But, as we well know, there is no holding back a popular movement that has the necessary momentum to start to roll. A Scot, James Logan, in 1831 published *The Scottish Gael,* which authenticated a number of tartans. This was followed by *The Clans of the Scottish Highlands,* in 1845 and 1847. In this two-volume work, the reputed costumes of the clans are illustrated in 72 magnificent, hand-coloured engravings from watercolour paintings by the artist Robert McIan. Hugh Cheape comments that this work further clouded the picture by "elaborating on the myth of clan tartan and providing fictions as compelling as any facts."[2]

Another "McIan," representing Clan "Mac Nicol," 10" x 14", $325.

Tartans: are they a part of ancient history or a later development heightened by the Victorian love of "Things Scottish"? Whichever it is, I'm sure it's of great interest and vital importance to the world of scholarly research. I leave it to the reader to draw his own conclusion. I, for one, care not. The tartans (whatever their age or origin) are part and parcel of Scotland, and sad it would be without the tartans, the kilt, the pipes, and the resulting images of old Scotia.

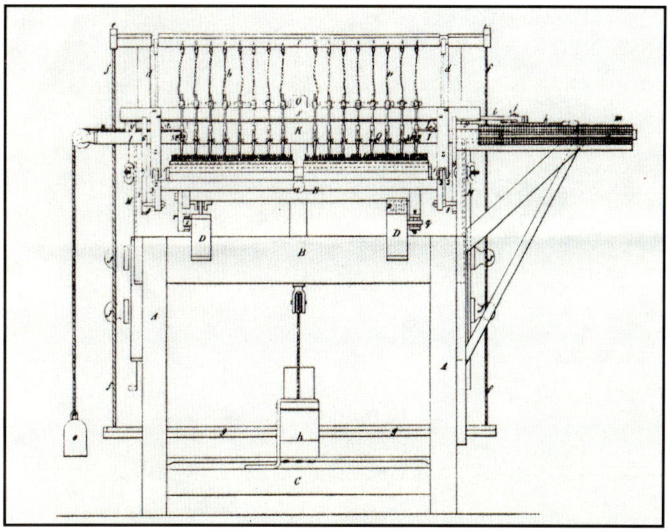

Schematic drawing of the apparatus for "machine painting," invented by W & A Smith, c. 1840.

Tartan Ware: A Form of Mauchline Ware

As was observed in Chapter Two, William and Andrew Smith were resourceful businessmen. When their first "main" product (snuff boxes) started to decline, they quickly replaced it with another, and another, and another. Among these was Tartan Ware.

Seizing on the popularity of tartans, they started to produce tartan-decorated items (including snuff boxes, early on) by hand-painting the tartans. Obviously, this was expensive and slow to produce, and didn't fulfill their need for volume. In the early 1840s, the Smith Brothers invented a machine which printed the tartans onto paper, which was glued onto the object being decorated. The machine was nothing but ingenious, particularly for its time. The machine had a series of pens, each fed by a reservoir holding a differently coloured ink. The distance between each pen could be "hand-programmed" to replicate the different tartan setts. They called their process "machine painting." In 1850, they did some pretty meticulous research and published a book, *Authenticated Tartans of the Clans and Families of Scotland*, in which they printed 69 different tartans of various clans and a brief history of each. Each of these tartans is printed on heavy stock and glued onto the page. There is also a preface, entitled "The Scottish Gael," which provides a history of tartans and glimpses into Scottish history.

Once the machine had been invented, the Smiths started to produce Tartan Ware.

Any object that had appeared originally as Mauchline Ware was now also able to be produced in the Tartan Ware format. (See Chapter One) There were, however, some significant differences. When the tartan paper was applied to round objects (such as an egg shape containing sewing articles), it was necessary to cut the paper in such a fashion as to allow the tartan pattern, or sett, to be aligned properly. This dilemma was solved by hiding the join with black paint covered by a wavy gold-painted line. Each tartan was "named," by stamping the name in small gold letters on the black painted background. Another difference was that the nature of Tartan Ware lent itself to some new forms. For example, a set of books (frequently Sir Walter Scott's works), each with a different hard-board Tartan Ware cover in a Tartan Ware presentation box, boxed sets of Tartan Ware snuff boxes in different tartans, and so on.

The Smiths had available to them a number of very competent painters who were highly skilled in painting "in miniature." A number of Tartan Ware snuff boxes, needle cases, and other boxes can be found with exquisitely executed paintings. Often these involved country (generally Scottish) scenes, a dog or other animal (game-birds were favourites). Because of the varnish "overcoat" the colours have remained true over the 150 or so years they have been in existence, just as have those of the tartans themselves. Incidentally, some of the finest Victorian landscape painters learned their "trade" as painters of snuff-boxes.

Tartan Ware string holder in close-up. Note name "M'Pherson" in tiny, hand-applied gold letters sometimes done by children, and the wavy gold-painted lines to disguise the joins in the tartan. Truly meticulous work. *Photo by William B. Bradley*

Needle case in knife box configuration, in distinctive "Rob Roy" tartan, with hand-painted scene on lid of "Ben A' Ann," c. 1860, 2.25" h., $750

From left: Wall-pocket in "Stuart" tartan. Back is scalloped shield shape with hole to insert screw/nail to hang on wall. Hinged lid on half round box has grey/green/yellow/black floral decoration and verse "To a friend". Inside lid is label for "Anchor Cottons". Black painted bottom has two ball feet and extended back to allow for free-standing alternative use. 4.25" x 5" x 2.25". $850. Centre: Round, lift-off domed-lid dresser powder box, with black painted round foot and rim edge. In attractive "Victoria" tartan. 2.75" x 3.38" base dia. $485. Right: Large round string-holder in "McPherson" tartan. Globe shape, with twist-off top to replenish string supply. On three black-painted ball feet. 4" dia. $850.

As was true in the case of Mauchline Ware, the Smiths required their workforce to be perfectionists. This was perhaps even more critical in the case of Tartan Ware, where a very minor mistake would be obvious. Great care was taken in all aspects of the manufacturing and finishing. The varnish coating was a particular concern. If not properly applied, the tartan paper could be exposed and torn, and the beauty of the object compromised. Other manufacturers, in addition to the Smiths, produced Tartan Ware, but the bulk appear to be the Smiths' output. The production continued until about the early 1900s; after that, some lesser quality pieces were produced but are easily detected by the obvious lower quality of both production and finish.

Needle case in knife box configuration, in green "Leslie" tartan, with hand-painted dog on lid, c 1860, 2.25" h., $750. *Photo by William B. Bradley*

Truly a one-of-a-kind early table snuff box in hand-painted Black Watch tartan. Interior (not shown) divided into four foil-lined compartments. Lid is hinged to box with secret hinge. Near front lock on box, rim is stamped "C. Stiven & Sons, Box-Makers to Her Majesty" together with two royal ciphers. On lid is hand-painted scene of Balmoral with Royal family in foreground. Balmoral is shown in it's original configuration, pre- 1853, dating box to c. 1848 when Balmoral was first discovered by the Queen, 11.5" x 8.5", $15,000.

Tartan Ware also lends itself to additional decoration. Like Mauchline Ware, one sees transfers and photographic scenes. Also, perhaps unique to Tartan Ware, the use of transfers of statuary was done. Several different transfers can be found, most notably "The Orphans," "Emily and the White Doe of Roylston," and "Venus and Cupid." While very little of the ordinary Mauchline Ware is found in the form of furniture (other than the occasional piece of FernWare decorated items), large Tartan Ware pieces are found: tea tables, small chests, mirrors, and the like. These seldom appear on the market, there being far fewer of them in comparison to the large numbers of smaller pieces, such as stamp boxes and sewing items.

Lift-off lid on powder box in "Albert" tartan. On lid is affixed the transfer of a statue of a woman with child in crib. 3.5" h x 4" dia., $450. *Photo by William B. Bradley*

Round lift-off lid thread container in "Victoria" tartan. On lid is oval sepia photograph of "Queen's View, Loch Tummel". Inside are three thread posts, with three bone/ivory portals on side to pull out thread. 3" dia. x 3" h. $650.

Round, lift-off lid thread container in "McBeth" tartan. Inside lid is label for "Clark Threads", and four thread posts, with bone/ivory portals on side to pull out thread. On lid is large vertical oval picture transfer, with title beneath "Sir Walter Scott Centenary, born 15 Aug 1771, died 21 Sept 1832", 4" dia. x 2.25" h. $485.

Values Today

Until a time in the early 1990s, Tartan Ware was more-or-less a "reasonably" priced collectible, selling usually for about twice the price of Mauchline Ware. As the century concluded, however, Tartan Ware was selling for three to four times that of a comparable Mauchline Ware piece, and in some cases of rare items, even more. Tartan Ware napkin rings, for example, sell for $60-80, compared to Mauchline ones at $20-30. Early hand-painted Tartan Ware snuff or other boxes can run $500 and up. Tartan Ware stamp boxes, card boxes, needle cases, small books, and the like are generally in the $250-750 range. A very large, rare Tartan Ware piece can easily go into the low thousands of dollars today.

As you can now discern, Tartan Ware had been "discovered" and, inevitably, prices rose. That fact has made it possible for the production of "fakes." Once a price gets to a certain point, reproduction is profitable for fakers. Some of the items being reproduced today include: picture frames, mirrors, and tea caddies. In the case of the tea caddies, the fakers are particularly clever, since they utilize old tea caddies covered with tartan paper. High-speed colour copiers make tartan paper difficult to differentiate from the real thing. Two possible clues, however: if the edge of the paper can be lifted a fraction of an inch and appears to be a rather new pure white, *beware*. Also, the new individual letters of the little gold name of the tartan, if rubbed with the finger, may be felt. Often fakers will add letters on top of the varnish. In old pieces the names were always added before the varnish was applied and they cannot be felt with the finger. Here are two good rules to follow: first, if the piece is "too good to be true," it probably is; second, buy only from a reputable dealer. Even he may occasionally be fooled, but at least he will refund your purchase price if the item turns out to be "not right."

A selection of Tartan Ware sewing articles. Front left: double-ended pincushion in "McPherson" tartan, 1.5" l., $425. Front right: Round pincushion in disc shape in "McLean" tartan. 1.38" dia., $285. Back row, from left: a compendium, consisting (from the top) of pincushion, retractable tape measure and waxer in "Caledonia" tartan. 2.38" h., $625. Large pincushion on black base in "McLean" tartan. Top lifts off for pin storage, 2.5" h. $425. Round pincushion on black base in "McBeth" tartan, 1" h., $285. *Photo by William B. Bradley*

From left: Round vertical match container "go-to-bed" in shape of military drum, with alternating panels of "Prince Charlie" (red) and "Gordon" (green) tartans. Top lifts off to access match storage, ivory finial to insert lit match; striker surface to bottom of box. 2.13" h. x 2.13" dia. $565. Round pin or sweetmeat dish on black-painted pedestal base. Note carefully joined tartan segments! 3" dia. x 2" h. $475.

Round milk-pail or wash-tub shaped pin-cushion, with side "carry-handles", in green "Gordon" tartan, with elaborate gold-embellished strapping. Original pin-cushion stuffing in place. 2.25" top dia. x 2.25"h. $625.

More small sewing articles. Front row, from left: Retractable tape measure in shape of crown, in "Stuart" tartan. 1.5" h., $525. Retractable tape measure in the shape of a beehive on round foot in "Caledonia" tartan, 1.5" h., $525. Barrel-shaped needle holder with lift-off lid, in "McLean" tartan, 1.75", $425. Rear, from left: Sewing egg with thimble, thread and needle storage on interior post, in "McPherson" tartan, 2' l., $625. Retractable tape measure in "Rob Roy" tartan and painted black edges, in form of butter churn. 2" h., $425. Bottle-shaped sewing kit with thread and needle interior storage, in "McBeth" tartan, 2.5" h., $425. Ring-box shaped hinged-lid thimble container in "McPherson" tartan. 1.5" h., $425. *Photo by William B. Bradley*

Urn-shaped match container "go-to-bed". Top lifts off to access matches, striker on bottom; ivory finial to hold lit match on top. "Hay" tartan with very elaborate gold embellishments and black-painted pedestal base. 3.25" h. x 1.75" top dia. $625.

From left: Thread holder/pin cushion on black pedestal base. At top is blue plush pin cushion which lifts off to access thread area. Thread pulls out from side ivory/bone portal. 3.5" h. x 1.5" dia. $485. Hexagonal hinged-lid thread container. Inside are three posts for spools, with side portals of ivory/bone to pull out threads. Inside lid is label for "Kerr's Threads". 3" x 2.75" across lid, x 2" h. $525.

A variety of thread boxes. Front row, from left: Lift-off lid round thread box in "Prince Charlie" tartan. On lid is sepia photo of "Lake View, United States Hotel, Saratoga"; around sides are ivory portals for thread, 2.25" h. x 4" dia., $425. Unusually shaped, oval hinged-lid thread box in "Stuart" tartan, with 6 ivory portals for thread. Inside lid is perfect "Clark Threads" label in colour. 5" dia., $750. Lift-off lid round thread box in colourful "McDonald" tartan, with 6 ivory portals for thread, 2.5" h. x 4" dia., $525. Rear, from left: Rectangular hinged-lid thread box in "Stuart" tartan with affixed transfer on lid of "St. John & The Lamb". Inside is fitted blue cardboard sleeve for storage of multiple rolls of thread. 7.5" x 3.5", $575. Round lift-off lid thread box in "McDuff" tartan, On lid is small ivory portal for thread, and small label indicating thread size. Inside lid is label for "Clark & Co" 2.75" h. x 3.25" dia., $525. *Photo by William B. Bradley*

Rectangular box, with elaborately scalloped ends in "McLean" tartan. Elaborately decorated around edges with gold painted embellishments. Lift-off lid accesses interior which is lined with red velvet. Decorated, front and back, with two gold "sunbursts". Catch release to front. On lip of box is legend "The Royal Exhibition Prize Medal Awarded to W&A Smith, Mauchline". Lid appears to have been hinged in past. Originally, possibly a tea caddy. 8" x 3.75" x 4". $2250.

Hinged-lid double-card box in "Caledonia" tartan, with card fan on domed lid. Inside is space for two decks, plus central covered section for storage of counters/chips. This storage area is accessed by interior lift-off lid in matching tartan. 7.25" x 4.25" x 1.75". $1350.

Front: Crochet hook, with steel impliment and Tartan Ware handle in "Prince Charlie" tartan. 4.5", $385. Back, from left: Patented darning mushroom with tartan facings, 4.75" l. x 2.25" mushroom dia., $385. Folding "book" needle case in "Stuart" tartan, with ivory bodkin in side-sleeve to act as closure. 2.5" x 3.5", $425. Folding "book" needle case in "McIntosh" tartan. Inside has scalloped tartan-edged storage for different size needles identified in gold numerals, 5" x 1.75", $425. *Photo by William B. Bradley*

A selection of Tartan Ware napkin rings, including: "McBeth," "Caledonia," "McLean," "MacFarlane," "Cameron," "Fraser," "Gordon," "McPherson," and "McFarlane," generally 2" x 1", priced from $60-80. *Photo by William B. Bradley*

A Tartan Ware variety. Front, from left: (top) Small, side-pinned hinged-lid nib box in "Caledonia" tartan, 2.38" x 1.25", $325. (under) Slip-off top card case in "Prince Charlie" tartan, 2" x 4", $385. Round, open-top barrel container for matches. Black painted interior, exterior in "McDuff". 2.5" h. x 2" dia., $425. Round lift-off top box for stamps in "Stuart" tartan. On lid is large Queen Victoria "penny red" stamp. 1.75" dia. x .5" h., $325. Round drum-shaped watch container, lift-off lid with ivory "pull". Exterior in alternating diamond-shaped panels of "Prince Charlie and 42nd or Sutherland" tartans. 2.25" dia. x 2.25" h., $625. Rear, from left: String-holder in "McPherson" tartan, and mounted on three black-painted ball feet. 4" dia., $875. Hanging wall-pocket, with optional-use three black ball feet, in "Stuart" tartan. Hinged lid to access, with "Anchor" cotton label inside lid. On lid exterior is elaborate floral decoration and legend "To a friend" 4.25" x 5" h., $925. *Photo by William B. Bradley*

Further Tartan Ware varieties: Front, from left: Folding pen-knife for opening letters. Ivory blade, "McPherson" tartan exterior. 4"., $450. (immediately above) Child's parasol handle in "McKenzie" tartan, 5.5 long, $525. Pair of bezique counters, each 3" x 2", $325. Middle row, from left: Round pin tray in "Prince Charlie" tartan, on black pedestal base, 2" h. x 3" dia., $525. Pair of glove stretchers in "McBeth" tartan, 7" l., $425. Pocket spectacle case, with flip-open end in "McBeth" tartan, 6" x 1.5", $495. Cribbage board in "Caledonia" tartan, with peg storage behind brass-end pins. 8" x 2.25", $625. Back row, from left: Eggcup in "McBeth" tartan, 2.75" h., $395. Large double card box in "Caledonia" tartan; centre compartment for pencils, etc., card "fan" on lid, 7.25" x 4.25", $1350. *Photo by William B. Bradley*

A selection of Tartan Ware smoking items: Front, from left: Vertical "go-to-bed" in "Caledonia" tartan, on painted black foot, 2.75" h. x 1.88" dia., $425. (bottom). Fine & rare pocket cigar case with slip-off lid in "Black Watch" tartan. Interior has four foil-lined slots and impressed legend "Stiven Laurencekirk," 5.5" x 2.88", $1250. (top) Small go-to-bed in "Robertson" tartan, 1.5" h., $225. Rear: Large foil-lined cigar case with pull-off top in "Stuart" tartan, 5.5" x 2.75", $825. *Photo by William B. Bradley*

As we observed in Chapter Two, Mauchline Ware collectors (and the same applies to Tartan Ware collectors), can decide to "specialize" in their collecting habits. For example, we have clients who collect solely sewing things, or tobacco-related items, or books, or egg cups or "shapes," and so on. In this regard, Tartan Ware lends another dimension: some collect only items with a certain clan name, such as all Gordon, or all McDuff, and so on, particularly if they are of Scottish ancestry of that name. My wife and I, for example, collect only Tartan Ware in the Munro tartan. This has created a hugh problem. After 15 years, we have found only three pieces in Munro; and we have four grandchildren.

Others collect only the "green" tartans. Far fewer tartans in hues of green were produced, compared to the "red" tartans (the ratio is about 1:8). Having said that, I have to admit that we don't really know the exact ratio. The general opinion is that the Smith's did not produce items in all 69 tartans shown in their book, how many they did of each (and which ones) is not known, for all the records went up in a 1933 fire. Tartan Ware collecting is a never-ending quest. You will never know when your specialized collecting area is complete.

---

[1]Hugh Cheape, *Tartan, The Highland Habit*, Edinburgh, The National Museums of Scotland, 1991, Pg 53-54.
[2]Ibid, Pg 58.

Bibliography

Cheape, Hugh, *Tartan, The Highland Habit*, Edinburgh, The National Museums of Scotland, 1991.

Grant, Neil, *Scottish Clans and Tartans*, Crescent Books, New York, 1987.

The Journal of The Mauchline Ware Collectors Club, Romsey, England, The Mauchlineware Collectors Club, 1986-2003.

Von Furstenberg, Princess Ira, *Tartanware, Souvenirs from Scotland*, London, Pavilion Books, Limited, 1996.

Way of Plean, George and Romilly Squire, *Scottish Clan and Family Encyclopedia*, New York, Barnes and Noble, 1998.

Tartan Ware desk items: From left: Book *Songs of Robert Burns*, red leather spine and tartan covers in "Prince Charlie" tartan, 133 pages, 2.75" x 4.5", $365. Pen tray, black painted exterior, "McBeth" tartan, 9" l., $850. Page-turner, sword-shape, in "Stuart" tartan, 9.5" l., $425. Letter-opener in "Prince Charlie" tartan, 7" l., $225. Straight pen with nib and tartan handle, 7.5", $325. Desk-box for nibs, etc., in "Clan Stuart" tartan. Lid has ivory pull, two interior divisions. 4.5" x 2", $650. Pencil case with slip-off top in "Prince Charlie" tartan. 7.75" l., x 1.75" dia., $425. Large vertical oval, slip-off top pencil case in "Caledonia" tartan 8" x 1.75", $950. *Photo by William B. Bradley*

Spectacular folding gameboard in alternating tartans of "Stuart" and "42nd" tartans. In form of a double book, with sides painted to resemble book pages. When opened up, there is a gold-tooled leather backgammon board. When book is laid out "flat" with the backgammon board underneath, the alternating 1.5" x 1.5" squares of tartan form a chessboard. 15.5" x 10.5" on each side x 3" thick. $7500

Game-board shown open to reveal backgammon board.

Rare standing obelisk thermometer with ivory scale and top ivory finial. Below is green plush padded receptacle for pocket-watch, flanked by decorated tartan pillars. All tartan is "Stuart". Base is oval in shape, with stud drawer above black-painted foot. Base is 5.5" x 4", thermometer and watch stand 12" h., $5000

Hinged game box in "Stuart" tartan, with interior divided into four sections. Box measures 5.25" x 3.38" x 2.5". One hundred and twenty Tartan Ware game counters are in box. Each is approximately .15" thick, and are in three different configurations as shown. $5000.

Chapter Four

Dirks and Sgian Dubhs

What Exactly Are They, You Ask?

Basically, and simply stated, they're knives. As you will recall from Chapter One, Scotland had a thousand plus years of violence, in which knives, swords and guns had a prominent part in daily life. No wonder then, that they continue, today, to be part of the Scottish scene, (and costume).

A dirk is a long knife, shaped much like a bayonet, worn on the hip, and suspended from the belt. Generally, the blade measures about 11 inches, with the grip adding another 6 inches, so the overall length is approximately 17-18 inches. The blade is protected by a scabbard.

A *sgian dubh* (pronounced "skean doo") is a small knife, also in a protective sheath, that is worn inside the top of the sock when wearing a kilt. The blade measures about 2-4 inches, and with the hilt, the overall length is about 7-9 inches. The name is spelled several different ways (*skean dhu*, for one) but the preferred spelling appears to be *sgian dubh.* The name in Gaelic literally means "black knife" (*sgian* for knife, *dubh* for black).

Three very early dirks. Top: wood hilt with interlace carving, 10" blade, c. 1650, $3500. Centre: brass hilted dirk, dated 1707, the date of the English-Scottish union, with "Prosperity to Schotland" motto on 10.5" blade, $4500. Bottom: Brass-mounted dirk with carved wood hilt, 10.5" blade, c. 1720, $3000. *Courtesy of James D. Forman*

History and origin

It would appear that the dirk has evolved into it's present form from a knife which was similarly shaped and called a *ballock* (also spelled *balloch*) knife. *Ballock* knives had been in existence for hundreds of years (in the days of body armour), and were basically stabbing weapons, with a pointed end and generally a triangular profile of the blade itself. Just below the grip (usually made of hardwood), two short "arms" came out to protect the hand. It was usually worn in a leather scabbard, hanging from the girdle (belt), in front of the body. Evidence appears on tombstones of such weapons in the 14th and 15th centuries, indicating that it was a weapon used by the nobility. As the days of armour drew to a close in the 16th century, the *ballock* knife started to take on a different character. A thinner blade, with a single sharpened edge (later both edges) became the norm, since it could function not only as a weapon, but as a hunting tool as well.

More evidence of the metamorphosis of the dirk is evident in 17th and 18th century portraits, in which the weapon appears in a leather sheath, with a small "byknife," a side-by-side knife and fork, or a pair of knives. Another development in this period was the use of cut-down sword-blades (a demonstration of good Scottish frugality, perhaps?). These were often of European origin, with well-tempered steel, less subject to damage at an inappropriate moment.

A short digression into the use of the dirk as a fighting weapon is appropriate. As you will recall from Chapter One, the highlanders were greatly feared for their downhill, all-out, screaming charge with claymores and dirks. In these attacks, the claymore would normally be wielded in the right hand, with the left hand holding a shield, called a *targe* (originally "*target*"). This was a round, wood and leather object, with brass studs and a 10 inch brass spike at the centre, with the left arm looped through a sling on the back to keep it erect in front of the body. In the left hand, behind the *targe*, was the dirk, with the blade protruding below and to the side of the *targe* to be used as a slicing/stabbing weapon in close combat. This era of the dirk as a true fighting weapon came to an end with the defeat at Culloden; from then on it was solely a decorative item, used both by the highland regiments and civilians, details of which will be discussed shortly.

The *sgian dubh*'s origin is a matter of some dispute. One possible explanation is that it evolved from a 17th and 18th century Scottish armpit dagger called a *sgian achlais*, which was about the same size and configuration. When entering into a friendly household, this weapon would be "un-concealed" by putting it into the top of the stocking. Another (and perhaps the more likely theory), is that it evolved from the use of the combination *ballock* knife (for butchering deer in the field) and the smaller bi-knife (for skinning purposes). In the process of skinning, the *ghillie* (game-keeper or servant) would perhaps stick the smaller bi-knife in the stocking-top to keep it readily available for use. It wasn't until the early part of the 19th century that we see portraits of gentlemen with *sgian dubhs*, until that time it appears to have been solely a utilitarian tool for field-skinning and other hunting use, principally by servants charged with that task, rather than as a weapon or a decorative accessory by noblemen.

From the early to the modern in *sgian dubhs*. Top: Early (c. 1820) functional *sgian dubh* with leather sheath, 2.5" blade and wood hilt carved in inter-lace pattern, $500. Centre: Wood hilted *sgian dubh*, notched back, 3" blade, c. 1810, $450. Bottom: 20th century *sgian dubh* by J. Hay, Edinburgh, 4.5" blade, $450. *Courtesy of James D. Forman*

The Dirk and *Sgian dubh* in 19th and 20th century Scotland

Until the early part of the 19th century, all members of highland regiments carried dirks, officers and privates alike. Gradually, the dirk became an officer's accouterment, and increasingly more of a "dress" item. Different regiments adopted different styles of dirks, generally silver mounted, and with distinctive regimental crests or badges. The grip became more ornate; often the shape was less utilitarian, carved in the image of a thistle or in a baluster configuration. Frequently the wood grip (ebony, boxwood, oak, or mahogany) was carved with Celtic inter-lace or basket-weave designs, and studded with silver or brass nails. At the top of the grip on the pommel typically would be a silver cover, often inlaid with an agate, a cut citrine or a cairngorm (a form of Scottish quartz from the Cairngorm mountains of central Scotland, with colours ranging from deep orange to smoky-gray). The sheath, still of leather (usually black), was strengthened with a shaped wood core, and the small bi-knife and fork housed in separate compartments vertically on the front of the sheath. Sometimes these auxiliary items were attached to the sheath with small silver chains, since they tended to slip out and get lost. These pieces also were decorated at the top of their pommels with a matching citrine or cairngorm, again silver-mounted. Regimental pipe-bands would be equipped with piper's dirks. These were relatively plain, with no auxiliary knife and fork, white metal fittings with embossed thistles, and blades acid-etched with thistles.

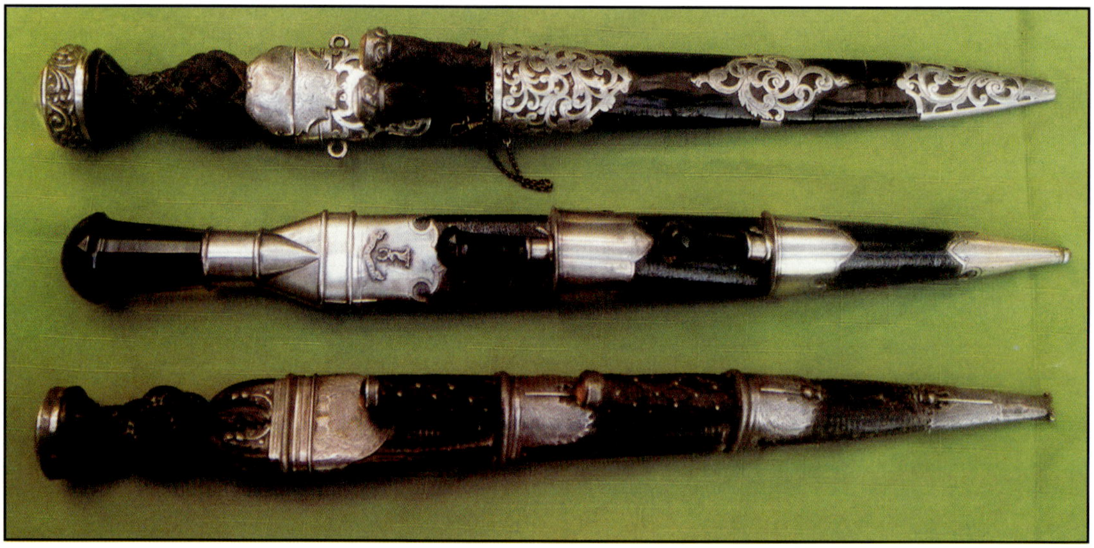

Top: Silver mounted Victorian dirk with side-mounted bi-knife and bi-fork, with safety chains. 11.5" blade, $2500. Centre: Rare, silver-mounted dress dirk, with the hilt on main blade and the bi-knife and bi-fork formed of cut dark smoky cairngorms, by Hamilton & Inches, Edinburgh, hallmarked 1913. 11.25" blade. $4500. Bottom: Baluster turned hilt on silver mounted dirk, c. 1810, $3500. *Courtesy of James D. Forman*

Three regimental dirks. Top: Pitlochry Highlanders, 12.5" blade, $2000. Centre: Gilt finished dirk for the 78th Highlanders (The Ross-shire Buffs), $3500. Bottom: Silver-mounted dirk for The Argyll & Sutherland Highlanders, blade by Wilkinson Sword Co., hallmarked 1970, 11.5" blade, $2000. *Courtesy of James D. Forman*

As the century wore on, the adornment process increased in ever spiraling increments. While military dirks were somewhat constrained by regulation, the civilian "market" knew no such bounds, and "bound" it did. As noted at the start of Chapter Three, King George set the early stage, aided and abetted later on by Queen Victoria. The silver mounts on dirks, executed by skilled silversmith craftsmen in Edinburgh (and later Glasgow), were elaborately embossed or chased in Celtic mythological designs (sea serpents and monsters), or Celtic geometric patterns. The stones at the top of the silver pommels became larger and larger. Some even appeared with hinged silver lids to access a small supply of snuff. Later, silver turned into gold, gold-mounted dirks appearing in the fashionable salons of the late Victorian era. Wood grips were replaced by ivory ones, studded with silver-mounted jewel studs. The "ultimate", perhaps, were the dirks with grips made entirely of carved agate or cairngorms, with elaborately chased silver mounts.

Matching officer's dirk and *sgian dubh* in gold-washed brass, to The Queen's Own Cameron Highlanders, with matched cut cairngorm stones. By Kirkwood of Edinburgh. Dirk is 17" overall, and *sgian dubh*, 7". 20th c., $3500.

Top: Ivory hilted dirk and *sgian dubh* (bottom of picture), both by R. W. Forsyth of Edinburgh, hallmarked silver, 1928, $6500. Second from top: ivory-hilted *sgian dubh*, 8" overall, $850. Second from bottom: Ivory-hilted dirk, late Victorian, $6000. *Courtesy of James D. Forman*

One of the foremost authorities on the dirk and *sgian dubh*, James Forman in his definitive booklet *The Scottish Dirk* notes:

> As late as 1915, one prominent figure still imagined a combat role for the dirk. John MacDonald, Lord Justice Clerk for Scotland wrote in the Times of London on November 29th, "Everything points to the advisability of a short knife or dirk being at instant command when the jump into the trench is made. And this not for thrusting forward as in striking a blow, but for backhanded action, the arm being swung with the blade protecting.
>
> The Lord Justice was dreaming old, old dreams in a world of flame throwers and phosgene gas. Specialized trench knives may have done more bloody work than puncturing cans of soup, but there is no evidence that the be-jewelled dirk of the Highland ball or the regimental parade ground ever made it into the trenches[1]

The *sgian dubh* underwent a parallel course as the dirk, from simple utilitarian form to elaborate adornment. Initially, it was difficult to entice the officers in highland regiments to adopt the *sgian dubh* (they considered it to be a servant's tool). Later, it became "matched" to the dirk, with similar mounts and regimental designations or badges. Regimental *sgian dubhs* were produced in silver, brass or gilt to match the dirk, with similar fittings of cairngorms (or sometimes glass with coloured foil-backing) at pommel top. Unlike the dirk, the *sgian dubh* became a regular part of the private's attire in some kilted highland regiments. Despite the widely held theory that it was once used as a fighting weapon, there seems to be no firm evidence to that effect.

In the case of Scottish civilian use, the *sgian dubh* became widely accepted in the countryside. In the field, it's use continued as a skinning and general utility knife, and was frequently found with deer antler handles, brown or black sheaths and simple silver, brass or white metal mounts. This, then, became the norm for daytime use. Like the military's aggrandizement of the dirk, the civilian version of the sgian dubh followed the same pattern. Silver mounts, elaborately pierced, fretted, embossed or chased with celtic designs, plus cut cairngorms on the pommel transformed a homely knife into male jewellery.

In the case of both military and civilian versions, dirks and *sgian dubs* began to appear in matched boxed sets, usually velvet fitted interiors, with the owner's name on an ivory label on the lid. These, even by the value of the currency of the day, were expensive articles, affordable only by the very wealthy. But the value of such a rare item today has soared. For example, one set, with royal provenance sold in 1987 for over $400,000. Queen Victoria had boxed sets made for her ghillies which contained silver-mounted dirks, *sgian dubhs*, plaid brooches, shoe buckles, kilt buttons and belt buckles. In about 1990, one of these was on offer at a Scottish antique dealer's shop for £18,000. (Then about $36,000; now probably valued at well over $75,000). Obviously, few of these ever come to market, they're passed down through the family as a "memory of Balmorality".

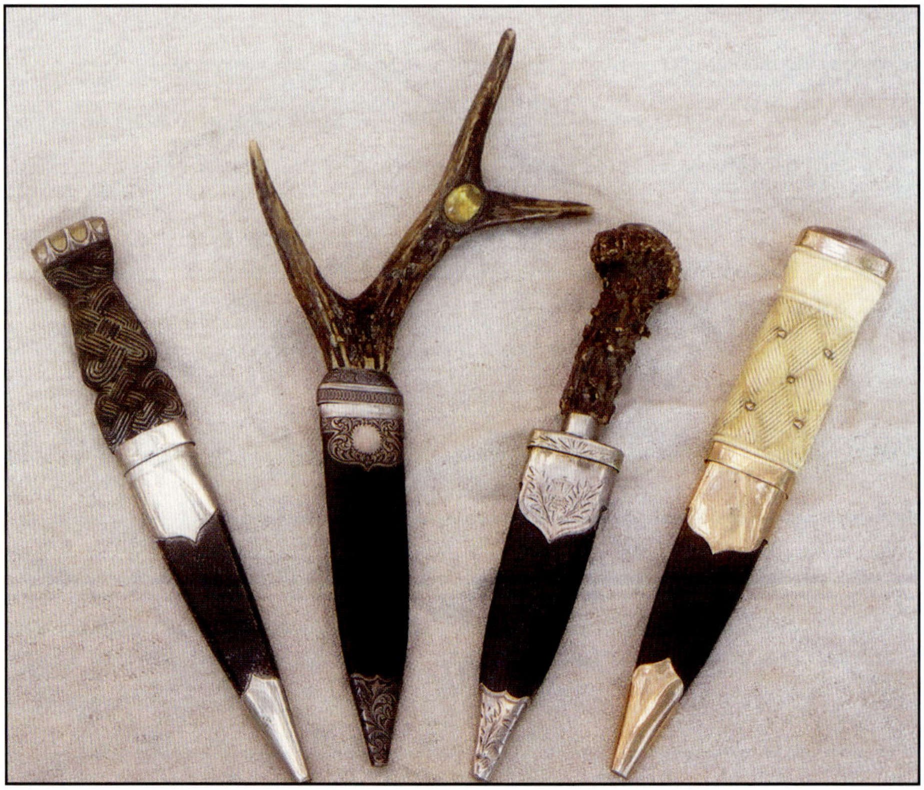

A range of *sgian dubhs*. From the left: Silver-mounted 20th c. *sgian dubh*, by Wilkinson Sword Co, $650. Ladies belt-hanging, silver-mounted *sgian dubh* with roe deer horn hilt, $600. Silver-mounted *sgian dubh* with stag horn hilt, $500. 20th c. gold-mounted, ivory-hilt *sgian dubh*, $1500. (All blades approx. 4"). *Courtesy of James D. Forman*

Close-up of blade in *sgian dubh* pictured above, with maker's stamp on blade.

Sgian dubh with brown leather sheath and wood hilt carved with inter-lace design. Silver mounts, with plain silver knob at top. Early 20th c., $750.

Close-up view of hallmarks: "F&M" for Ferguson & McBean, and "Invs" the town mark for Inverness. At centre (barely visible) is the unusual symbol for Inverness hallmarked silver, a dromedary. Why a camel? No one seems to know.

Two military sgian dubhs. From left: Silver-mounted sgian dubh to "The Argyll & Sutherland Highlanders". Ebony handle with silver studs. Affixed to handle is regimental emblem of coronet over reversed cipher of Princess Louise (The Regiment having attended her at her wedding to The Duke of Argyll). Greek key design on handle silver mounts, celtic serpent & inter-lacing on sheath. Pale cairngorm at top of pommel. Stamped on back of sheath silver mount is legend "Anderson & Sons, George Street, Edinburgh". Hallmarked, Edinburgh 1915. One of the few silver regimental sgian dubs for "other ranks", and arguably the most attractive. 7.5". $900. Brass gilt sgian dubh for the "Black Watch Highlanders". African blackwood handle with brass studs. Cut cairngorm mounted at top of pommel. Blade has notched back, single fuller. 7.5". $675.

The young members of society were by no means neglected when it came to these male adornments. Every self-respecting Victorian child had to be "just like Daddy". *Sgian dubhs* and dirks appeared in smaller scaled versions for the younger set, and they were very faithful replicas of the "real thing", with one significant modification. The child's version generally had no blades in either item. Sometimes a wooden blade would be found, but more often than not, the dirk and *sgian dubh* was a one-piece, non-lethal toy. Several surviving portraits of young Victorians show these junior versions. (They were not, as one person advised at a recent antique show, a "salesman's sample.")

For the last 150 years, there has been a steady diminution/amalgamation of the Scottish regiments, and with it, the number of distinctively different regimental dirks and *sgain dubhs* has also been reduced. A wave of amalgamations took place in 1881, another in 1960, and a further one in the late 20th century. As in the case of any antique "collectible", this decrease in supply can only drive up the prices of those remaining available to the market. So, if you're sitting on a collection of Scottish military dirks, just hang on, and you'll do just fine.

Values Today

The last ten years demonstrates the trend. In early 1990, a decent Scottish military dirk, c. 1890 would sell for $300-500. A military *sgian dubh* was in the region of $100-250. Today, the prices are $1500-2500 and $500-1000, respectively. "Typical" (if there is such a thing) Victorian civilian silver-mounted three-piece dirks and *sgian dubhs* have had the same sort of appreciation, but command values perhaps a quarter more than their military counterparts. Rarer items with ivory or elaborate cairngorm adornments would run up to twice the "normal" price. On the other hand, a person with a "modest" budget can find modern replica pieces, with plastic handles, pewter or sheet-silver decoration and foil stones in tourist shops for $300-800 for a dirk and about $100-300 for a *sgian dubh*. (Obviously, these are for wearing, rather than as collectibles.). In an article in *The Highlander*, author Joe D. Huddleston made an interesting comment:

> Like the kilt, the dirk is unique in western culture. Although it comes in an infinite variety, it has always been recognizable as a Scottish Dirk. It differs from other large sheath knives in that it has been in continuous use and wear since the early 1600s. After all, where else in western society is it considered high-fashion to stroll into a formal dinner dance wearing a knife with a 13-inch blade?[2]

Two questions which we are asked frequently at shows are: "Where can I look for an antique dirk or *sgian dubh*?" and "Are there any fakes about?" In addition to the occasional dirk or *sgian dubh* which may crop up at an estate

An assembly of a child's dirk (no blades), a functional sporran with white horse-hair, and a child's *sgian dubh* (no blade). All three are late Victorian, mounted on tartan, with a handcarved Scottish pine shadowbox frame entitled "Just Like Daddy's," $750.

sale (check copies of the *Maine Antique Digest* or similar trade journal), sometimes they're available at gun or knife shows. There are also on-line auctions such as "e-Bay"®, (subject to the usual caveats of "long-distance" buying). One or two British specialists have auctions two or three times a year, and offer elaborate full-colour catalogues (Wallis and Wallis, and Bosley's come to mind). As to "fakes," I've never run across one, but I would raise one caution. A "Victorian, Queen's crown, piper's dirk" (and priced as such) may be a more recent Indian-made piece. Get an expert's advice to make sure.

There are many silver-mounted dirks and *sgian dubhs* that are not "hallmarked." While silver hallmarks are often found on silver mounts, their absence does not necessarily mean that they are not made of silver. Obviously, one has to be able to distinguish, from the look, between silverplate and silver. When marks are present, a useful little portable reference book is available, *English Silver Hall-Marks* by Judith Banister (see bibliography following).

Further, one cannot underestimate the value of seeing the "real thing." If on vacation in Scotland (an experience not to be missed), visit the Black Watch Museum in Perth or other regimental museums elsewhere in the country, The National Portrait Gallery of Scotland, or The National Museum of Antiquities of Scotland, both in Edinburgh.

Finally, lest I be called on the carpet for an embarrassing omission, I should quickly point out that dirks and *sgian dubhs*, while clearly native to Scotland, are also in use in other countries in which the kilt is worn. Canadian and Indian regiments, which served the Empire in days gone by, proudly wore old Scotia's finery, and continue, in the case of the former, to this day. And, let's not forget the literally hundreds of members of bagpipe bands around the world. If you recall, in Chapter One, we pointed out that one of Scotland's major "exports" were her people and their skills. One early 20th century commentator, whose name has long passed into history, observed that "the further away from his homeland that a Scot travels, the more Scottish he becomes." May the traditions continue.

---

[1]James D. Forman. *The Scottish Dirk*, Alexandria Bay, New York, Museum Restoration Service, 1991, pg 50.
[2]Joe D. Huddleston. *The Scottish Dirk*, Kansas City, Missouri, The Highlander, Mar/Apr 1997, pg 22.

Bibliography

Banister, Jane, *English Silver Hall-Marks*, London, England, W. Foulsham and Co. Ltd., 1990.

Forman, James D. *The Scottish Dirk*, Alexandria Bay, New York, Museum Restoration Service, 1991, pg 50.

Forman, James D, *Sgian Dubh: Fact and Fancy*, Lincoln, R.I., Man At Arms, Jan/Feb 1985.

Forman, James D., *Evolution of The Scottish Dirk*, Lincoln, R.I.,Man At Arms, Mar/Apr 1982.

Huddleston, Joe D. *The Scottish Dirk*, Kansas City, Missouri, The Highlander, Mar/Apr 1997, pg 22.

Huddleston, Joe D., *The Sgian Dubh*, Kansas City, Mo., The Highlander, Nov 1996, pg 10.

Wood, Stephen, *The Scottish Soldier*, Edinburgh, Scotland, Archive Publications, Ltd, in association with The National Museums of Scotland, 1987.

Chapter Five

Militaria

Sporrans

Military sporrans, literally, come in all shapes and sizes. Similar to the dirk and the *sgian dubh* as detailed in the preceding chapter, each regiment "personalized" their sporrans to conform with the rest of their uniform, usually with their regimental badge or other identifying devices, but also with distinctive differences in style and colour.

First, however, is a short primer on sporrans, for those to whom this is a new word.

A sporran is the pouch-like article of clothing that hangs from the belt on the front of the kilt. The vast majority have a leather pouch, faced with horse-hair (white, gray or black), and often a series of 2 to 6 round or elongated tassels of contrasting horse-hair suspended from metal cones, which are in turn, attached to the sporran with small chains. At the top of the sporran is a metal piece, called the cantle. The cantle can be curved or squared-off at the top. The dimensions vary widely, but a rough guide would be to say that the cantle measures about 6" across by 3" deep, and the length of the sporran from cantle-top to bottom of hair about 16"-18". The sporran has a practical, as well as a decorative use, since most have access to an internal storage area for money, handkerchief, car-keys or whatever. Sometimes there's a release button at the top of the cantle to pop it open, in other cases access is achieved by lifting a leather flap on the back of the sporran pouch. The sporran is held in place by a chain-linked metal/leather belt attached to the back of the purse, looped through two loops on either side of the kilt at the waist, and fastened in the middle of the back. (The sporran is not only a useful article, it is an essential one, there being no pockets in a kilt.)

Depending on the regiment, the metal in the cantle and cones can be silver, silver-plate, white metal, or brass. Often, enlisted ranks have a base metal, while officers have silver. Frequently the cantles are elaborately decorated with repoussé work of thistles and foliage. Other cantles have a metal surround and a facing of patent leather-like material. Officer's sporrans frequently have a separate set of "evening-wear" tassels, cones and chains, where the tassels are formed of twisted gold bullion which are used in replacement of the regular "day-time" ones.

A collection of Scottish sporrans can make a most attractive display, either in glass-fronted cases or just hanging on a den wall. The variety in style, shape and colour is extensive, when you consider that, at the height of the "Empire", there were probably close to 25 Scottish regiments and volunteer battalions, all with their own ideas of how a sporran should look. Prices for antique sporrans usually are in the $500 to $1000 range. As with any other collectible, however, the rarer items command the top prices. A fine, silver-mounted officer's regimental sporran with name identification, c.1880, could easily run $2500. For sources, please refer back to Chapter Four on dirks and *sgian dubhs*.

Print, hand-coloured, of piper in front of Edinburgh Castle. Published by William Miller, Albermarle Street, London, Jan 1 1805. Later in book *Costumes of Great Britain*, as #60 in series, by W. H. Pyne, 1809. 9" x 12", matted & framed to 15.5" x 19". $525.

Piper's sporran to The Argyll & Sutherland Highlanders, 20th c. Brown horsehair, black tails, gilded cantle with white metal Regimental insignia affixed. $850

Piper's sporran to The Black Watch Highlanders. White horsehair with black tassels and cones. Gilt cantle with St Andrew's cross at centre. 20th c. $950

Three sporrans. Top: Regimental sporran to Royal Scots. White horsehair with black tassels, white metal cantle with black leather centre. Stamped 1939, Glasgow. $750. Lower left: Very early sporran, c. 1700. Brown leather pouch, brass cantle. $3000. Lower right: Unmarked, 20th c. silver-plate cantle, white horsehair and black tails. $300. *Courtesy of James D. Forman*

Plaid Brooches, Belt Buckles, and Shoulder-belt Plates

One of the more distinctive elements of Scottish kilted soldiers is their plaid brooch. Not all kilted regiments wear a plaid; in some regiments only the band members do. The plaid, in a tartan matched to that of the kilt, is a length of fabric attached to the back of the waist, and drawn through the epaulet on the left shoulder. To keep this in place, a round metal brooch is attached to the jacket. These plaid brooches generally measure about 3" in diameter, can be silver, silver-plate, or brass (to match the other accouterments such as the sporran, dirks, etc). Again, they are distinctive to the regiment in terms of both design and content. Some have large cut cairngorms or foil-backed glass at the centre. Frequently they are decorated with repoussé thistles and foliage; others have the regimental badge affixed, battle honours listed, and so on. Within the regiment, plaid brooches can differ in size and execution according to the wearer's rank. Generally, the plaid brooches worn by pipe-majors and drum-majors were more "magnificent" than those of the ordinary piper or "other rank". Needless to say, the officer's ones were always fancier than that of anyone else.

Belt-buckles and shoulder-belt plate buckles usually followed along in style with the plaid brooch and the other pieces; however, being somewhat more utilitarian in nature, they did not get "fancied-up" with cairngorms and the like. Once again, they were different between each regiment, so the "collectible range" is extensive. Plaid brooches, with a "bit of age" on them, range from roughly $100 (for the plain white metal variety), to about $1000 for an unusual one. Rare, silver-mounted, hallmarked pieces from the 1800s would sell for $1500 and UP. Belt-buckles and shoulder-belt plate buckles are a bit more mundane in price terms, but still an attractive collectible "niche." Prices are in the $50-250 range, save for the great rarities.

Round white-metal plaid brooch to The Black Watch Highlanders, 20th c.. 3" dia.. $400.

Three regimental plaid brooches, all 20th c. From left: Highland Light Infantry, $400. Royal Scots Fusileers, $400. Argyll & Sutherland, $400. *Courtesy of James D. Forman*

Belt buckle of brass with white metal badge affixed. The Argyll & Sutherland Highlanders. 20th c. $300.

Two regimental belt-buckles. From left: Brass buckle to The 72nd Highlanders, (Duke of Albany's Own) $300, white metal belt buckle to The Royal Scots, $300. *Courtesy of James D. Forman*

Bonnet Badges, Buttons, and Swagger Sticks

These three items are a most affordable and interesting "niche" of Militaria collecting.

Bonnet Badges

Any person in proper military form will have his head covered when out-of-doors. In the case of Scottish regiments, the head covering varies from the well-known balmoral (named after "you-know-where"), which is basically a beret-style bonnet, with a contrasting colour tourie, "pom-pom" on the top, short ribbons streamed from the back, and a headband often in a red and white diced pattern. Again, the colours vary by regiments. Some regiments (and frequently the bandsmen), will wear a large feather bonnet, made of ostrich feathers, usually black, about 18" in height, with a diced headband, a series of "tails" of feathers from the back, and a 9" plume of contrasting colour on the side of the bonnet. On the left side of both the bonnet and the balmoral is pinned a bonnet badge, which identifies the regiment of the wearer. These bonnet badges are found in various metals, silver, silver-plate, brass and white metal, enameled and so on. They frequently have repoussé work of thistles and foliage, The Cross of Saint Andrew, the unit's regimental number, and/or their motto. Taken all together, they are both distinctive and attractive. The members of some Scottish regiments wear a peaked cap, or a forage cap, or a shako (a peaked cap with a high crowned top, sometimes plumed). All will have some sort of regimental "bonnet badge" to identify the wearer's regiment.

A selection of Scottish regimental bonnet badges mounted on tartan fabric. $50-75 each.

Three bonnet badges, all 20th c. From left: The Argyll & Sutherland Highlanders, The Royal Scots, London & Scottish. $75 each.

Selection of nine bonnet badges. Top, from left: Highland Light Infantry, Argyll & Sutherland Highlanders, same. Centre: three variations of badges to The Black Watch Highlanders. Bottom from left: The Royal Scots, The Gordon Highlanders. $50-75 each.

As we noted in Chapter Four, in the last 150 years, Scottish regiments underwent a series of amalgamations; some regiments were absorbed into others; some were phased out completely. The point of the matter is that there was a constantly changing scene in terms of uniforms and "their bits and pieces", a heaven-sent opportunity for a collector if there ever was one. Bonnet badges came and went; as regimental numbers changed, so did the badge. It's entirely possible that one of the regiments in existence today, e.g. The Black Watch (the one in longest continuous service), and it's various volunteer battalions raised in time of war, could have had possibly 50 different bonnet badges worn by it's members over it's history. Multiply that by the fact that badges differed, at the same point in time, both by rank and by the individual's function, and the "badge universe" soars. Generally, pre-World War II badges run in the range of $35-100, with older, rarer ones more in the $100-200 range. Post-World War II badges should not run more than $50. But, BEWARE re-strikes. These are increasingly common and frequently difficult to tell from the "real thing". Buying from an established, reputable dealer is about the only defence.

Sweetheart Pins

There is also an interesting adjunct to bonnet-badges, and their regimental provenance. Soldiers, since time immemorial, when they "went off to war" left behind a mother, wife or girlfriend. To give them something to "hold onto" during their prolonged dangerous, and (for the lady) terrifying absence, they frequently would give their favourite a sweetheart pin to remember them by. These were, more often than not, a miniature replica of the bonnet badge, or a similar distinctive pin with the regiment's motto or other device thereon. Quite frequently these were very finely crafted of silver or gold, often with enameling, or with semi-precious or precious stones. World Wars I and II sweetheart pins can be found at reasonable prices, ranging from $40-$200. A collection of these, in an attractively framed display box makes a most handsome wallhanging.

Selection of "sweetheart badges" (smaller versions of bonnet badge). Top, from left: Argyll & Sutherland Highlanders, The Seaforth Highlanders, The Highland Light Infantry. Bottom, from left: The Black Watch Highlanders, The Gordon Highlanders. $50-200. *Photo by William B. Bradley*

Buttons

The same sort of phenomenon that we noted in bonnet badges also exists in the case of uniform buttons. The styles, colours, rank differentials noted for bonnet badges all apply equally, if not more so, to buttons. And, if you don't feel like chasing bonnet badges or buttons, you could concentrate on shoulder titles, collar badges and other regimental insignia identification, such as badges used on document boxes, saddle cloths, pouches, holster covers and the like. A decent selection of individual buttons can be found for under $25 in most cases. One good source for all militaria items mentioned in this chapter is London's Camden Military market, held on Wednesdays and Saturdays. Often items can be purchased via e-Bay™ or other on-line auctions.

Swagger Sticks

Swagger sticks are often over-looked by collectors of militaria, but they, too, can make for an impressive collection when arrayed on a wall-rack or similar display method. A swagger stick is pretty much what the name says it is. It's a stick which, while perhaps no longer as utilitarian in nature as it once was, provides it's user with a certain panache and stature. The swagger stick typically measures about two feet in length, and about 1/2"-3/4" in diameter. The top is frequently in the shape of a metal "golf-ball", with the regiment's insignia embossed thereon. At the other end of the stick is a small metal protective tip. The wood is often bamboo or malacca; somtimes varnished or ebonized. The metal varies by regiment and rank, from white metal to hallmarked silver.

Four swagger sticks. From left: London & Scottish, Durham Light Infantry (English), 42nd Black Watch Highlanders, Highland Light Infantry. $50-250. *Courtesy of James D. Forman*

Swagger sticks are only carried by officers and NCOs, not "other ranks." They are usually tucked under the left arm (leaving the right hand and arm to deliver and acknowledge salutes), but I would have to assume that they are often transferred to the right hand and "twitched" to emphasize a point the bearer wishes to make. Although, fortunately, I have no first hand knowledge of the fact, I have been led to believe that the corporal of the guard was want to use his swagger stick on the kneecaps of a less-than-fully-alert kilted sentry, or for other similiar disciplinary measures—I'm sure it was extremely effective. Modern swagger sticks are generally in the "under $100" bracket; older ones can range up to $250, more for the rare personalized and silver hall-marked pieces.

Regimental Swords

I should be clear that this brief section can only skim the topic, both because of space and knowledge considerations. The reader may recall from Chapter One some brief comments about the highlander's use of the massive cross-hilted claymore, and the conversion in the 17th century to the lighter Continental basket-hilt sword. Because of their age and value, the chance of stumbling across a genuine claymore is almost non-existent, any self-respecting claymore is already comfortably ensconced in a museum of its choice.

Right: Shell guard Claymore, 53" long, c. 1600, $12000. Left: Quatrefoil guard Claymore, 53.5" long, found near Battle of Kindallachon. Narwhale grip probably a later embellishment. $15000. *Courtesy of James D. Forman*

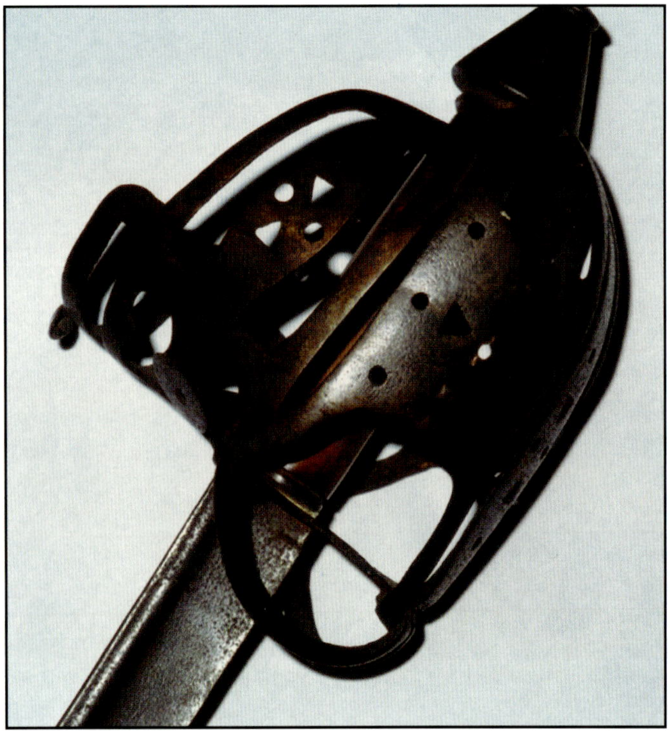

Close-up of basket of West Highland "beaknose" basket-hilt, 17th c., $7500.

In the pre-Culloden days, a Scottish gentleman normally would wear a sword (and pistol) for self-protection. Post-Culloden, swords were largely the prerogative of the military. The Scottish regiments had adopted the basket-hilt sword as their "aine," but, in truth, it wasn't really a very popular combat weapon. In his excellent paper, "Blades of Glory, Swords of The Scottish Infantry," author Stephen Wood states:

> By 1863, therefore, when the new pattern of broadsword was introduced, it arrived at a time when Highland officers, for a variety of motives, were increasingly finding reasons not to wear the basket-hilt. These reasons and motives must have led to increased personal expense too, as officers would have found that they needed several swords, one for each different function or order of dress. In addition to field officers' and adjutants' bowl-hilted swords, light-weight swords were increasingly being carried for wear at Court or on evening piquet duty and broadswords with simple cross hilts were being adopted for wear with undress uniform.[1]

Unfortunately, the illustrators of the 19th century furthered the mythological Highland officer's use of the basket-hilt sword in combat. In reality, a more effective, heavier bladed weapon was probably the norm. Nevertheless, Scottish regiments continue to this day to use the 1863 pattern basket-hilt, and, indeed, it is a handsome part of the uniform. The curved metal of the basket, with the distinctive "Jacobite heart" cut-outs, the red buff leather basket lining, with blue thread edging, and blue thread fringe at pommel top, combine with the fish skin grip wrapped with brass wire to make a most impressive appearance. The blade is typically acid-etched with thistles and foliage, frequently with the Royal Cypher of the monarch on the throne when the sword was produced. Also, the makers' name appears just below the ricasso, along with the ordnance mark signifying the weapon "passed inspection" for quality. The blade was single-edged and had two fullers, sometimes referred to as "blood-gutters." In some cases, the sword was engraved with the owner's name, rank and regiment, sometimes solely the regiment's identification is found. In rare cases, the sword will be a presentation piece (and so engraved) from fellow-officers on the owner's promotion or retirement.

Three different Scottish regimental swords. Right to left: Victorian basket-hilt regimental sword, with 1856 presentation etched on 32" blade. $5000. Silver-mounted basket-hilt sword with leather scabbard. c. 1830, 32.5" blade. $7500. West Highland "beaknose" sword, with 28.5" long, broad blade, c. 1680. $7500. *Courtesy of James D. Forman*

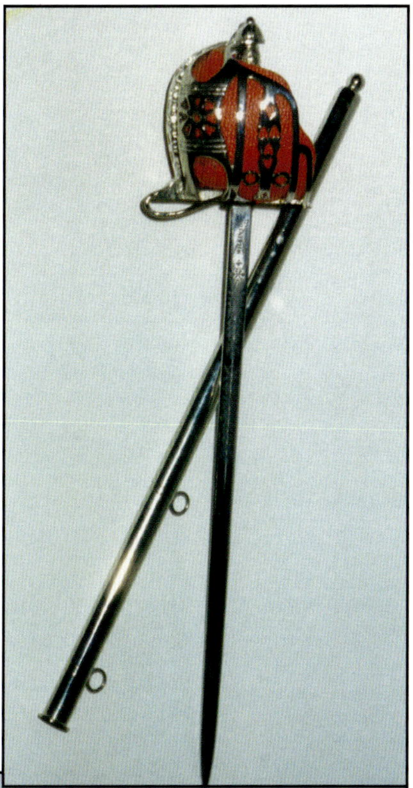

20th c. version of Scottish regimental basket-hilt sword, 1863 pattern, with stainless steel scabbard. Blade stamped "Wilkinson Sword". $2000.

Another Scottish regimental basket-hilt sword, from World War I, and signed to "The Calcutta Scottish," with George V King's crown etched on blade and maker's name "Walton & Co. Calcutta," in brown leather scabbard. $2000.

Placing price parameters on Scottish swords is particularly difficult for it depends to a very high degree on the provenance. Presentation or "named" pieces basically set their own prices. Regulation issue 1863 pattern basket hilts can run from $1000-2500. Condition is paramount; a small amount of blade discolouration is acceptable, extensive pitting or rust is not. Any blade damage or breaks/repairs in the basket structure severely decrease value; some loss of leather basket lining is "normal wear and tear", except to the extreme purist. However, a Scottish basket-hilt sword in reasonable condition can be a fantastic centre-piece for a display of Scottish memorabilia.

Pistols

It appears that while canon and firearms were in use in Scotland since the 14th century, there was no substantial "organized" firearm manufacturing until the 17th century. This brief discussion on the Scottish pistol does not intend to give the reader an encyclopedic knowledge of the genre; rather, merely an overview. The earliest pistols had a firing mechanism called a "snaphance" and the towns of Dundee and Edinburgh were quite often their "birthplace." Rifles with similar mechanisms were manufactured and were deemed "long-guns." Later, in what became the centre of 17th and 18th century Scottish arms manufacture in the Perthshire town of Doune, a new firing mechanism appeared, the highland lock. The flintlock firing mechanism was also used on Scottish pistols.

Gun/pistol manufacture was as much a craft/art as anything, and families became established as the "experts" in the field. Among them were the Murdochs, Campbells, Christies, and Caddells, all of Doune. The pistols were crafted out of sheet steel. At various times the pistol butts assumed different shapes, including the fishtail butt, lemon butt, heart butt, ram's horn butt and lobe butt, all names fairly descriptive of their configuration. In their book, *Scottish Firearms*, authors Blair and Woosnam-Savage note, referring to the Scottish pistol:

> The finest examples, most of which are by Doune makers, are characterized by their elegance of form and decoration, the restrained use of engraved Celtic designs combined with silver inlays being particularly pleasing.[2]

After the disaster at Culloden, Scottish pistol manufacturing went into a terminal decline. Cheaper versions were being produced in England's industrial Midlands with which to equip the highland regiments. Fortunately, however, there still exists a fair number of these beautifully crafted weapons for the weapons collector and connoisseur to admire and covet. The finer ones are found in museums all over England and Scotland, particularly the Scottish regimental museums in the regiment's "home" town. The auction houses of Wallis and Wallis and Bosley's will have the occasional "all-steel Scottish flintlock pistol" (sometimes from an estate or de-accessioned from a museum), but the price will "*nae* be cheap." A decent pistol, made and signed by John Murdoch of Doune, c. 1790, will command a price in the $4500-7500 range; a matched pair, closer to $15000. Once more, with provenance, the price increases. But, if you run across one at a dealer or at an auction, spend a minute or two in contemplation, if not necessarily in anticipation of buying; they are things of beauty, and who knows when (if ever), you'll have a chance to hold another.

All-steel, silver inlay flintlock pistol, signed by John Murdoch of Doune. All original with ram's horn butt, 12" overall. c. 1760, $6500.

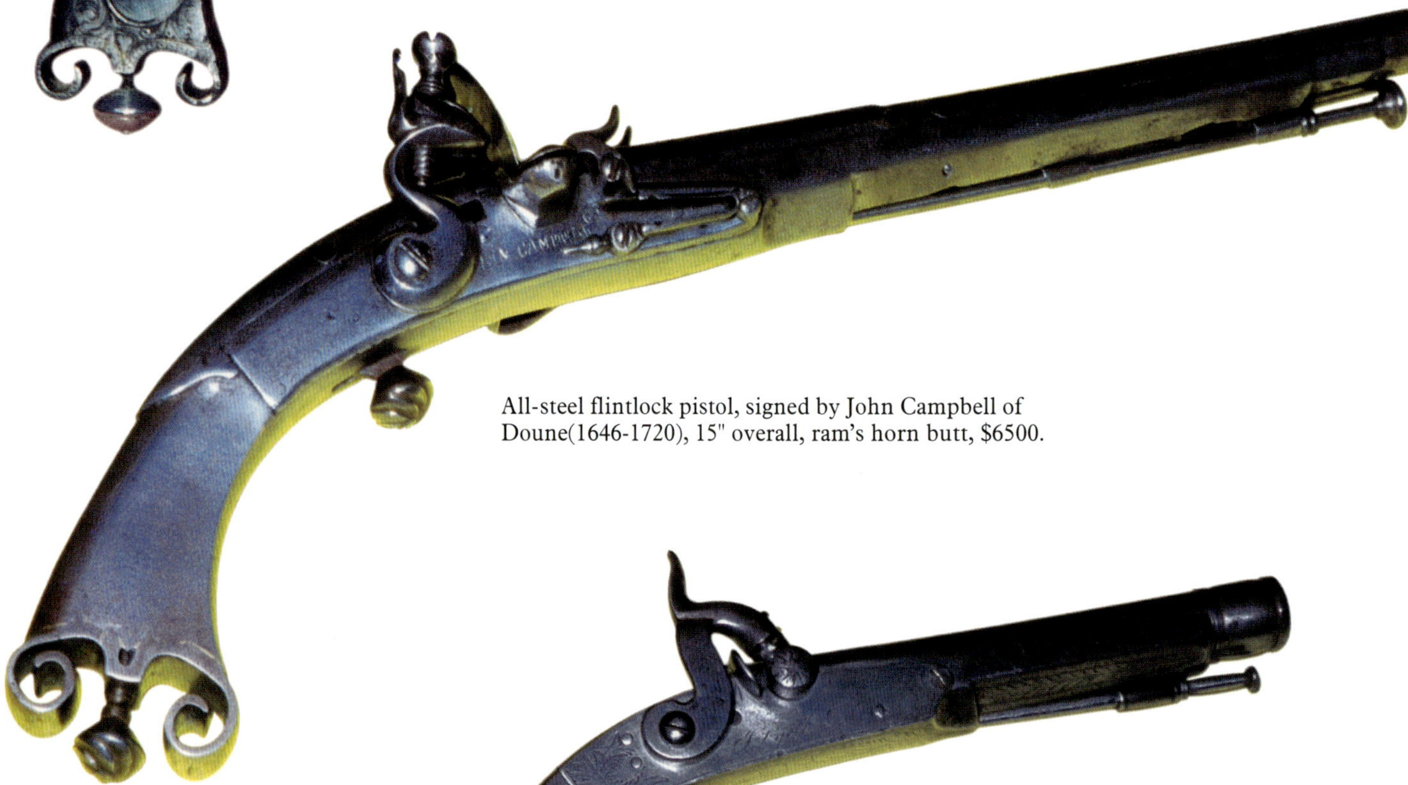

All-steel flintlock pistol, signed by John Campbell of Doune(1646-1720), 15" overall, ram's horn butt, $6500.

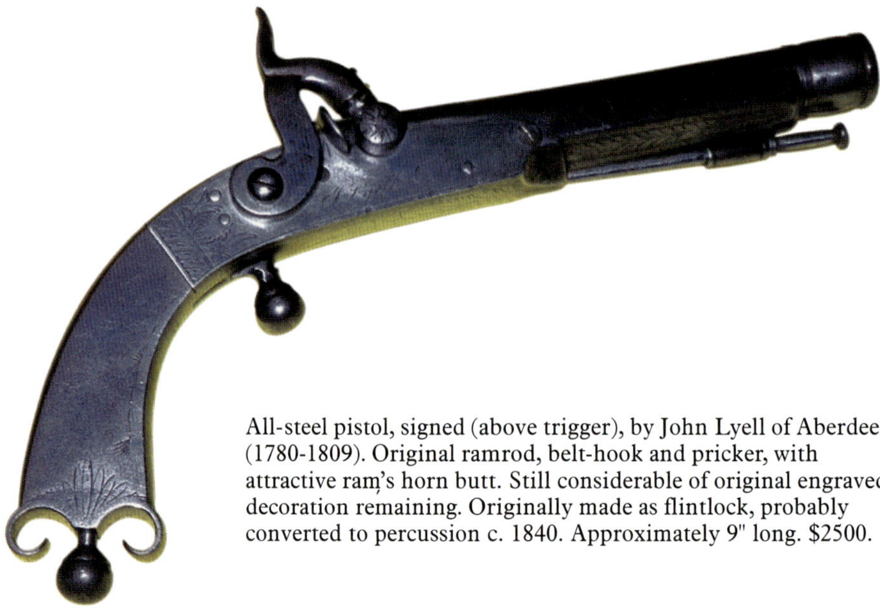

All-steel pistol, signed (above trigger), by John Lyell of Aberdeen (1780-1809). Original ramrod, belt-hook and pricker, with attractive ram's horn butt. Still considerable of original engraved decoration remaining. Originally made as flintlock, probably converted to percussion c. 1840. Approximately 9" long. $2500.

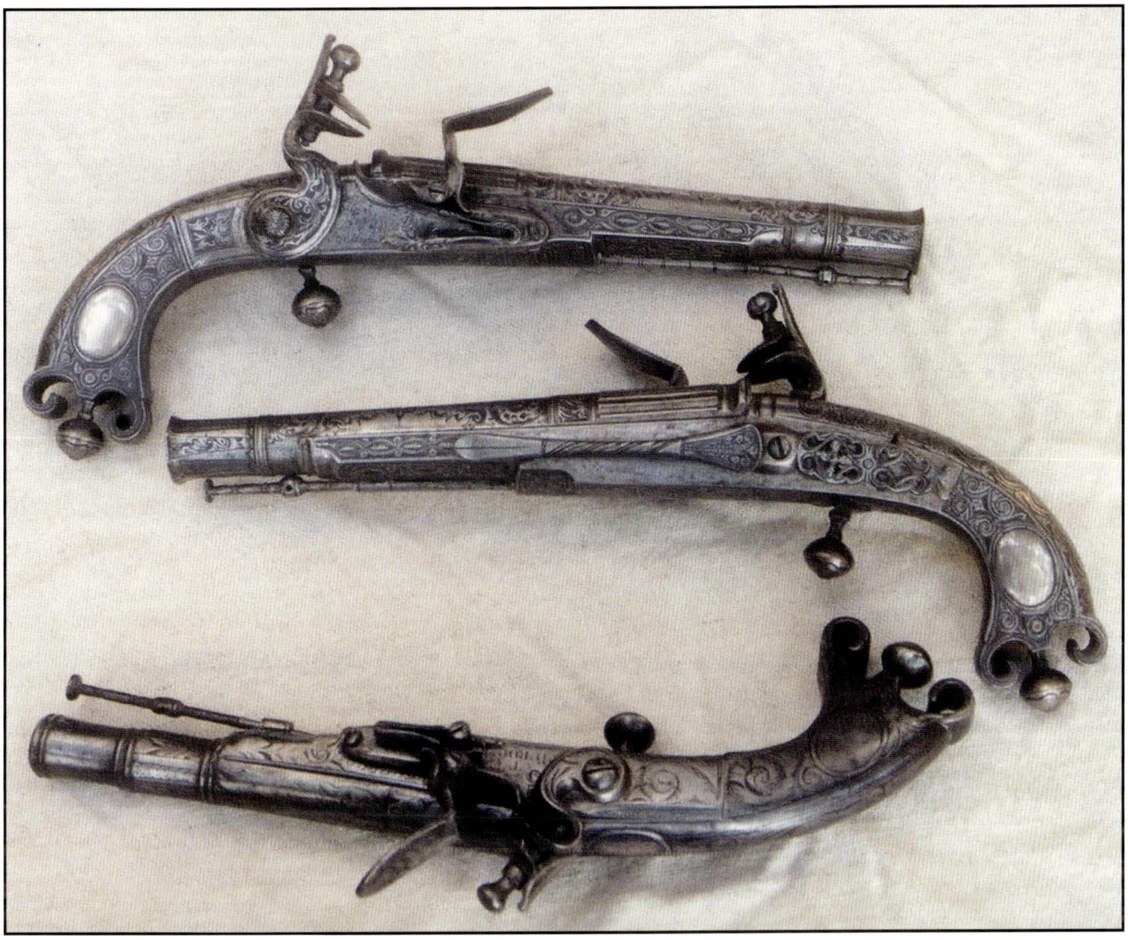

Top: Rare matched pair of all-steel flintlock pistols by Jo Christie of Stirling (Ex Litchfield Collection), 6.75" barrels, ram's horn butts, $15000/pair. Bottom: All-steel flintlock pistol by T. Murdoch of Doune, inscribed to Seargent in 42nd (Black Watch Highanders Regiment). 5.75" barrel. $6500. *Courtesy of James D. Forman*

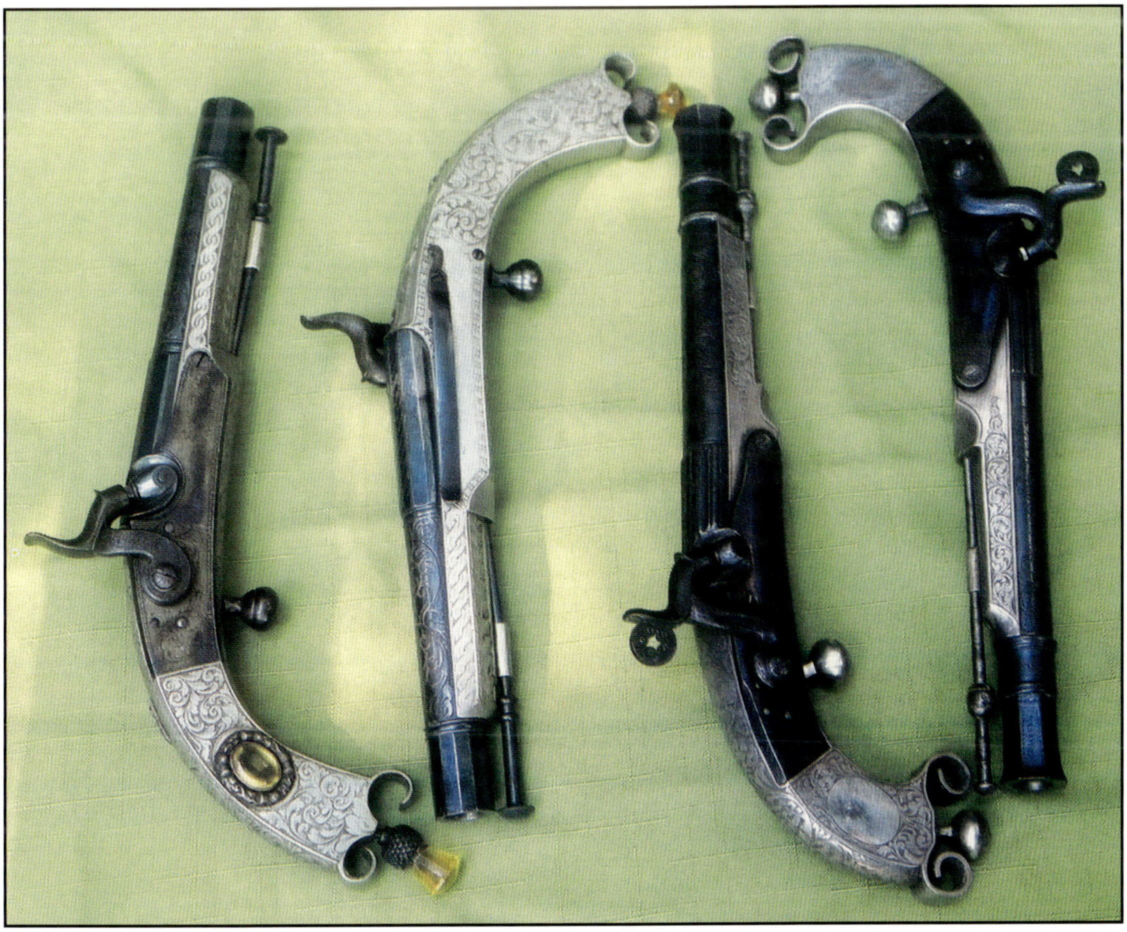

Left: Pair of percussion pistols with rams-horn butts, crystal or cairngorm adornments and silver inlays. Decorated with two different family crests. Probably a wedding pair. 6.5" barrel. $15000. Right: Pair of costume percussion pistols, silver inlay and ram's horn butts, Edinburgh, 7" barrels. $7500. *Courtesy of James D. Forman*

Miscellaneous Militaria

As you perhaps have surmised, the Scottish military by-passed very few opportunities to be-deck themselves or their surroundings with attractive, distinctive and unique objects, .many of which have become the subject of some spectacular and interesting collections. A few examples follow and more are to be found in subsequent chapters. (E.g. Chapter Ten contains some examples of several regimental smoking-related articles):

Medals- a field unto itself, and requiring the tutelage of a real expert in the field, and that description does not apply to me. Nevertheless, because of the Scottish military's half-a-millennium existence as global warriors, there were sufficient wars and sufficient Scottish gallantry to provide medals galore. And, this is one area in which the provenance is more often the rule than the exception, providing a most interesting historical perspective, in addition to the attractiveness of the object itself.

Paper Ephemera- the military always found it necessary to "record" things, and fortunate for us they did so. Diaries and letters from the battlefield are fascinating insights into their thoughts and lives, not filtered as in a historical document, but a genuine "human" experience. I, for example, have a collection of an ancestor's letters written home from the Crimea.. In re-reviewing them in the course of writing this book, I was struck by the writing and descriptive skill of the writer, Brevet-Major Hugh F. Drummond, who was killed in action on August 13th, 1855. These letters were later privately published in 1855, by Norris and Son, London. The last few letters were those of condolence from his fellow-officers to his parents. One was from Lieutenant-Colonel W. F. Scarlett, of The Scots Fusileer Guards, his commanding officer. Colonel Scarlett also returned to his parents Drummond's "field note-book," containing orders, troop dispositions and the like together with this poignant note from Scarlett:

> This pocket book was taken out of his jacket by me after his death. He wrote the detail the day previous to his death. W. F. Scarlett, August 17th, 1855.

I now have the notebook in my collection. It is a fascinating piece of nostalgia.

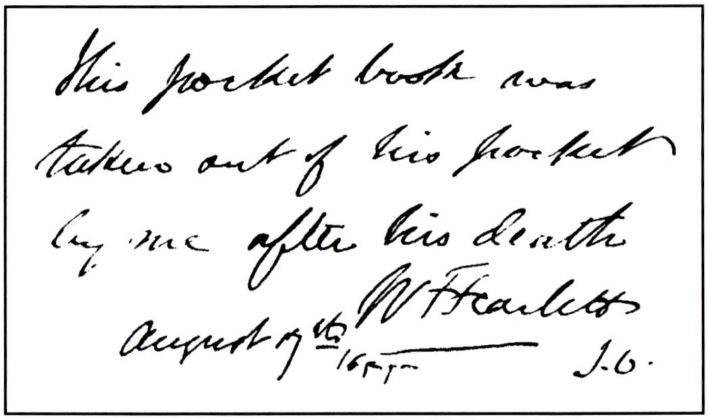

Inscription on the last page of Major Drummond's pocket notebook!

Menu holder for Scottish regimental officer's mess, 20th c., $200.

Old field maps and cigarette cards depicting military leaders or regimental uniforms are other areas of interest.

Mess gear- The equipment used in the process of eating can be most interesting. The "other ranks" had their mess gear of tin, while the officers' eating utensils were more often of silver. The Officer's Mess, a time-honoured tradition in the British forces is a marvelous source of good collectible "stuff." Hallmarked, and regimentally marked serving silver and silver platters, plus glassware, china, and other "mess" items, such as menu card holders, all distinctive to the regiment, can form the cornerstones of a fascinating display.

---

[1]Stephen Wood. "Blades of Glory, Swords of the Scottish Infantry, 1756-1900," The American Society of Arms Collectors, *Bulletin #72*, Spring 1995.

[2]Claude Blair and Robert Woosnam-Savage, *Scottish Firearms*, Alexandria Bay, New York, Museum Restoration Services, 1995, pg. 33.

Bibliography

Blair, Claude and Robert Woosnam-Savage, *Scottish Firearms*, Alexandria Bay, NewYork, Museum Restoration Services, 1995.

Bloomer, William and Kathleen. *Badges of the Highland and Lowland Regiments, including volunteer and territorial battalions*, East Dulwich, England, 1982.

Caldwell, David H. "The Art of Scottish Firearms," *Man at Arms*, Lincoln, Rhode Island, Jan/Feb 1985.

Claydon, Richard T., "The Traditional Pistols of Scotland," *The Canadian Journal of Arms Collecting*, Ottawa, Canada, Museum Restoration Services, Vol 8, No 2.

Darling, Anthony D., "Weapons of the Highland Regiments, 1740-1780," *Historical Arms Series*, No.33, Alexandria Bay, N.Y., Museum Restoration Services, 1970,1995.

Forman, James. "The Ifs, Ands, And Butts of Scottish Pistols," *Man at Arms*, Lincoln, Rhode Island, Nov/Dec 1994.

McKerracher, A. C., "The Pistol-Makers of Doune," *The Highlander*, Kansas City, Missouri, , Vol 20, No 2, Mar/Apr 1982.

Whitelaw, Charles E., "Scottish Arms Makers." *Man at Arms*, Lincoln, RhodeIsland, July/Aug 1975.

Wilkinson-Latham, R. J., *Discovering British Military Badges and Buttons*, Princes Risborough, Bucks, England, Shire Publications, No 148, 1994.

Wood, Stephen, "Blades of Glory, Swords of the Scottish Infantry, 1756-1900," The American Society of Arms Collectors, *Bulletin #72*, Spring 1995.

Chapter Six

Civilian Dress

Much of the detail previously reviewed in Chapters Four and Five applies equally to Scottish civilian dress as to the military, but there are some differences, of which we should make brief note.

Since they're not being worn "on parade," civilian sporrans tend to be less differentiated than the military ones. There are basically two types, a day and an evening sporran. Typically, the day sporran would be relatively simple and utilitarian, a pouch for the necessities and some exterior decoration. Perhaps the pouch would be all leather, with two or three woven leather tassels, or perhaps a brass cantle with a short-haired face of pony hide or seal-skin, and simple tassels to match. The evening sporran, however, was considerably more elaborate. A typical evening sporran would have silver cantle and cones and perhaps sealskin or leopard face, with two to three tassels of silver chain with fur tassels below the cones. Very occasionally one will run across an antique one with some "collectible" value. I have seen one in bear fur in its original tin box, with a date of 1780, if I recall correctly.

Dressy Victorian sporran of white horsehair with black tassels. Cantle of embossed thistles and cones are very fine quality silver-plate. c. 1890. $750.

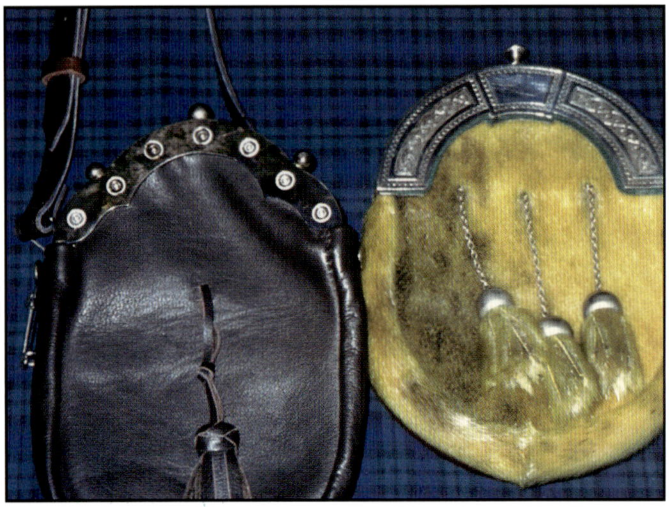

Two civilian sporrans. On left: Old cantle of plated brass, mounted on new pouch of brown leather. $250. On right: Silver cantle with Celtic designs, pouch of sealskin. 20th c., $600.

Dressy Victorian sporran of white horsehair with black tassels. Cantle and cones are white metal. c. 1900. $350.

Custom sporran featuring a badger head after the Argyll & Sutherland style. Brass cantle, leather pouch, gold bullion and red leather cones on white fur tassels. Very dressy. 20th c., $800.

Civilian evening sporran of brown fur with fur tassels. Cantle and cones are silver. Celtic geometric designs on cantle. 20th c. $750.

Child's Victorian dress sporran. Silver-plate cantle with claw-set faux amethyst at centre. Pouch is faced with angora goat hair. 12" high. c. 1890, $550

Day and Evening Dress

In the daytime, at home and in the field, a Scottish gentleman would wear a sports shirt, sweater or ski jacket, hunting tartan kilt (see below), a day sporran with leather belt, dark knee-high wool stockings with red flashes, and brogues. Flashes are the "suspenders" holding up the stockings, with the tail ends hanging down. In town, or for any semi-formal activity, the sport shirt and sweater would be replaced by shirt and tie and Harris tweed jacket. In keeping with military tradition, a balmoral would be worn, but out-of-doors only.

In the evening, for men, a dinner jacket (probably the style known as a "Prince Charlie"), black tie, white shirt with gold studs and cuff-links, dress tartan kilt, evening sporran, white or tartan stockings with flashes, and black dancing shoes with long-laces looped around the ankle. The shoes were sometimes black patent leather with silver buckles. Hats were not part of the gentleman's evening dress. For a Highland Ball, a white tie would be worn with a dress dirk and *sgian dubh*, and sometimes a plaid brooch.

For casual wear, ladies would typically wear a blouse with sweater and jacket or ski jacket over a tweed or hunting tartan skirt (not a kilt), "sensible" hose, and comfortable shoes. For a bit more proper attire for tea, or a trip into town, day-time dresses would be the order of the day, with dressier ones for non-formal evening wear. On the occasion of a Highland Ball, however, all the stops were pulled full out! Formal long evening dresses, with silk tartan sashes, dancing slippers, and all the "good" jewellery that the family could afford would be on m'lady's person (including a tiara if one were possessed or could be borrowed).

Tartans, Kilts, and Customs

Each clan normally has both a hunting tartan and a dress tartan. The hunting tartan was often in muted colours, so as not to be too obvious to whatever the wearer was hunting. The dress tartan, on the other hand, was the opposite, being the tartan that supposedly "came down through the ages." Sometimes the dress tartan is found in two variations, modern (usually brighter) and ancient (of the same colours but less brilliant in hue). It was traditional, in the old days (50 years ago), that you did not, under any circumstances, wear a tartan that you were not entitled to wear. Ladies could wear either their own family tartan or that of their husband. Womens' tartan skirts were just skirts, not pleated kilts which were the prerogative of the male, solely.

Clan Badges

One of the few, but very attractive, items of Scottish civilian dress, for the "antique collector," are clan badges. These are very similar in size, shape, and use to bonnet badges, discussed in Chapter Five. Clan badges are worn by the gentleman on his balmoral, and sometimes by the ladies as a jacket pin for non-formal activities. In the same fashion as the bonnet badges had the regimental motto, unit number, or similar device, so do clan badges have similar devices to enable clansmen and women to recognize one another. They act as a mark of family association, loyalty, and a visible tie to the past. Quite often the clan badge has the chief's crest or arms set in the centre of a "garter and buckle" surround, on which would be the clan's motto, war-cry, or other suitable clan expression. Sometimes, behind the badge pinned onto the side of the balmoral would be a sprig of a plant associated with that individual clan, such as heather or club moss.

Selection of silver clan badges, all featuring the "garter and buckle" surround. *Courtesy of Samuel Spencer, photographer*

Clan badges differed over time, just as did bonnet badges. Each chief had his own set of arms and his followers would have his arms, motto, etc. on their clan badges.

Badges can be found in many types of metal; seldom brass but more frequently silver or pewter. Sizes vary; a

Three clan badges to Clan Munro, vividly demonstrating the variations in size and design of badges within just one clan.

chief's badge properly was a bit larger than anyone else's. If not, these days, there is not much point in being a chief, is there? His followers' badges were usually about 3" in diameter. If the badge was silver, frequently, but not always, it would be hallmarked so a date can be established for when it was made. Also, dates can be established by researching the different arms, mottos, and crests on the badge. A facility for the serious researcher can be found in Edinburgh, at the office of The Lyon Clerk and Keeper of Records, since this office is responsible for registering all Scottish armorial bearings. Excellent sources for information are books on Scottish clans (available in any good Scottish apparel shop) and *The Book of Crests* (see the bibliography at this chapter's end).

Clan badges of silver can range in price from $75-250, depending on their age and rarity. Pewter or white metal ones should run roughly $35-125. Any shop selling Scottish clothing will have a line or two of clan badges; they are not yet collectibles but are available for "wannabe" Scots.

A good guess would be that there are probably 400 or so different clan badges that an assiduous and dedicated collector might find, certainly enough to keep one busy for a few years. A display of old silver clan badges is desirable to many collectors of "Things Scottish."

In the preceding chapter, Chapter Five, we explained the military use of the plaid brooch. A Scotsman, wearing the kilt at a "dress-up" affair (say, a clan gathering or a Tartan Ball or Burns' dinner) might wear a plaid as well. The plaid would be held in place on the left shoulder by a plaid brooch or pin, a civilian version of the military one. Usually in silver or silver-plate, most have a cairngorm at the centre and a silver surround of thistles, incised or embossed. While a plain plaid pin dating to the early part of the 20th Century can be found for $200-300, the fancier versions of hallmarked silver with large, well-cut cairngorms or citrines can command prices up to $2500. These are finding favour with ladies as "fashion statements" to be worn in the day-time on jacket lapels.

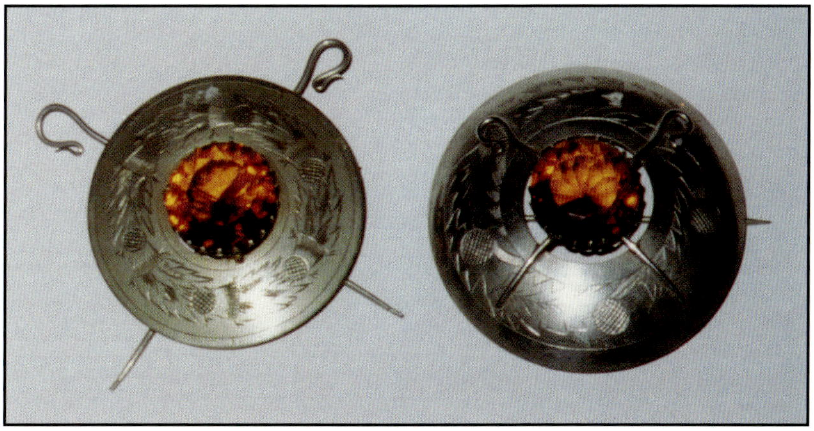

Two civilian plaid brooches, both in silverplate with claw-set centre, facetted orange stones, and with shepherd's crooks as part of their motif. 20th c. $200-300.

Two outstanding large civilian plaid brooches. Left: Large cut, very pale yellow cairngorm in claw mount and open back; stone alone measures 1.5" in diameter. Silver surround is embossed with thistles and four bosses or helmets. Old C-style pin, hallmarked Edinburgh, 1912. Overall 3.5" dia. $1650. Right: Large cut, yellow cairngormin with silver mount and open back, stone is 1.5" dia., .5" deep. Silver surround is chased with Celtic interlace design, hallmarked 1927, Edinburgh. Vendor stamp for R. W Forsyth, 3" dia., large old C- pin. $1850. *Photo by William B. Bradley*

Bibliography

Martine, Roddy. *Scottish Clan & Family Names*, Edinburgh, Scotland, John Bartholomew & Son, Limited, 1987.

McLaren, Mike, *The Book of Crests, Scottish American Clans*, Bowie, Maryland, Heritage Books, 1990.

Chapter Seven

Jewellery

Selection of bracelets and brooches, showing the wide diversity of materials, forms and motifs used in *pebble jewellery* in the late 19th century.

Background

Early in Chapter One, we noted that there were early Celtic patterns and designs found on tombstones and reliquaries dating back to the pagan days of the first and second centuries. Similar patterns are found on Scottish jewellery produced over the centuries and even those being produced today.

One of the earliest forms of Scottish jewellery is the pin (or brooch). Well before buttons were used, pins held two pieces of cloth together. In early Scotland, large, heavy ring pins were used which had a one-piece surround with a pin to attach to the cloth. Alternately, the pin had a gap in the surround to make piercing the cloth easier, and this type is called a "penanular" pin.

One early brooch that dates to the eighth century is known as the Hunterston brooch. Another brass ring brooch, found in Banffshire and known as the Tomintoul brooch, dates to 1650. It is a beautiful example of the genre. Yet another, dating to about 1550, is the Ballochyle brooch in which one can see a similarity to a man's plaid pin, that has been worn with Highland dress from the seventeenth century onwards.

A variety of ring brooches were made throughout Scotland during the seventeenth and eighteenth centuries, frequently by itinerant craftsmen known as "tinkers." The designs of these ring brooches followed those of earlier ring brooches, including running scroll motifs, geometrics, serpents and other animals, often grotesque birds, foliage and interlace. These same designs were evident during the period on *targes* (shields) and powderhorns.

Many early Scottish settlers in America brought with them and later produced, for their own use, ring and penanular pins with the same designs. These were often traded with local Indians, who found the designs interesting enough to copy, and very adroitly. It is sometimes difficult to tell an Indian-made brooch from a Scottish-made brooch. The New York State Museum, in Albany, has an interesting display of Indian-made "Scottish" jewellery.

Luckenbooth Pins

In the eighteenth and nineteenth centuries there emerged a unique form of Scottish jewellery which became known as luckenbooth pins. The name comes from the locked booths used by jewellers near St Gile's Kirk (church) on Edinburgh's High Street, often called The Royal Mile. Early versions of the pin consisted of a rather small single heart, under one inch long, usually made of cast silver and frequently decorated with cut, clear, quartz stones. Later versions consisted of a pair of intertwined hearts which a man traditionally purchased for his fiancée when they became betrothed. There is also some evidence that a similar heart-shaped pin was used as a lucky charm when pinned to a baby's clothing as protection against the child being stolen by the wee folk (i.e. fairies).

Twin-heart luckenbooth pins evolved over time. A crown or coronet was added to the pin at the top. The silver surrounding the crown was often cross-hatched. Many were inscribed on the back with dates when the gift was given and the donor and recipients' names or initials. By the end of the nineteenth century, luckenbooth pins had become larger in size, some measuring over 3 inches long. Semi-precious stones were added, as well as elaborate foliate chasing and other similar embellishments. Early luckenbooth pins should cost in the range of $300-500; nineteenth and twentieth century examples can be found for $200-350. Examples in gold would be roughly one and a half to twice as much more, since very few were made.

Two early round brooches of brass with typical Celtic designs, c. 1680. Larger one $600; smaller $450. *Courtesy of James D. Forman*

Mary Pins

Gradually, from the luckenbooth pin the Mary pin developed with a niche of it's own. Sometimes the double heart in the luckenbooth pin resembled an "M," and the jeweller would add a large, elaborate crown over the pin; the sides became extended, so that the pin was more oval than vertical. On the sides, a thistle design was added on one side and a *fleur-de-lys* on the other. The *fleur-de-lys* commemorated the "auld alliance" with France, as well as Mary Queen of Scots' position as Queen of France. Later, Mary pins would be decorated with agate stones.

A broad selection of silver Luckenbooth pins. In centre, the smallest pin set with cut clear quartz crystals dates to c. 1780. Right, the largest from the Edwardian era, c. 1910. Others set with blue enamel, amethysts, or cairngorms range in age from early 19th c. to late 20th c. *Photo by William B. Bradley*

Pebble Jewellery

During the late seventeenth and early eighteenth centuries, Scottish women began to wear what they called "pebble" jewellery. These were pins, brooches, and other forms of jewellery, usually made of silver (more rarely gold) set with polished stones which originally came from Scottish rivers and streams.

Example of a Mary pin in silver and agate. Note the *fleur-de-lys* and thistle. *Photograph by Tom Dawes*

A selection of pebble jewellery. Note the use of cairngorms as well as a variety of agate. The round circle brooch at lower left contains an interesting mix of agate and granite. The variety in design was limited solely to the jeweller's imagination and the supply of materials at hand. *Photo by William B. Bradley*

Another great variety in design and materials. *Photo by William B. Bradley*

Queen Victoria's love of Scotland and all "Things Scottish" set in motion the growth of this fashion. As tourism from England to Scotland mushroomed in the mid-1850s, Scottish jewellers were quick to assure that there was a goodly supply of (what was now called) "Scottish agate" jewellery for tourists to purchase and take home. Not only was the silver and agate jewellery, with soft colours of the Scottish countryside, made in the forms of ladies' pins, but also bracelets, rings, earrings, hatpins, pendants, belt-buckles, cuff-links, and the more rare necklaces. The taste even extended to pebble-decorated match safes, match boxes, chatelaines, stamp boxes, napkin rings, etc. In their excellent book *Victorian Jewelry, Unexplored Treasures*, authors Ginny Reddington Dawes and Corinne Davidov describe agate as follows:

> Agate is a variety of quartz, a mineral composed of silicon dioxide. It can be clear and colorless or have variegated color arranged in layered stripes such as banded agate (usually black or brown and white) or Montrose agate (gray striated). It can have cloudlike or moss-like formations, as in moss agate (milky white agate with green inclusions) or mocha agate (brown inclusions). There are three distinct categories of quartz:
>
> Transparent—crystalline stones such as amethysts (pale purple),citrines (pale yellow), and cairngorms (smoky orange brown).
>
> Translucent—chalcedony (usually milky white or bluish), carnelian or cornelian (translucent red orange), and bloodstone (dark green with tiny red flecks).
>
> Opaque—jasper (usually red, mustard or brown).

A very finely executed mid-Victorian, c. 1860, modification of the ancient Tara brooch set with cairngorms, varied agates, and finely chased silver fittings. $1250. *Photo by William B. Bradley*

Two very fine and different brooches. On left: round pinwheel of tubular silver inset with agates and claw-set cairngorms. $850. Right: striking garter and buckle pin with varied agates. $750. *Photo by William B. Bradley*

Rectangular pin on left has unusual combination of enamel, silver, and cairngorm. $575. Pin on right has agate (jasper), silver, and cairngorms. $465. *Photo by William B. Bradley*

Another type of stone used in the making of agate jewelry was granite, a combination of quartz and microcline. Mined in Aberdeen, Scotland, it had a unique pink and gray coloring, and it was never mixed with other stones.

Malachite, a vivid green mineral composed of alternating bands of light and dark green, was in great demand by makers of agate jewelry. Found nowhere in Scotland, it was imported from Siberia by way of Germany".[1]

Three silver and malachite pins. Note intricate silver roping design on the centre pin. *Photo by William B. Bradley*

Different shapes and sizes, but all brooches featuring gray, striated, Montrose agate. *Photo by William B. Bradley*

Cairngorms are mined in the Cairngorm mountains of central Scotland. Another form of granite used in Scottish agate jewellery is Peterhead granite, from Scotland's east coast. It has a unique pink colouration. Aberdeen granite is more predominantly gray in colour.

It has been estimated that there were over 1000 people working in the Scottish tourist jewellery trade at its peak in 1870, mostly in Edinburgh. Scotland's jewellery industry could not supply the growing demand for Scottish agate. England's jewellery centre in Birmingham rose to the occasion. By scanning some of the catalogues published by Birmingham jewellers in the last quarter of the nineteenth century, it becomes apparent that Birmingham jewellers imported agate stones from sources such as Africa and even shipped silver settings to Germany where the polished stones were set. See a catalogue from Joseph Cook & Sons, Ltd, Birmingham, in the Appendix. After the "fashion craze" for agate jewellery diminished following Queen Victoria's death in 1901, more austere Edwardian fashions became popular.

Many "themes" quickly become apparent when you view an extensive collection of Scottish agate jewellery. The endless knot is one form that recurs time and again in pins and bracelets. Various versions of a star theme are also found. Hearts, in an endless variety of shapes and sizes, were extremely popular. The Cross of Saint Andrew, Scotland's national symbol, is well represented in Scottish agate pieces. Other popular variations include axes, arrows, anchors (a symbol of hope), horseshoes (good luck charms), butterflies, seashells, bows, and leaves. Particularly favoured for bracelets were snakes and serpents. Another popular bracelet and pin format featured the buckle and garter form that derived

A wide variety of styles and materials with designs including St Andrew's Cross, Maltese Cross, arrow, shield, endless knot, and anchor. *Photo by William B. Bradley*

from the aristocracy's crests and badges, which were traditionally surrounded with a silver band featuring the Royal Order of the Garter with a buckled strap. Finally, a myriad of pins can be found in figural patterns, including golf clubs and tennis racquets, sailboats, and musical instruments (harps, banjos, violins, etc). The list was limited solely by the jeweller's imagination and public demand.

Another very popular Scottish agate pin style was the *sgian dubh*, or dirk (see Chapter Four). These miniature knife designs came in all sizes. Those under 2" in length were probably for a lady to wear on her jacket or blouse. Those measuring 3" to 6" long were destined to be worn as kilt pins. Some of the larger dirk pins, being exact copies of the full-size ones, even had little auxiliary knives and forks that came out of the sheath. One even turned out to have a pair of sewing scissors deployed from the sheath. Another, illustrated in Dawes and Davidov's book, was a small fruit knife.

The subjects for Victorian jewellery appear endless. Here a variety of musical instruments, an umbrella, sailboat, and golf club. *Photo by William B. Bradley*

Pendant crosses were quite popular. From left: silver and Montrose agate cross, Celtic cross of jasper and bloodstone on chain, St Andrew's Cross of silver and agate with crown at centre. $300-500 each. *Photo by William B. Bradley*

Very rare silver and agate snake brooch demonstrating incredible jeweller's skill. c. 1860, $2000.

Kilt pins, generally 4"-6". Note the pin, third from left, in configuration of a deer's foreleg with hoof of amethyst, $475. Note also pin, third from right. a faithful replication of an officer's basket-hilt sword with jasper and bloodstone. On the back is a distinctive British Patent Office diamond registration mark for 1864. $950. *Photo by William B. Bradley*

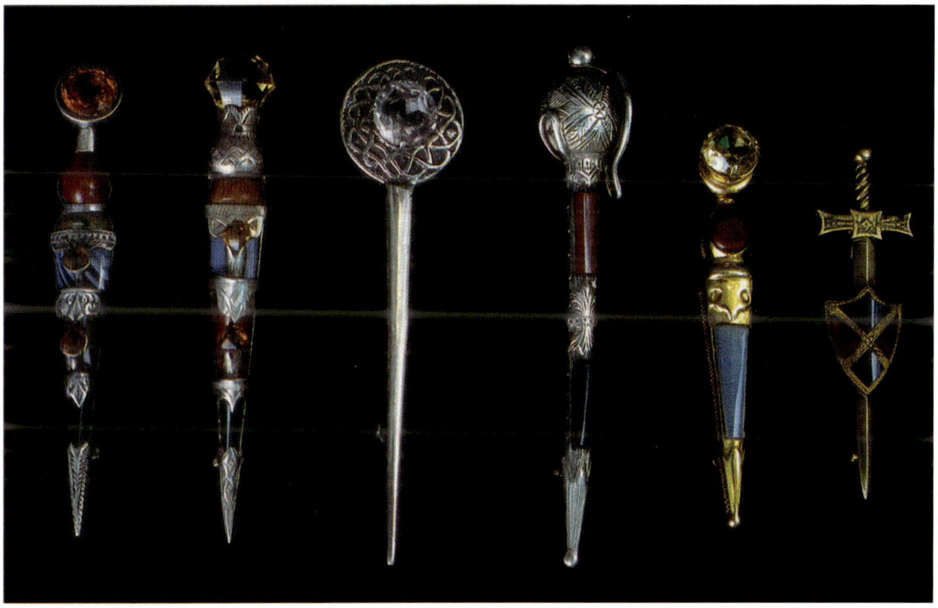

A variety of small dirk and sword pins, approx. 3" and under, worn on jackets or as lapel pins. *Photo by William B. Bradley*

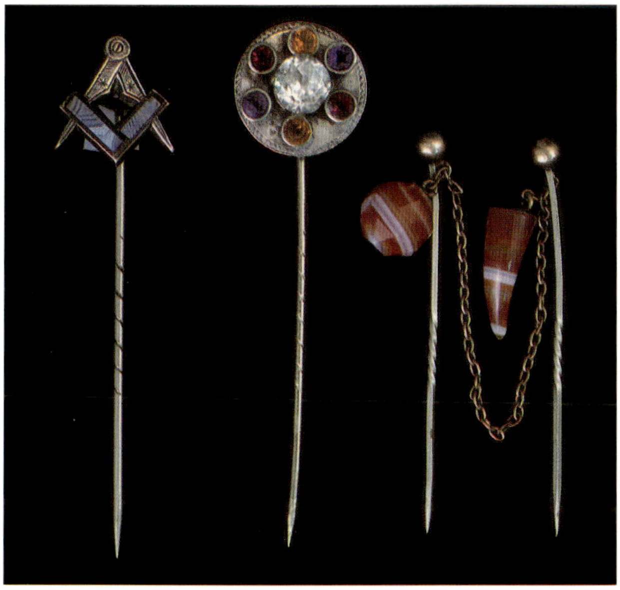

From left: A Masonic stickpin in silver and agate. A silver stickpin with clear quartz and tourmalines. A silver cloak pin with variegated agates. $175-185. *Photo by William B. Bradley*

Markings

Scottish agate jewellery makers were not known for signing their work. Some specific patterns were registered with the British Registry Office and bear the distinctive diamond mark, which provides date of registry, etc. The major makers appear to have been Muirhead of Glasgow, G. & M. Chrichton, McKay and Cunningham, Marshall and Sons, and Meyer & Mortimer, all from Edinburgh, plus Jamieson & Rettie and Sons from Aberdeen.

Most of the Scottish agate jewellery that can be found today is silver engraved with Victorian foliate designs, occasionally thistles. Some can also be found with geometric or Celtic pattern chasing. Gold settings are found far less frequently for two good reasons: there were fewer gold pieces made, and families who could afford gold were more likely to hang onto them over the succeeding generations. Quite often, early pins can be identified by their slate backs onto which "slices" of agate were adhered. Early pins also typically had a "c" pin stem, which extended beyond the edge of the pin itself. (The first "safety" locking device as part of the pin-stem didn't come about until about the end of the nineteenth century).

Unusual and dressy bracelet with alternating claw-set cairngorms and end-capped carved agates, all in gold. The crowning touch is the exquisite agate garter and buckle padlock. $3,250. *Photo by William B. Bradley*

Gold and agate round brooch, with Saint Andrew's Cross and crown at center with unusual agate. $1750.

Handsome bracelet with hinged closure and cairngorms featured.

Exceptional gold and agate bracelet, c. 1860. $5000.

Values Today

As you might expect, the value range for agate jewellery is extremely wide. A simple, small bar pin in silver with one or two pieces of agate could run about $200. A wide choice of pins is in the $300 to 700 range. A very fine large ring pin, with agates and cairngorms, can cost up to $1500. If set in gold, it could be twice as much.

Two specific bracelet forms are worthy of a quick note. The barrel bracelet consists of a series of small cylinders of cut agate or granite, each end capped in silver, with silver chain links connecting them. Usually, barrel bracelets date to the mid-1800s.

The medallion or locket bracelet consists of a series of hinged silver sections, each set with agate, and with a larger oval silver section at the centre. This centre section often had a hinged glass panel, behind which a lock of hair or a photo were placed. Quite frequently these and other bracelets had a "padlock" closure to secure the catch. The padlocks, sometimes of plain chased silver and sometimes mounted with agates or malachite, are things of beauty in their own right. A relatively simple bracelet with linked agates set in silver could cost from $500 to 750. An elaborate silver and agate bracelet with central locket or medallion could cost as much as $2500.

Silver and agate linked bracelet with centre medallion on a pivot to provide two pictures in the locket. c. 1850. $1850.

Silver, agate, and cairngorm bracelets and a silver and malachite witch's heart bracelet at top. All 19th c., $350-650. *Photo by William B. Bradley*

Animal Jewellery

One of the favourite pastimes in Victorian Scotland (and still today) is the enjoyment of the phenomenally attractive countryside and it's many opportunities for sports of all types. Elsewhere in this book we consider fishing, hunting, and shooting. A by-product of a sporting life created a bizarre form of Scottish jewellery. The Scottish red grouse was not only sought for its delicious (if a bit gamy) meat, but also for its feet. Cured and mounted in a silver setting with a silver ring on its centre claw and a cairngorm at the top, it made a pin widely accepted as a lucky charm. Worn by both men (as a kilt pin) and women (as a lapel pin), it received wide approval among all social classes. Sometimes, the larger, somewhat scaly foot of a pheasant was also used in such jewellery. Also, a young man could have a kilt pin fashioned from the hoof of his "first deer kill" (a coming of age ritual). A badger or otter foot, silver-mounted and properly inscribed for the occasion of giving, was also used as a kilt pin. Lucky grouse pins are today being mass-produced with fake rabbit fur, but are quite easy to distinguish from authentic old pins. A nice silver-mounted, c. 1890, real grouse foot pin could cost around $200; an otter or badger foot kilt pin might be about $300 to 400.

From left: Victorian pheasant claw with silver and cairngorms. A silver mounted kilt pin of otter foot. A grouse claw with silver and amethyst. $185-400 each. *Photo by William B. Bradley*

Iona Jewellery

As part of the Arts and Crafts movement in the early years of the twentieth century, we recognize the work of Alexander Ritchie of Iona, a small island off Scotland's west coast. Iona, the "sacred isle" and a home of the Gaelic culture and language, was the site of a small jewellery shop opened by Ritchie in 1900. Virtually single-handedly, he and his wife revived the old Celtic patterns and motifs for a variety of gifts and most specifically for silver jewellery. His maker's mark "AR" or "AER" can be found on jewellery at antique shops today. More importantly, he paved the way for similar designs produced today in Scotland that are available at countless gift shops throughout the country.

Other Victorian Jewellery

Scotland, of course, participated in the manufacture and use of other types of jewellery besides those with indigenous Scottish agate. Niello, for example, which is an amalgam of metals poured into incised areas on silver, can be found with Scottish motifs such as thistles and the like. Mourning and hair jewellery commemorating lost loved ones, a most Victorian genre, is also found. Other jewellery made of gunmetal, cut steel, aluminum, pewter, and polished steel also were in use in Scotland as the fashion dictated.

A Tartan Ware stretch bracelet in "Prince Charlie" tartan. Quite rare. c. 1890. $1000.

Unique to Scotland is jewellery made from Mauchline Ware and Tartan Ware (see Chapters Two and Three). Small round pins in a variety of tartans can occasionally be found. They may have a British Registry diamond mark on the back, and are usually quite early in date. Finding one in good condition can be difficult, however, given the propensity to damage from everyday usage. Tartan Ware bracelets consist of small, shield-shaped segments of Tartan Ware strung on stretch-cord to slip over the wrist. Frequently the stretch cord is replaced. Usually there are six or seven segments, typically in the same tartan. Occasionally one in all different tartans, each named, can be found. Rarely, Tartan Ware cuff links are seen. Pins or brooches were also made in Mauchline Ware, frequently with a transfer scene relating to Rabbie Burns; somewhat rare, they command a price of around $200 to $400. Round Tartan Ware pins are available in the $500-1000 range. Tartan Ware bracelets in top condition command prices in the range of $1000-2000.

Charles Horner Jewellery

Late in Queen Victoria's reign, a silversmith in Chester, England, made silver pins, hatpins, and lavalieres specifically for the Scottish market. Charles Horner created a most distinctive style. Virtually all his pieces featured one or more thistles, with the "blossom" executed in purple or yellow, sometimes glass, sometimes amethysts and citrines. The silver usually was twisted in distinctive curlique patterns. He was one of the few jewellers of the time who signed virtually all his pieces. The Chester hallmark and date mark will be there also, right next to his "CH" stamp. His work can be found with dates ranging from the early 1890s to the mid-1920s. Prices are usually in the $200 to $400 range.

A small selection of silver thistle pieces by Charles Horner of Chester, 1870-1920. A unique style. *Photo by William B. Bradley*

Miracle Jewellery

Yet another form of Scottish jewellery should be noted, even though it is actually English. In the late 1940s and 1950s, jewellery was produced under the brand name "Miracle." These pins, bracelets, necklaces, etc. were copies of traditional forms of Victorian pebble jewellery. In their own right, they are quite attractive, but no match for their older counterparts. Using various base metals and molten glass, they replicate the kilt pins in the forms of dirks, penanular pins, and so on. Prices generally are in the $75-200 range. Occasional collectors look specifically for Miracle jewellery. As with other things no longer being produced, it is reasonable to assume that prices of these pieces will rise.

A selection of Miracle costume jewellery, including (at top) a replica of a Scottish flintlock pistol. $175-300. *Photo by William B. Bradley*

A group of *pebble jewellery*. Note the heart brooch and matching earrings at the top, and selection of green malachite jewellery which proved to be very popular in the Victorian era (even though malachite was not native to Scotland).

---

[1]Ginny Reddington Dawes and Corinne Davidov, *Victorian Jewelery, Unexplored Treasures*, New York, New York, Abbeville Press, 1991, p. 61.

More Miracle costume jewellery, all knock-offs of Scottish pebble jewellery. $125-225.

Bibliography

Dawes, Ginny Reddington and Corinne Davidov, *Victorian Jewelery, Unexplored Treasures*, New York, New York, Abbeville Press, 1991.

James, Duncan, *Old Jewellery*, Haverfordwest, England, Shire Publications, Ltd, 1989.

Marshall, Rosiland K. and Dalgleish, George R., *The Art of Jewellery in Scotland*, Edinburgh, Scotland, Scottish National Portrait Gallery, HMSO, 1991.

MacArthur, E. Mairi, "The Ritchies of Iona," *The Highlander*, Winnetka, Illinois, USA, Angus J. Ray and Associates, May/June 1997.

National Museum of Antiquities of Scotland, *Brooches in Scotland*, Edinburgh, Her Majesty's Stationary Office Press, 1979.

Nimlin, Jock, *Let's Look at Scottish Gemstones*, Norwich, England , Jarrold and Sons, Ltd.

Wingrove, Susan, "Scottish Ring Brooches and Scottish Heart Brooches," *The Highlander*, Winnetka, Illinois, Angus J. Ray Associates, 1987.

Chapter Eight

Kitchen Wares

Over the ages, any society develops a group of items that are in everyday use, usually with a character uniquely shaped to the climate, societal habits and other formative parameters. And Scotland is no different. One of the most interesting areas to examine, and one that is ready-made for an "antiquer," is that which in today's vernacular has been cleverly christened *kitchenalia*, or kitchen wares.

An 18th or 19th century Scottish kitchen was a pretty primitive affair. In those days, most of the cooking was done in a fireplace, (earlier over an open fire in the centre of the family's one-room turf-roof home) with food-preparation at a kitchen table. Later in the period, coal stoves came on the scene, and acted as both a source of heat and a means of cooking. Over time, some very specific and practical utensils were developed to facilitate the daily chores of preparing the family meal(s). This chapter will review some of these.

The Spurtle

One of the main-stays of the at-times meager Scottish diet was porridge, which, together with soups of various types, might be the main course of any given meal. Porridge was cooked in an iron pot hung from a pivoting metal arm over the fire or on top of the stove. The utensil used to stir the cooking porridge was called a "spurtle". Very simply, it is a turned piece of wood, about 9-15" in length, with the bottom ("stirring end") rounded, and the top (handle) often carved in the shape of a thistle blossom. These continued in use well into the 20th century, and new ones can still be purchased in some of the older ironmonger's shops (hardware stores). Nice, older spurtles with a good dark "used" patina can be found at reasonable prices, say $20-50.

The Girdle

A Scottish girdle refers to a small iron cooking utensil. It is generally round, about 6"-20" in diameter, with an attached ring that can be hung from a pot-hanger over the fire in the fireplace. The smaller girdles were used to bake pancakes, bannocks and scones (all small biscuit type foods); the larger ones were used to bake the family bread. I'm pretty certain these are no longer being manufactured; nicely "seasoned" old ones can be found in the $50-100 range and make a most attractive addition to a collection of kitchenalia.

From left: a pair of spurtles (porridge stirrers), a bone spoon from highland cattle horn, a stag horn handle knife, and a telescoping toast fork. $35-185.

A souvenir copy, in brass, of the traditional iron girdle. $125. *Photo by William B. Bradley*

The Kettle

While by no means unique to Scotland, the kettle was a water-heating vessel that has probably seen more universal use in Scotland than perhaps any other country. The reason is the Scots' fondness for tea. Tea, in the 18th century, was a prohibitively expensive luxury, affordable only by the upper classes. As the Empire grew and commercial shipping and importing more prevalent, tea became affordable to the middle classes and, ultimately, everyone. Every household had its kettle. These were usually made of a heavy iron, with a distinctive curved pouring spout, and curved top handle (well removed from the top of the kettle itself, to keep fingers from being burned) and complete with removable lid. The kettles were in use 24 hours a day. They never left the fireplace or stove, so that the visitor could be offered a bit of highland hospitality with a "cuppa." (See Chapter Eleven for information on Scottish teapots.) Sadly, the iron kettle has fallen to the axe of progress, with the coming of aluminum and electric kettles. Few old kettles can still be found, since they did tend to rust out, and were just thrown into the *midden* (the garbage-dump). If you run across one, it should run you about \$50-75. There are also some copper teakettles, from the early 20th century, which make handsome decorative pieces on top of a cupboard in a country-style kitchen. They follow the same basic shape as the early iron ones, but are usually a bit more elaborate in handle-turnings and decorative finials.

Tea kettle. This example is in brass and a bit more decorative than the traditional iron one, c. 1880. \$225.

The Trivet

The preceding notes on the tea-kettle lead very naturally into the trivet, again not native to Scotland but an essential part of any Scottish fireside or kitchen. Once the tea was brewed and in the teapot, one had to keep it warm for the second (and third) cup. The trivet was often placed on the fireplace hearth and on it was placed the teapot, close enough to the fire to keep warm; and far enough away not to crack the teapot. The trivet was also used to keep the bottom of the teapot from burning the kitchen table, and also on the edge of the stove itself to keep the teapot away from the direct heat. These trivets are found in brass or iron, usually with three or four short 1" to 2" legs. Frequently, they are triangular in shape (like a clothes iron) and have a handle with a wooden grip to protect the fingers. They measure about 4" to 6", plus the handle. The manufacturers would emboss the lattice-like metal stand (to allow heat to reach the teapot bottom) with a folksy motto, such as "our aine fireside." Trivets are usually in the \$50 to \$100 price bracket and they come in a myriad of shapes and sizes.

Pair of brass trivets on three legs featuring thistles, St Andrew's Cross, and good-luck horseshoe. Early 20th c., \$75 each. *Photo by William B. Bradley*

The Salt Box

Quite frequently, a Scottish kitchen would have a wall-hanging salt box next to the fireplace or stove. These were usually wooden, with a shield-shaped back or top with a hole to suspend it from a nail, and a hinged lid. Thus, a pinch of salt was always readily available to toss into the pot, be it soup or stew. Some salt boxes, c. 1890-1930, were square, dark stained pine with a pinned or hinged lid. Earlier ones, c. 1840-90, had a half-round shape of stave construction with alternating vertical sections of light (sycamore) and dark (laburnum) wood. Sometimes the vertical strips would be glued together and some were held together by horizontal woven willow bands without glue. Both types had the hinged or pinned lids to keep the salt dry. Later salt boxes can be found today for $100-200, but the stave type, being older and more difficult to come by, are generally in the $400 and up range.

The Luggie

A *luggie* is a dipper used to scoop milk out of the bucket after milking the family *cooe* (cow). The body is round with straight sides of stave construction and alternating strips of wood, secured by woven willow bands. A high vertical handle enables the bowl to be dipped in the milk pail. Some *luggies* have one other unique construction feature, a double bottom containing several dried peas from the vegetable garden. When shaken by the children dipping their morning milk, it makes a most satisfying rattling sound. *Luggies* are becoming quite difficult to find nowadays; and prices are generally in the $500 and up category.

Left: A luggie with stave construction bound in willow, early 19th c., 5" dia., rare in this fine condition, $650. Right: Hanging salt box with alternating strips of ash (light) and laburnam (dark) woods, stave construction, 9.5" h., $575. *Photo by William B. Bradley*

Close-up of luggie showing stave construction and willow banding. Not a drop of glue or a nail in the piece.

Spoons, Skimmers, and Ladles

These articles tend not to have a unique Scottish character in the same fashion as some of the items noted above do. Nevertheless, one can find some handsome old large wooden spoons, iron-handled brass pot-skimmers, and other such at some of the Scottish antique shops and flea markets.

Butter Pats and Molds

Quite frequently butter pats and molds are found with the national Scottish flower, the thistle, as their imprint motif. These come in all shapes and sizes, and are generally round with the stamp 2" to 4" in diameter. Older examples (ones that have seen their full day of use) can be found with a handsome dark patina to the wood (generally a grained wood such as oak) for prices in the area of $100 to $200. Attention purists: Just because they have a thistle imprint does not necessarily mean that they are of Scottish origin; but we accept all things with thistles as Scottish enough to qualify for inclusion.

Three traditional Scottish butter stamps or molds, all with a thistle motif, 19th c., $125-225.

Toasting Forks

With an open fireplace and no electric toaster at hand, how can we prepare the morning toast? Simple, to the Victorians who, faced with this dilemma, invented the telescoping toasting fork. A small 2" to 3" wide brass trident was attached to a 12" long black-painted metal tubular handle. A slice of bread was impaled on the fork and held to the heat of the fire. When your fingers were too close to the heat and were also toasting, you pulled out the inner telescoping handle until your fingers were a comfortable 18" or so from the heat. At the top of the handle is a round hook (sometimes with a thistle-blossom finial) to hang the fork next to the fireplace. A nice toasting fork, c. 1900, will set you back a modest $50 or so.

Shortbread Molds

One of Scotland's most loved culinary delicacies is shortbread, a delectable, full-of-calories, butter and sugar confection. To shape the shortbread, a wood or ceramic device similar to a butter mold was pressed into the dough, leaving an impression, sometimes a thistle blossom and foliage or a series of fluted lines or other decorative pattern. Generally, wooden shortbread molds are round, approximately 6" in diameter, and hang from a hook at the back. They make an attractive wallhanging. Ceramic ones, round with about a 6" diameter or square, were often advertising pieces for a flour manufacturer whose name and logo were printed on the mold with a transfer. Plain wood molds should be in the $35 to $75 price range; ceramic ones in the $100 to $275 range.

Top: China shortbread mold with traditional fluted edging and thistle motif. A late 19th c. advertising piece, $365. Bottom: China jelly mold with thistle, late 19th c., $225.

Jelly Molds

The Scots are very much into sweet desserts and *blamanges*, a form of jelly, and similar molded foods like aspics and gelatin-based concoctions. These were a part of Victorian culture in Scotland. To present a good table-side appearance, the jelly molds for prepared foods were often made in a container that had an attractive pattern at the bottom, so that when the food was turned out of the container onto a serving-plate it had the pattern of a thistle or other motif on the top. Even ice cream could be molded and served this way. Today, molds of tin or copper are prized by collectors and can be found for prices around $100 to $300. They make attractive wall hangings. The occasional pewter jelly molds have a removable top and bottom so that the ends can easily be removed and the jelly turned out onto a serving plate. See also Chapter Eighteen.

Other Scottish kitchenalia items include pots and pans, mixing bowls, kitchen knives, spoons, forks, and other essentials to a kitchen. We have detailed only those things that possessed a unique Scottish flair. Additional items with true Scottish kitchen-connections also are covered in subsequent chapters, such as stoneware cream pots, milk jugs, jam jars, biscuit tins, horn spoons and scoops, and napkin rings; and the list could go on.

Chapter Nine

Desk-Related Items

In the 21st century, we tend to take for granted our communication systems, forgetting the art of letter-writing which preceded the telegraph, telephone, television, radio, internet, and e-mails. Upper and middle class Scottish Victorians perfected the art form of writing letters. To do so, they required a desk and all the special paraphernalia that went with it. This chapter considers the desk paraphernalia that was produced individually or in sets. Not all of the desk items discussed here would be exclusively Scottish, but they were in daily use in Scotland and often were decorated with Scottish motifs.

Desk Sets

Very few complete desk sets can be found today, since the various pieces often became separated over time. A full set might comprise the following: a desk portfolio, writing surface lined with blotting paper, rocker blotter, hinged-lid divided stationary holder, desk calendar, inkwell, page turner, letter opener, scissors (often encased), pen tray, container for pen nibs, and stamp-box. Sets were made in an infinite variety of materials, but usually the pieces in the set would match. You might find sets of leather, other animal skins (elephant, rhino, alligator, ostrich, shark), ivory, and wood, such as burl-wood. Decorations include silver, silver plate, other metals, and Scottish agate. Specialist London antique dealers may occasionally have a full set that would cost $1000 and up. If you are extremely lucky, you might find a presentation set with the donor's and recipient's details engraved thereon. Realistically, however, you are more likely to find bits and pieces, as detailed below. A considerable number of desk paraphernalia were made in Tartan Ware and Mauchline Ware, see Chapters Two and Three.

Desk Portfolios

This is a book-shaped, 9"x 11" folder with hard covers in which paper and "works-in-progress" could be stored. Interior covers were frequently lined in a silk moiré and some portfolios had multiple interior dividers. The covers are the most attractive feature, elaborately decorated with silver, silver plate, or another metal sometimes bearing the owner's initials or name. Today, a fairly simple desk portfolio could be available for approximately $100, while a silver-mounted ivory one might command upwards of $500.

Blotters

Blotters appear in two formats. The first is a rectangular writing surface at the center of the desktop. The edges could be in the shape of a tray, about 18" x 16", and the bottom or interior fitted with blotting paper. When you finish writing your letter with liquid ink, turn the letter over on the blotter and blot the excess ink. The second type of blotter is the rocker blotter. This is a small (6" x 3" x 3") object with a top knob to hold and a curved bottom fitted with blotting paper. Lift this blotter, apply it to the finished letter, and rock it back and forth gently to blot any excess ink. Rocker-blotters can be found in the $50 to $150 range. Tartan Ware rocker blotters are more towards the $350 to $500 range. For illustrations, refer to photographs in Chapters Two and Three.

Inkwells

Here is a collector's dream; the variety of inkwells is almost endless. This desk item was frequently pro-

Round spherical brass inkwell; hinged lid with original glass container inside, saucer base. Decorated with four matching agate marbles and foliate incising. c. 1880. $650. *Photo by William B. Bradley*

duced and sold alone, not only with desk sets. They were favourite presentation and retirement gifts, so they are often available at a good antiques shop. In addition to the finishes noted with the desk sets above, inkwells also were made of porcelain, glass, horn, and other materials, even horse hooves. A typical inkwell might consist of a four-footed oval metal tray with two fitted receptacles for glass cups for ink and between them a modelled stag's head with a rack for pens. The price range is wide, depending on quality, age, and rarity. If you see one and it appeals to you, go for it!

Inscribed presentation silver-plated inkstand, dated 1912. Glass inkwells are missing covers. Modelled stag head at centre with horns for straight-pen storage. On four claw feet. 6" h., $350.

Silver-mounted inkstand of horse's hoof. Central silver inkwell with lid. Hallmarked Birmingham 1899. 2.5" h. $475.

Pens and Pen Trays

A storage facility for the pens was sometimes provided at the front of the inkstand, but more often the pen had its own home in the pen tray. Typically 11" x 3" x 2" high, the pen tray had a dish-like interior (frequently glass-lined to prevent ink from soiling the finish). The opportunity for affixing a presentation plate to a pen tray was often utilized. Until the invention of the fountain pen, straight (or dip) pens were the norm, usually 7" to 9" in length, and consisting of the pen handle and the nib holder. The pen might be silver, ivory, wood, or whatever an owner could afford. Pen nibs were fitted into a slot at the bottom of the handle. Prices could run approximately $75 to $250 for a pen tray and $25 to $100 for a straight pen.

Solid cast brass Scottish red deer with antlers shaped to store straight pens. 19th c., 6" h., $650.

Two desk items in Mauchline Ware. Top: Combination stamp and nib box in configuration of butler's tray, $295. Below: rounded-end pen tray, $185.

Stamp and Nib Boxes

Stamp boxes were somewhat special to the early Victorians (Scots included), since postage stamps did not become available until the 1850s. Clearly, boxes made for postage stamps were made solely for that purpose. They are rectangular with a lid, either hinged or lift-off, and one, two, or even three divided interior compartments for different denomination stamps. Often the compartments have sloped bottoms to more easily withdraw the stamps. Lids were sometimes decorated with a full-sized or miniature stamp design, typically a Queen Victoria "2d red.". Stamp boxes also are found in a small round shape with lift lid. Nib boxes are usually quite small, with hinged lid, measuring roughly 3" x 2" x 1". Sometimes, stamp boxes and nib boxes appear as a unit with separate compartments for nibs and stamps. Stamp boxes are highly collectible and are found in a broad variety of materials: silver, silver plate, wood, Tartan Ware, Mauchline Ware, horn, metal, and so on. Those with stamps affixed to the tops can be found with different colours, ages, and denomination stamps, enlarging the collecting range even further. Prices start at about $50 and a nice selection can be found in the $100 to $250 range.

Mauchline Ware desk calendar with hand-programmable cards, a complete set, c. 1880. $325.

Stationery Holders, Card Holders, and Calendars

A typical desk set stationery holder measures approximately 8" x 5" x 8", with hinged lid or open top. There would be three to four horizontal dividers to separate the stationery, envelopes, and post-cards. A miniature version of this was used to hold calling cards. A similarly shaped box was a desk calendar. It had three horizontal divisions: the front one contained a series of cardboard cards with days of the week, the middle one had cards for the date (1-31), and the back one had cards for the month. The cards required hand-placement, in true Victorian fashion. Another style desk calendar also required "hand-programming," but was a bit more inventive. It had a series of turning knobs to line up the correct day of week, date, and month. Price ranges today are wide. Any one of the items noted should be able to be found for about $50 and up. Seldom do you find a complete calendar of the cardboard insert type. There is always one card missing!

Miniature letter-rack in "McGregor" tartan on rectangular foot. This was probably used as a calendar with cards "hand-programmed" to reflect day-of-week, date & month. Sadly, in this Tartan Ware example, the date cards are missing! On base is label for original vendor "Guerrier, Rue St Honore, 205" (Paris). 4.25" x 1.25" x 3.25". $650.

Rulers

Many different styles of rulers were made, and three are worth a quick look. First, the traditional flat ruler, normally found in 12" and 15" lengths, has varying scales and a brass edge. A second type is triangular with a variety of scales, often listed as "English inches" and "French centimeters." A third type is round, shaped like a rolling pin, about 9" in length. Sometimes the knob ends of these pull out to access an eraser and pencil. The round ruler's popularity was secured when drawing an ink line with a nib pen; the ink did not smear by leaking under the brass edge, as was frequently the case with a flat ruler. Materials used were wood, brass, Tartan Ware, and Mauchline Ware. Rulers were a popular form of advertising for stationers who would imprint their logos. Quite frequently rulers were imprinted with the current postal rates, allowing a collector to fairly accurately date the ruler. There are folding carpenters' rulers, too. A nice advertising ruler, c.1890, could cost about $25 and up.

String Holders

Before the advent of Scotch brand cellophane tape (which has no known Scottish connection that we are aware of), packages were done up with string. In true Victorian style, the string was kept in a purpose-built container, usually referred to as a string holder. String holders were usually made of wood, were globe shaped with a hole at the top through which to draw the string, and often had a hanging cord to place on a hook beneath a utility shelf. The globe would twist apart at the middle to inset a new ball of string. String holders were usually about 4" in diameter and were popular in Tartan Ware and Mauchline Ware, but they also are found in other wooden forms. Prices start at about $50.

Paper Knives, Letter Openers, Bookmarks, and Page Turners

In addition to a letter opener, a well equipped Scottish Victorian desk would also have a paper knife. In the early 19th century, books were bound without the page edges being cut. The owner of a new book would cut each page open by hand. To do this, a fairly blunt-edged, wooden paper knife was used, being usually 9" to 15" in length. A similarly shaped "pagenator" was used to turn the pages of the book while reading, to avoid getting destructive skin oil and dirt from fingers onto the pages. A boomark, similar to a large paperclip, was also a regular inhabitant of the desk area. Most paper knives and pagenators are made of wood, often in Tartan Ware and Mauchline Ware finishes, and some have advertising logos. Letter openers can be found in silver, silver plate, white metal, ivory, and wood. Sometimes the handles are decorated with Scottish banded agate marbles. Bookmarks were also produced in a variety of materials, including wood, metal, and agate trowel-shaped devices.

Exquisite silver and agate desk letter opener with cut thistle-shaped citrine at top. Extremely fine silver chasing. c. 1880, 6", $750.

Seals, Sealing Wax, and Match Holders

To assure that the letter being posted was not opened en-route, the sender often would seal the envelope flap with a dab of sealing wax. To doubly reassure the receiver that the privacy of the letter had not been compromised, the sender could imprint the seal with his crest or initials. The process could take several forms, but generally proceeded as follows. A match, taken from a *match holder*, would be ignited by drawing it across the striker at the front of the holder. The lighted match was held under a stick of sealing wax, held in a *sealing wax holder*, and molten wax dripped onto the join of the envelope flap. The sender then pressed his *signet ring* onto the warm wax, leaving an imprint. Lacking a signet ring, he could utilize a standing seal with crest or initials. Finally, the letter was ready to post.

As the reader will note, there are three specific purpose-made articles involved in this relatively simple process. The match holder assumed a variety of shapes and was made of a variety of materials, typically being a small goblet-shaped container on a pedestal and a striker on the base. Prices today, $75 to $150. A sealing wax holder was shaped like a small, double-ended pincushion with the interior hollow to accept a stick of hard sealing wax. Again, they were made from a variety of materials, and today's prices are in the area of $100. Signet rings were usually gold and frequently a gift from father to son when he came of age, twenty-one. Prices for old signet rings could be around $100 and up. Standing seals were made of silver, agate, silver plate or brass. There was a round base, 1/2" in diameter, with a 2" to 3" vertical handle. On the base was the owner's initials or crest. The range is enormous, and prices could start at about $75.

Small brass chamber stick with saucer base; side thumb-holder, and snuffer. c. 1890, $325.

Scissors Sets, Chamber Sticks, and Photo Frames

A set of scissors is an essential tool at a desk. Often a large and a small pair of scissors, usually made of steel or stainless steel, would be enclosed in a scissors case. Some have a folding cover and some a wooden sleeve into which scissors would be slid for safekeeping. A matching letter opener was sometimes included. You could find a nice set today in the $50 and up range. Before the introduction of electricity, and other than gas lighting, candles furnished the usual illumination. Desk sets often came with matching candleholders and smallchamber sticks. They had about 4" diameter saucer bases, side finger holds, and 5"vertical candle holders. These are found in various shapes of wood, with "barley-twist" stems and brass *bobechés*, saucers to catch dripping wax. Today they would be roughly $100 to $300. Also, small brass chamber sticks and candleholders can be found in the shape of a thistle, c.1890, priced today in the $75 to $250 range. In the last quarter of the 19th century, photography became popular and studio portraits would be displayed at every opportunity. Easel-back photo frames were found on every stretch of flat table and the desk was not immune. Some very fine 5" x 7" frames can be found in silver, wood, leather, etc. There are also attractive little oval frames of pressed brass or white metal with elaborate thistle and foliage surrounds measuring roughly 5" x 3" with folding easel backs, so they could be taken on a visit. Prices today are in the $150 and up range.

From top: Pull-off top spectacle case in rare green "MacKenzie" tartan. With Original (?) gold-filled "specs". 5". $425. "Sleeve" scissors case in "McPherson" tartan, with leather sides and open ends. Sterling scissors have heavily embossed handles. Scissors measure 4" x 2". Case is 5" x 1.25". $525.

Pair of small, brass, thistle-shaped chamber sticks with saucer base and side finger-hold, on three feet, 19th c., $135.

Pair of brass Victorian candlesticks, 5" h., in the shape of standing thistles with foliage stem, 19th c., $195.

Small pressed metal desk photo frame with easel backstand, 5" h. c.1900, $185.

Chapter Ten

Snuff and Tobacco Smoking

Snuff is the powder residue remaining after grinding up the stalks of tobacco. The Scots called it *sneesh*, and appear to have adopted the habit of "sneeshing" shortly after tobacco was brought to The British Isles after its discovery in the New World in the 16th century. The taking of snuff was widely prevalent in Scotland across all spectrums of society. It was not a cheap habit, by any means, but the habitué found ways to pay for it.

Snuff was inhaled through the nostrils, not the most endearing sight to be sure. Not only was it expensive, but the light powder form also was difficult to contain and isolate from moisture.

Snuff Boxes

The invention of a "secret hinge" (see John Sandy's hinge discussed at the beginning of Chapter Two) on snuff boxes provided a means to contain the snuff in air-tight conditions. Snuff boxes were made from many materials and all had some sort of tight closure, often with a form of over-lipped lid. Early boxes were wood. Later, as the use became a societal art form and ritual, boxes were made of silver, gold, brass, ivory, etc., often being elaborately decorated with cairngorms or other jewels.

Snuff boxes were made small for carrying in the pocket and large ones, in the shape of a round vase, were made for table use. Vase-shaped ones were often made with stave construction in different woods, panels of ivory and ebony, etc. (See Chapter Eight for details on stave construction.) Later, snuff boxes, now being termed snuff-mulls, were made from the horns of Scottish sheep. A group of skilled craftsmen, called "horners,"developed the technique of curling a sheep's horns by means of heating them in hot water. (See also Chapter Sixteen.) Small snuff-mulls, also termed pocket snuffs, measure about 5" to 6" end to end. The hinged lids, often made from silver, pewter, or brass, might be decorated with the owner's crest, initials, a thistle, and often a cairngorm. They can also be found inscribed from an individual or organization. Many pocket snuff boxes date back to the end of the 17th century, and they are truly works of art.

Typical silver-mounted Scottish horn pocket snuff mull, Inscribed date on silver shield 1788. Note intricately curved tail. Approx 3.5", $650.

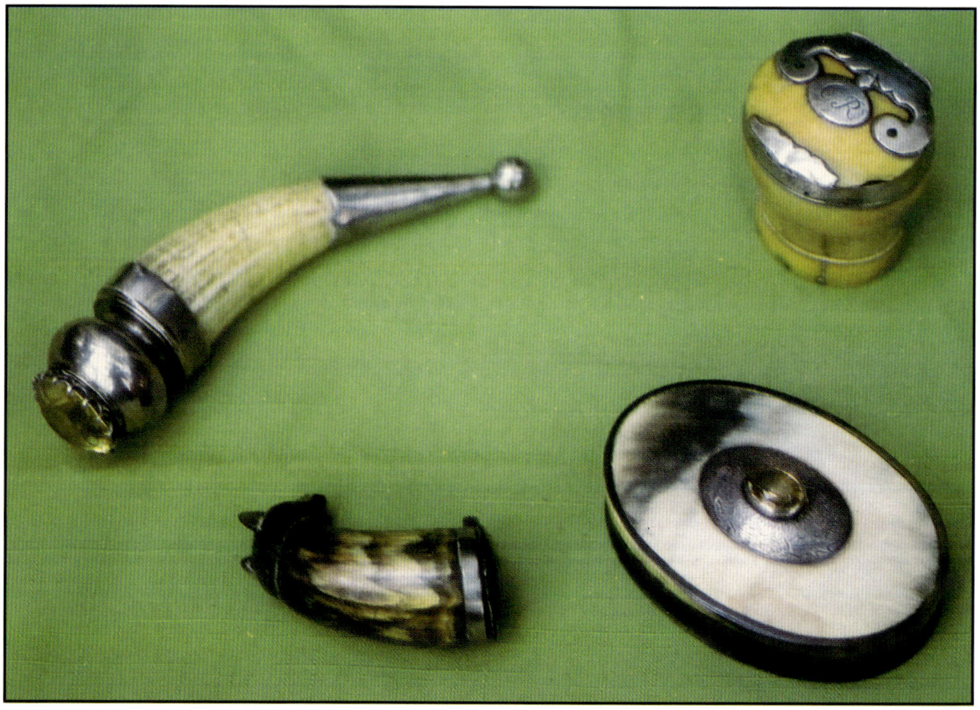

Four different snuff mull configurations. Clockwise, from left: Silver-mounted whale's tooth with claw-set citrine, 19th c., $650. Vase-shaped ivory and silver mounted table snuff mull, early 18th c., $850. Round table snuff of cattle-horn with silver and citrine mounts, $500. Early 19th c. horn pocket snuff mull, with carved dog head, silver-mounts, $500. *Courtesy of James D. Forman*

Close-up of top of pressed horn table snuff mull with silver fittings, large cut citrine and silver affixed thistle/foliage. Air-tight lid with cork lining. mid-19th. c. $950.

Larger snuff mulls were made towards the end of the 18th century. Some were made from flattened cow-horn with silver-mounted lids and thistle or cairngorm decorations; they could lay flat on the table. Others were mounted on a stand and employed a similarly decorated cow horn in its original, conical configuration. The ultimate in snuff mulls were a few magnificent specimens found in gentlemen's city clubs and the officers' messes of Scottish regiments. These utilized an entire ram's head, suitably preserved by a taxidermist, mounted on a three-wheeled tray for ease in passing it from place to place. Into the top of the skull was recessed a silver-hinged box handsomely decorated with repoussé thistles and a large, smoky-gray cut cairngorm. At the end of the ram's horns were matching silver-mounted cairngorms. Attached to a silver ring on the head were five silver chains with a small tool for the proper preparation of the snuff at the end of each chain. An ivory hammer, to break up the lumps, a probe to dig out reluctant snuff, a scoop or spoon, a small rake, and a rabbit's foot to sweep up the residue were all attached. Naturally, there was a silver presentation shield detailing the regiment, the donor, and/or the date.

Horn table snuff mull with silver mounts and side-affixed silver Jacobite rose. Hallmarks for London, 1830. $750.

Powderhorn, converted to table snuff mull. Originally carried by chain from fittings below lid and above tail. On sterling silver hinged top is a smoky cairngorm; at the tip is silver thistle finial with amethyst. Early 19th c., $1000.

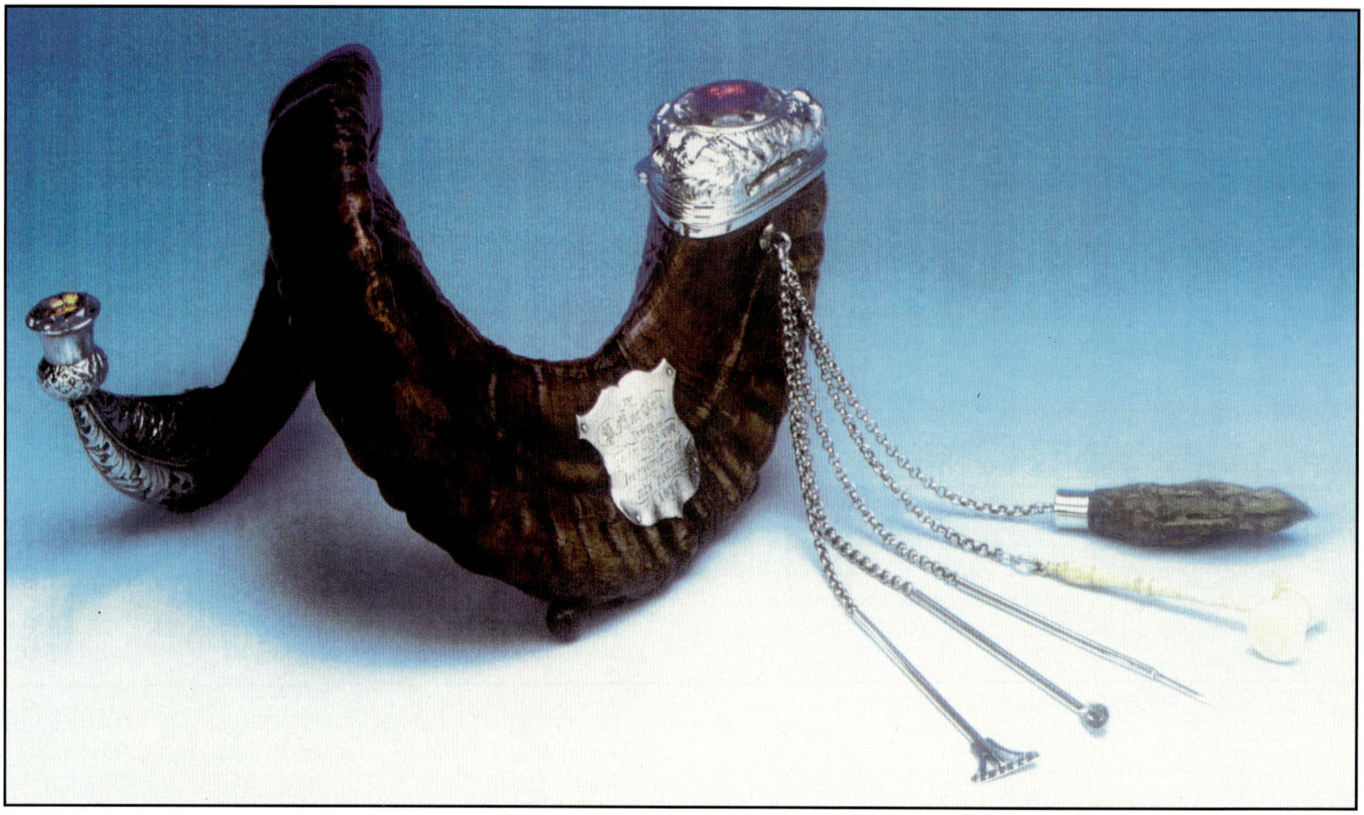

Large ram's horn table snuff mull. Elaborately embossed silver mounts with foil-backed quartz stones in thistle tail finial and hinged-lid cover. Presentation inscription for 1878. Silver chains with attached implements of rake, scoop, pick, ivory hammer, and rabbit's foot. $3000.

Ram's horn table snuff mull, with detailed silver embossing on hinged lid and thistle tail finial. Beautiful dark smoky cairngorm mounted on lid. $3000.

The *piece de resistance*! Full ram's head table snuff mull with gold mounts, utensils, amethysts in hinged lid snuff container and at horn tips, complete with rack to hold cigars, c. 1880. $10000.
Courtesy of James D. Forman

Small, hinged-lid tobacco tin, "Tam O'Shanter Tobacco", with curious cut access flap in bottom. c. 1920s. 3.5" x 2.25" x 1.25", $40.

Early tobacconist's figure of Scottish regimental officer taking a pinch of snuff. 42" high, carved gesso and original old paint. $6000-7000. *Courtesy of Kaja Veilleux Antiques, Inc.*

Because of the relatively large numbers produced, snuff boxes are still relatively available, with prices for a simple, undecorated wood box about $100 and ranging well into the thousands for an elaborate gold or silver jewel-encrusted example. Small table-snuffs would run today in the $250 to $750 range. Pocket horn snuff mulls are findable today at about $500 to $1000. Elaborate and larger horn table snuffs could be $750 and up. The rarest of the rare, a fully accessorized ram's head table snuff, with full provenance, could be approximately $5000 to $10,000. They are seldom seen unless one comes up to auction.

Before departing the world of snuff, one must recognize the tobacconist's Highlander display figure. As American tobacconists had their cigar store Indian to advertise their wares in the 19th century, so the sellers of snuff in the 18th and 19th centuries in Scotland had their display figures of 3'- to 4'-high carved wooden Highlanders, complete with snuff mull in one hand and a "wee pinch" on the way to his nostrils in the other. Very occasionally one of these may come up at auction. Make sure of its provenance and be prepared to pay $5000 or more. By the mid-1800s, snuff taking was completely out of favour in Scotland.

Tobacco-related "bad habits" persisted into the late 19th and 20th centuries with the smoking of cigars, cigarettes, and pipes. Tobacco products have inspired all sorts of interesting niches into which antique enthusiasts can probe.

Cigarette and Cigar Boxes and Cases

Two forms of cigarette boxes exist, those for the pocket and those for the table. Table styles in wood, silver, pewter, gold, or whatever offered opportunities for personalization to commemorate an occasion, wedding, anniversary, promotion, retirement, or similar event. The same is true of pocket cases. Both forms, if Scottish, could have a thistle motif or other Scottish association emblem in inlaid agate, cairngorms, or the like. One popular outside covering in Scotland was *shagreen*, sharkskin, often found on cases and other smoking articles, finished to a green or white-grained surface and frequently with ivory embellishments. Today, a plain cigarette case, c. 1900 and with a bit of character, could cost in the area of $75. A nice *shagreen* case could be $300, and silver or gold cases could start at about $100 and go up in value from there.

Cigar boxes and cases are not very different in character, description, and pricing from cigarette ones, save for the obvious difference in size to accept the larger cigar shape. Humidors for loose tobacco must exist as uniquely Scottish, but we haven't run across one; if you have, do let us know.

Match Safes or Vestas

Before the advent of safety matches, the cardboard match box, and even later paper matches, wooden striking matches were subject to instantaneous combustion and were therefore kept in air-tight containers referred to as match safes or *vestas*. (Oddly, some of these are not dissimilar in appearance to even-later ZIPPO™ lighters). Match safes are found in various materials, including wood, Mauchline Ware, Tartan Ware, and even (more frequently) metal: silver, brass, pewter, or gold. A typical Scottish version, c. 1890-1900, is hallmarked silver with an elaborate inlaid jasper and bloodstone agate design in the shape of a thistle, measuring about 2" x 1" x 1/2". It has a flip lid to access the matches and a ridged silver striking surface on the bottom. This type has a round loop at the top which could be attached to a man's watch-chain, a lady's *chatelaine*, or be worn as a pendant on a chain around the neck. Of course, the more practical method was just to slip it into the pocket (for naughty ladies who smoked cigarettes, very forward in those days). A plain wood match safe, or *vesta*, can be found today for under $100 and a more elaborate one, as described above, can be $500 to $750.

Silver and agate match-safe or vesta, incised silver and agate-inlaid thistle, hallmarked Birmingham, 1922. $650. *Photo by William B. Bradley*

Table Cigarette Holders and Ashtrays

In the early 20th century, smoking of cigarettes became more prevalent. It became fashionable to place an open vertical container containing cigarettes on the dining room table, along with a match container. When the gentlemen retired from the table to the billiard or smoking room for their post-prandial cigar and glass of vintage port, the ladies stayed behind in the dining room for their own puff. These holders were often done in silver, marble, granite, china or glass. Prices should be in the $50-200 range. Ashtrays range very broadly in character. We have seen "mini" portable pocket/purse ashtrays with a closeable top, all the way to a massive chair-side ashtray on stand. Some rather nice silver "presentation" ashtrays can be found, with the owner's crest on them, or commemorating an anniversary, shooting or fishing prize, etc. These are nice, because the date is usually inscribed. There are also some very handsome china or cut glass ashtrays that were made in the early 20th century, with transfer figures of Scottish regiments, or thistles etched into the glass, respectively. Prices range from $35-250.

Match box containing a box of safety matches on four bun feet with silver mounts and inlaid agate top, hallmarked, Birmingham, 1916. $600.

Tobacco Jars

Prior to the days of our familiar rolled cigarettes, one had to roll-your-own and of course the tobacco for these "butts" had to be kept in air-tight containers, usually the pocket-tin in which the "'baccy" was purchased. Sometimes, however, the frugal Scot would wish to buy his supply in larger volumes (at a saving.). He very probably kept it in the same containers which were being used for pipe tobacco. Any airtight material served, but wood and china seem to have been preferred.

Wood tobacco jar, c. 1830. Stave construction with lift-off top. Alternating strips of ash (light) and laburnam (dark) wood. 6" h. $500.

Barrel-shaped wood tobacco box, 19th c., $415 *Courtesy of June and Tony Snow*

Pipes

Scottish pipes (as in smoking, not musical bagpipes) can be found dating back to the 19th century. Often made of briar or other native wood, they sometimes had a hinged top, perforated, to act as a windscreen to avoid spreading dangerous sparks around the countryside. We are not very "into" pipes, so we will refrain from attempting to establish any price parameters. Another version of Scottish pipes, which we do see once in a while, are clay-pipes. These are often incised on the side "Made in Scotland" "Glasgow" or other reference to the point of origin. They often have a small "stand" below the bowl to allow resting on the table in between puffs. These are relatively fragile, and it's a wonder any have survived from the turn of the 20th century (or earlier), particularly since most were used for smoking in the local tavern or pub. They're nice little pieces, however, and are a reasonable $25-50.

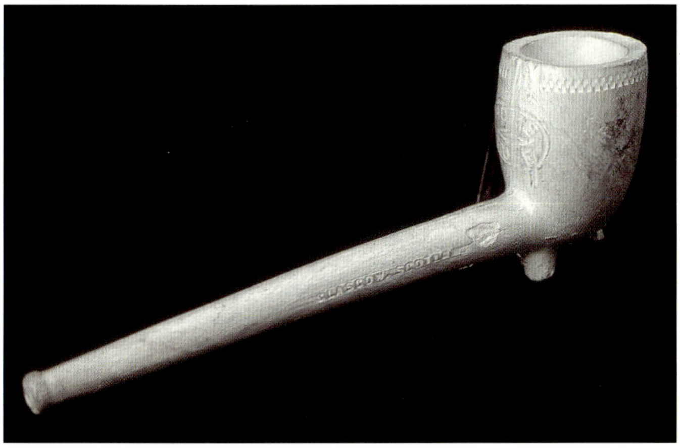

Clay pipe with standing foot, marked Glasgow. 19th c., $75. *Photo by William B. Bradley*

Cigarette and Cigar Holders

These are attractive pieces made in a variety of materials: horn, ivory, silver, tortoiseshell, you name it. This is one area in which we are unaware of any true Scottish examples. They may very well exist, but we have not run across them.

Lighters

We will not dwell on the entire category of lighters which started to appear c.WWI. The English firm of Dunhill™ is probably one of the more famous ones. One early lighter bears mention, however. About 9" high and made of molded pot-metal, this lighter is a beautifully crafted and painted figure of a Gordon Highlander officer in full kit. His head is hinged, and once pushed back, one can access a small brass rod, with wick and striker at the bottom. Drawn sharply across the striker fitted into the base on which the figure stands, the lighted wick is then used to light the evening's cigar. We are advised by a reliable source that these lighters were found in the officer's mess of the Scottish regiments; although we've never run across another, save the Gordon's. At the obvious (and accepted) risk of being accused of punning, one could truly say that this is a striking antique.

Officer's mess cigar lighter in the form of a figure of a Gordon Highlander officer. Head hinges back to access metal striker with wick. 19th c., $950.

Chapter Eleven

Ceramics

An Overview

Scottish ceramics production dates back to the earliest settlements and continued through medieval times. Two sites in Lothian, near Edinburgh, have been identified by pottery shards recovered from archeological digs. Occasional records of later pottery-making in Scotland have been found, but with all of Scotland's troubles in the fifteenth through seventeenth centuries, it was, to say the least, sporadic and disorganized.

All that changed, however, in the second half of the eighteenth century, with the industrial revolution and the coming of the factory system. Scotland, fortunately, had the necessary infrastructure to build upon. Graeme Cruickshank, in his book *Scottish Pottery*, explains:

> Pottery making tended to gravitate towards those areas which could supply it's basic needs: clay to make the pots, and coal to fire them; sufficient labour not only to man the factories but also possessing the aptitude to learn new skills; a ready means of transporting the finished ware in bulk, which in those days generally meant going by sea, coupled with a proximity to population centres and the markets which they could provide.[1]

The earliest Scottish potteries were established in the Glasgow area and the East Lothian areas to the east of Edinburgh. Despite a few rocky starts, by the end of the eighteenth century Scotland's potteries were off and walking, if not exactly yet running. Ceramics also started to be produced, principally in the eastern environs of Edinburgh, at Portobello, Musselburgh, and Prestonpans.

A brief lesson in the different terms involved in the next few pages is in order. **Pottery**, a generic catchall term, is made from clay and is opaque, not very suitable for decoration, and not expensive to produce.

Porcelain, or china, is a translucent, "hard paste" ware fired at high temperatures. It can be shaped into elaborate forms, takes well to decoration, and is fairly expensive. The Chinese and Japanese kept the making of porcelain a secret until chemists in Meissen, Germany, uncovered the technique in the early eighteenth century. Hard paste porcelain was not made in Britain, where a soft paste type was developed using Cornish china clay (kaolin) and china stone (petuntse).

White salt-glazed stoneware was one of the early products of the Edinburgh factories.

Delftware, a pottery glazed with a reduction from tin (much of which came from Cornwall), and produced in Glasgow, became a prolific export to the American Colonies in the second half of the eighteenth century.

The factory also produced **stoneware**, dense, heavy, and fired at high temperatures, and **creamware**, light, strong, and very workable.

Spongeware, a Scottish pottery decorated by sponge-printing, was another later product.

The nineteenth century, particularly the second half, was the hey-day of Scottish pottery. The range was enormous, including dainty tea-services, decorated table-pieces, Victorian souvenir items such as miniature cups and vases, sometimes decorated with the arms and mottoes of holiday towns, classically shaped jugs and ewers, bowls, platters, punchbowls, *ashets* (Scottish for serving platters, after the French *assiette*), porridge bowls, plates and saucers. Also a host of domestic stoneware items were made, such as dairy cream pots, hot water foot warmers, cider jars, beer and ginger beer bottles, butter crocks, ink bottles, kitchen containers, tobacconist's jars, jam jars, clay pipes, and so on. Several of these items will be reviewed in more detail in this chapter.

Armorial Porcelain

While not originally produced in Scotland, Chinese-made armorial porcelain was most popular at the end of the eighteenth and well into the nineteenth centuries. Any self-respecting Scottish family of means and with a large house had their own sets of china services, for breakfast, luncheon, dinner, tea, and coffee, decorated with their family coat of arms. If the family had no coat of arms, they borrowed or invented one. Sets of porcelain were expensive and took up to three years to be made and transported from China to Scotland on clipper ships. British and continental factories started to produce armorial porcelain about the second quarter of the nineteenth century. Obviously, with the passage of time, a lot of these old sets have been broken up or just plain broken. Either way, they are rare today and an individual un-chipped plate or dish, clearly dating to around 1800, would sell today for $500 to $750. Large platters, soup tureens, and the like could be much more. Old services may have had one or two "fill-in" pieces of later manufacture produced in the late nineteenth or twentieth centuries, to replace missing items. Coats of arms may have been added at later dates. Examine pieces carefully, ask questions, and deal with reputable dealers who will stand behind their written invoice.

Armorial plate bearing the arms of Munro of Lindertis, 9" dia. Part of a dinner set, sadly now mostly dispersed, c. 1820. $500. *Photo by William B. Bradley*

Victorian Figures and Souvenir Items

In Chapter One, we related how Scotland became a tourist attraction, starting in the mid-nineteenth century, thanks to Queen Victoria, Sir Walter Scott's novels, the coming of the railroad, and the improved road system. One of the requirements for sustaining tourism is a supply of souvenir items to memorialize the excursion. Scottish potteries were quick to fill this need. The best known region in England that produced commemorative Victorian china figures is Staffordshire, yet many ceramic figures also were made in Scotland, rather than England. Factories at Glasgow, Pollockshaws, Edinburgh, Portobello, and Prestonpans all produced the figures. Animals and famous people were favourite subjects, including Queen Victoria and her family, military heroes, politicians, theatre personalities, and—above all—highland cattle and dogs. In Scotland, the china dogs claiming their position of honour on the family mantlepiece were called *wally dugs*, "wally" being Scots for china. These figures were rather crudely made but are in considerable demand by collectors today. The minimum price for a Staffordshire figure would be approximately $250. Rare figures or top condition multiple figure groups run well into four figures.

In a fashion closely paralleling the growth of the Mauchline Ware souvenir trade, the Scottish pottery factories produced a mass of small china pieces decorated with heather, thistles, a verse from Burns, and most popularly the arms and mottoes of towns all over Scotland. These pieces often took the forms of small vases, thimbles, cups and saucers, plates, and ashtrays or replicated a Scottish *quaich* or *luggie*. Colourful, inexpensive, and small enough to slip in the pocket, these items continued to be produced into the twentieth century. They are probably still being turned out in the twenty-first century, as well. You should be able to find the older souvenir novelties today starting at about $50. New ones could be $10 to $20 maximum.

Staffordshire figure of a Highlander, 16" h. Estimate $250-400. *Courtesy of Phillips Auctioneers, Edinburgh*

Jugs and Ewers

Classical-styled jugs and ewers were popular products from about 1850 onwards. These utilitarian table pieces were used to pour milk and other liquids at the dining table. Bell's Pottery of Glasgow turned out many of the designs, and some of their shapes and painted decorations were registered. John and Matthew Bell started their factory on the banks of the Forth and Clyde canal. They became wealthy men, not only by selling their broad range of Victorian china to their own contrymen, but also by enjoying substantial sales to the Far East and particularly to the American market. Their ever-popular "willow pattern" was a successful blue and white earthernware table pattern, as was their "triumphal car" pattern, showing a chariot drawn by leopards and other animals surrounded by temples, palms, and palaces. On the backs of the plates was Bell's distinctive logo and the name of the pattern. The "willow pattern" was produced at a number of other Scottish factories, as well. Other table items produced by both the Bell's and Edinburgh potteries such as William Reid of Musselborough, included punch bowls, compotes, and serving dishes. Jugs, such as one with a picture of Robbie Burns and a verse from his poems, can be found today for prices in the neighborhood of $275. Plates in good condition in the "willow pattern" and with Bell's logo are about $175.

Ironstone jug in white glaze with duplicate colour transfer on each side. Gold stippled top and bottom portions. 8" h. Mark on bottom for David Lockhart of Pollockshaws. 1896. $375.

Tin, enamelled "tooth-mug" honoring Queen Victoria on her sixty years on the throne. (1837-1897). Has pictures of her at both these significant years. 4.5" h. x 3.5" dia. $135.

Relief molded jug with side handle and depiction of "Rabbie" Burns on both sides. Earthernware in pale blue, from Scottish pottery (not marked), last half 19th c. $285.

Over-size souvenir cup and saucer with Burns' verse in mulberry, late 19th c., $185.

Oval platter, scalloped edges, with multiple Scottish hunting scenes. Stamped on back "Caledonia, Middlesboro Pottery". c.1840. 10.5" x 9". $365.

One dish of a set of eight, plus three serving platters in Wedgwood creamware "Thistle pattern," late 19th c. $1000/set.

Single dinner plate in flow-blue willow pattern, with distinctive mark(blue wreath, bell and crown) for J & MP Bell & Co., Glasgow, 10.25" dia., c. 1870, $115.

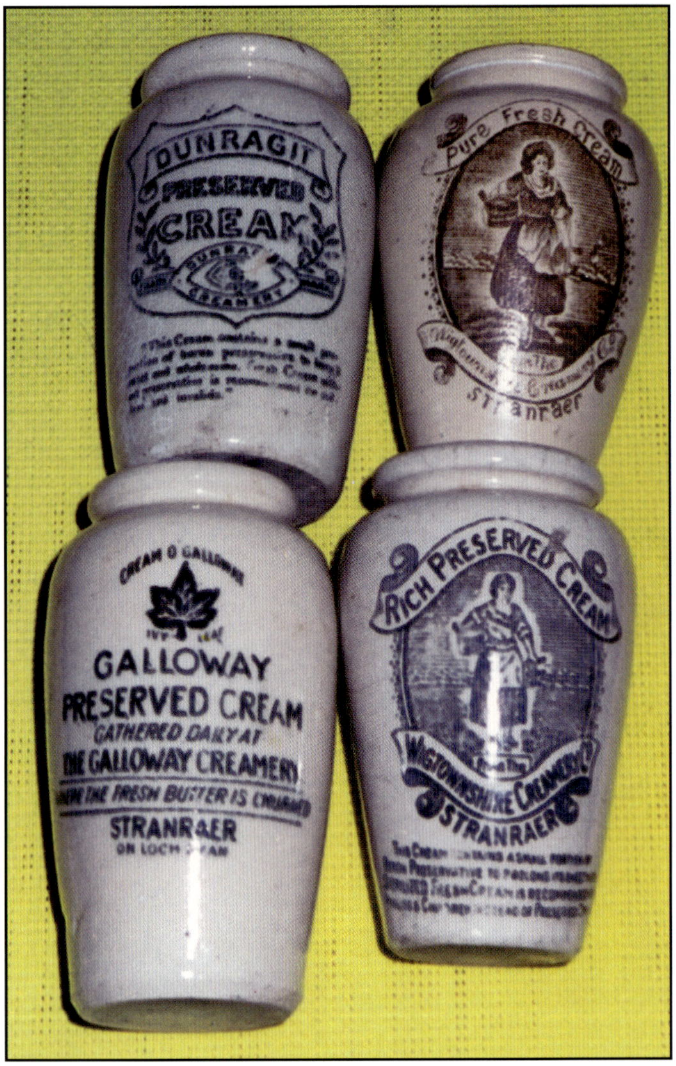

Four different cream pots; note sepia and black transfers for "Stranraer" on right.

Dairy Cream Pots

A less formal product of Scotland's potteries was a stoneware object known as a dairy cream pot. These cream pots, as we will henceforth refer to them, came about as the result of refrigeration and the invention of the cream separator, all in the last half of the nineteenth century. From then until the 1920s, cream pots were used to deliver the household's daily cream order. Once used, the cream pots were tossed into the *midden*, only to be dug up by latter-day collectors.

Three cream pots, all with black transfers and brown painted shoulders and necks.

Cream pots come in a great variety of shapes along with the printed name of the dairy that distributed the cream. In some cases, the name of the cream pot manufacturer was incised on the side of the pot near the base before firing; however by far the greater number produced were not marked. The name, logo, and product information of the dairy was either applied with a printed label or was added by underglaze printing. The design was stamped on before glazing or it was transfer printed from a hand-engraved copper plate. Since a number of highly skilled engravers were available, the designs on some of these cream pots were most attractive, illustrating cows, milkmaids, foliate patterns, thistles, and so forth. Normally, cream pots were produced in off-white, gray, or cream glazes. Occasionally, the shoulders and neck would be light or dark brown. Transfers appeared most frequently in black, in sepia, and more rarely in blue. Sizes ranged from 3" to 7" high; by far the majority were in the 3.5" to 4.5" range. Oddly, no volume content was stated—what you saw is what you got!

Four more cream pots. Note differences in transfers on the two "Dunragit" items.

Two more cream pots. Note slight discolouration on necks and shoulders, acceptable to this degree since these items were excavated.

Cream pots were manufactured by various Scottish potteries, and collectors should be able to find examples with incised marks from Port Dundas Pottery, Govancroft, Possil Pottery, and Kennedy, all of Glasgow; Caledonian of Rutherglen, Buchan of Portobello, Price of Bristol, England, and Priest Canton of Cardiff, Wales. Pots were sealed with cork, tinfoil, or a waxed fibre disc, which fitted into the recessed neck of custom-made pots. By far the largest number of cream pots were produced at the Scottish factories, as were most of the pots with English dairy stamps.

Scottish dairies that distributed included Craigmillar, Dalbeattie, Dunragit, Galloway, Dairy School Kilmarnock, Saltburn, Strathbogie, Wigtownshire, Cooper's, Cameron of Ayr, Imperial Creamery of Glasgow, Huntly Creamery, and Stranraer Creamery. Many had several different sizes and transfer designs.

These comprise a wonderful collector's niche, being relatively inexpensive and with a variety of approaches to the challenge of forming a collection. You could acquire one from each dairy, one from each manufacturer, concentrate on one dairy and try to get all the different transfers and sizes, or any combination of the above. The number of new sources being uncovered (dumps, *middens*) appears to be dwindling.

An ordinary Scottish cream pot with a simple logo in transfer black, and no incised mark, can still be found for $35. A nice one with attractive transfer of figures in black and an incised mark could be about $55. A rare blue transfer design with incised mark and brown top and shoulders could be $100 or so. Some firing blemishes and discolouration are acceptable, but chips and severe brown discolouration are not.

Domestic Stoneware

Stoneware products were churned out profusely by Scottish potteries in the nineteenth and early twentieth centuries. Most came from the Portobello area (Buchan and Gray) and several independent potteries in the Glasgow area. Some of the more interesting items (but by no means all of them) include the following:

Jam and Marmalade Jars

Usually in white-grey stoneware, these straight jars with wide tops had a colourful printed label or a black printed transfer, such as the familiar Keiller's Dundee Marmalade™. The latter comes in at least three sizes: a mini at 2" high used on trains and in hotels for individual servings, the normal at 5.5" high, and the large at 8" high. Current prices are $20 to $40 (the mini being rarer, costs more). These jars were later copied in plastics.

Keiller & Sons Dundee marmalade jars; all stoneware. One full size and two miniatures.

Not all marmalade came from Dundee. Here is a jar from Moir's of Aberdeen.

Ginger Beer and Beer Bottles

The styles of stoneware and the different transfers used on these echo those of the cream pots. Generally they are off-white, gray, or cream and some have light or dark brown shoulders and necks. Some early bottles were dark brown earthenware with both the bottles' manufacturer and the beer-maker's name incised. In the traditional bottle shape, they are about 9" high, some with long necks and others with short shoulders. Sealers included cork, metal-hinged rubber stoppers, and rubber screw tops. Transfers tended to be even more elaborate than those on cream pots, with very imaginative calligraphy style and fanciful logos. Transfers appeared in blue, sepia, and black, and occasionally a green might be found. Prices start at about $65.

Four ginger beer stoneware bottles from various Scottish locales.

Three stoneware bottles, centre with transfer vendor information and the others with incised vendor markings.

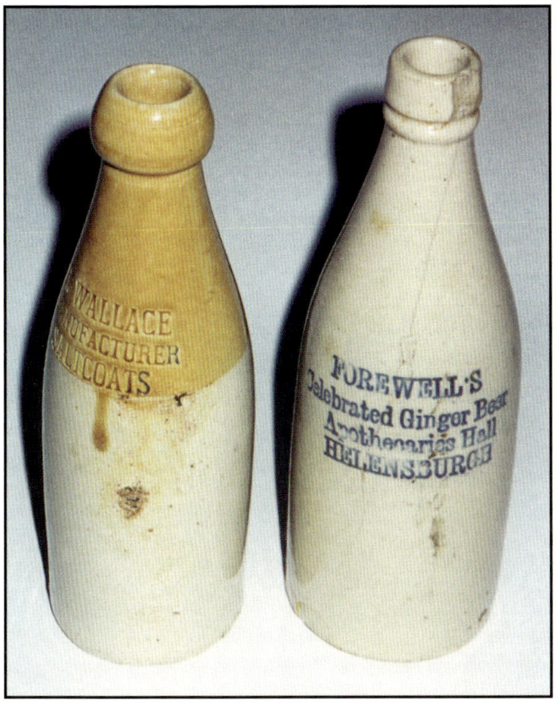

Firing defects (on left) and minor chips (on right) are acceptable if the transfers are sufficiently rare.

Foot Warmers

Also called water bottles, and sometimes by the Scots, pigs. These were stoneware containers in a variety of configurations, which were filled with hot water from the kettle on the stove and taken up to warm the ice-cold sheets at the bottom of the bed. This was pre-central heating; if you were extremely lucky, you had a bedroom. If you were really lucky, you had one with a fireplace. Most did not. The foot-warmer, more often than not had a wooden handle, a rubber cork to plug the fill hole, hopefully, but not always with a rubber o-ring that worked, and held about a gallon of water, which became cold much too quickly. Every manufacturer seemed to have a different design, military canteen configuration, a doctor's bag shape, for example, but the usual seemed to be oblong, with a flat bottom and curved sides. Each was stamped with a "catchy" name, the distributor's name and frequently the manufacturer's name incised on the side. Prices could be in the $250-400 range.

Typical stoneware foot warmer called a "pig," which is probably a very good analogy. $225

Stoneware foot warmer in shape of doctor's bag. Note the typical Victorian humour in the initials on the side. $275

Crocks and Flagons

There are some very attractive butter crocks which were produced by the Scottish pottery industry in the last half of the nineteenth century. The distributor's name was either stamped (transfer) or incised into the stoneware, and often some sort of design was incised before firing, a Greek key pattern, for example. The crock usually had an outward turning lip, often in a light or dark brown colour, contrasting with the usual gray, off-white or cream of the body of the crock. As often as not, any patterning was found either around the base and the lip. Lids? Sometimes they can still be found, but usually the crock is found without. Whisky, beer, cider and all manner of other liquids were sold and/or transported in large stoneware flagons and jugs. Cork or rubber stoppers were used. Frequently, these flagons had a small "finger-hold" integral handle on the top shoulder, just under the top; also the top was frequently manufactured with a pouring lip. Incised manufacturer's names, and distributor's names, either incised or transfer labels, are usually found on these large stoneware pieces, generally in the 2-5 gallon sizes.

Large stoneware trade bottle with a side handle, 16" h. $285

Attractively shaped stoneware whisky jug from Dunoon. $300.

Stoneware whisky jug with attractive black transfer. $150.

Large butter crock (holds 6 lbs) with black transfer. $285.

Kirkaldy Potteries and Wemyss Ware

At the same time that the Glasgow and Edinburgh potteries were churning out stoneware and other pottery products, another nearby Scottish locale was also active manufacturing similar items to those previously reviewed and also producing another very distinctive and collectible Scottish ceramic product. At the end of the nineteenth century, Kirkaldy, in the kingdom of Fife, on the north shore of the Firth of Forth, had a number of producing potteries, including Fife Pottery of Robert Heron and Son, and Kirkaldy Pottery of David Methven and Sons. Sometime around 1880, Heron and Son first came out with a line of pottery, which they called Wemyss ware after attractive continental ceramics found in Wemyss Castle in Fife. This rather bold and brightly coloured treatment was applied to a whole range of ceramics: dishes, garden planters, jugs, candle sticks, etc. Bohemian artist Karel Nekola was responsible for the designs which, while quite varied, all had the same look. In his 35 years at the factory, until his death in 1915, he trained many artists, including his own children who carried on his distinctive handpainting of Wemyss ceramic articles. Fruit, particularly apples and cherries, and flowers, all brightly coloured and sometimes with an attractive apple-green glaze, were some of his design hallmarks. One of the reasons for the popularity of Wemyss ware at the end of the nineteenth century was its endorsement by Royalty and the aristocracy. Today, Prince Charles is believed to be a keen collector, as was the late beloved Queen Mum.

Ceramic animals also were popular with the aristocracy. Wemyss developed a highly distinctive seated cat, as well as pigs in varied poses. These were all done with a whimsical touch, both in the beast's pose and expression and in the painted execution. Black hens and cockerels, dragonflies, rosebuds, irises, thistles and the cabbage rose were also favoured subjects. Wemyss ware was sold from a showroom at the factory but also through selected agents throughout the country. One of the larger agents was Thomas Goode and Son of London. Accord-

Small Weymss plate with typical rose and foliage, 5" dia. $285.

"Clover," a large, 17", Weymss pig from the Bovey Tracey period. $4000. *Courtesy of Phillips Auctioneers, Edinburgh*

Most attractive Weymss small dresser comb tray, 10". $575. *Photo by William B. Bradley*

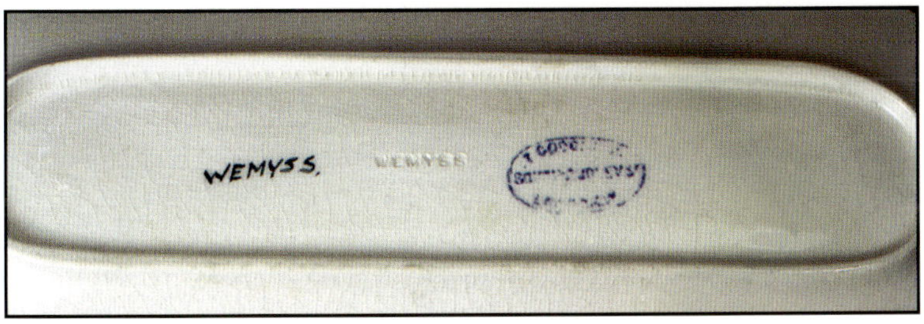

Reverse of comb tray pictured above, showing incised mark for Weymss, the painter's Weymss mark in green paint, and the vendor's imprint "T. Goode & Sons, Scottish Weymss, London." *Photo by William B. Bradley*

ing to a definitive work on Wemyss, *Kirkaldy Potteries* by Carol McNeill:

> Virtually all pieces of Wemyss Ware were marked. Earlier pieces had a semi-circular Wemyss Ware stamp and R.H. and S. impressed on the foot of the piece before it was fired. Other marks include the word Wemyss impressed in a straight line, or "Wemyss" inscribed by the decorator using the last colour on the paintbrush — and sometimes a combination of both. Pieces sold by Thomas Goode in their London shop had the firm's name rubber-stamped or painted on them as well. Karel Nekola, David Grinton and John Brown occasionally signed or initialled some of their work, especially major pieces, and the way in which "Wemyss" is written is a reliable way of identifying different artists.[2]

Production of Wemyss continued until 1928, when the factory closed down as a result of the Depression and lack of demand. Production rights were bought by Bovey Pottery in Devon, where Weymss hand-painted pieces were made and painted by Nekola's son, Joseph, until 1957. More recently, the Wemyss tradition has been continued, back in Fife, by Griselda Hill Pottery, where the same hand-painting and under-glaze techniques are still used.

Before the 1950s, Wemyss ware was priced not far above any other ceramic product with decent lines and execution. Then, Wemyss was discovered by collectors and the price reacted accordingly. The world record price for a Wemyss piece to date is £12,650, or over $20,000 at the $/£ exchange rate in 1996 when an oriental garden seat painted by Karl Nekola was sold at Sotheby's. A Wemyss cat and a pair of pigs have also achieved the same lofty level. But there are less expensive pieces available. A nice small cup and saucer in cabbage rose can be found for approximately $500 or a small dresser comb tray in red rose pattern for $600, complete with painted and incised Wemyss marks and the Goode stamp.

Pot Lids

Just a quick mention of another collectible, though not necessarily all of Scottish manufacture, but certainly with strong Scottish association. In the nineteenth century many small pots were made to hold gentlemen's relish, a pickle-like concoction, anchovy paste, as well as toothpaste and other cosmetic products. These china pots, generally about 3" in diameter and 1.5" to 2.0" in height, had a lift-off lid to access the contents. Some were decorated with thistles or other Scottish motifs. English Staffordshire potteries produced some very interesting pots with lids decorated with typical Victorian themes. One of the leading manufacturers was Pratt Brothers of Fenton, England, who produced a variety of these lids in the 1847-1880 period. Frequently, and some times incorrectly, all these lids are generically called "Pratt lids". The designs were painted in watercolour and then etched on copper, frequently copying famous artists of the era. There are at least three with Scottish scenes. "The Return of The Chieftains," showing hill ponies with dead red deer being taken off the hill, kilted Scots, and their deerhounds in attendance. A second is "42nd Embarking for the East," showing members of the Black Watch regiment boarding a ship for the Crimea, escorted by tearful family members. A third is a copy of the Landseer painting "Snow Drift," with sheepdog and sheep trapped in a snowdrift. All date to the last half of the nineteenth century.

Pratt pot lid with colour transfer "Return of the Chieftains," $275.

Prices, while having increased in the last five years, are still manageable. One of the pot lids noted above, in prime condition, can be found for $200 to $300. A simple Anchovy Paste pot lid, with thistle decor, could be under $100. Lids should be free of chips and discolouration, but some mild glaze crackling is acceptable. The underlying pot is almost optional, in a sense, since you're buying the artwork, rather than the entire object. However, it is nice to have both. Add $10 to $15 for the pot bottom. Watch for photographic reproductions glued onto an old pot lid. If the edge pulls up, that's a dead giveaway every time.

---

[1]Graeme Cruickshank. *Scottish Pottery*, Princes Risborough, Aylesbury, Bucks, England, Shire Publications, Ltd (Shire Album #191). 1987, pg 5.

[2]Carol McNeill. *Kirkaldy Potteries*, Fife, Scotland, Fife Publicity, 1998, pg 92.

Pratt pot lid with colour transfer "Embarking for the East," (42nd Black Watch Highland Regiment enroute to Crimea, 1864). $275.

Pratt jam jar with transfer of red deer stag and hind, after Landseer's painting, 5" h., $225.

Bibliography

Copeland, Robert, *Blue and White, Transfer-printed Pottery*, Haverfordwest, England, Shire Publications, Ltd., (Shire Album #97). 1994.

Cruickshank, Graeme, *Scottish Pottery*, Princes Risborough, Aylesbury, Bucks, England, Shire Publications, Ltd (Shire Album #191). 1987.

Freeman, Lisa, "Starting To Collect Pot Lids," *Living with Antiques*, Belmont, Vermont, Fiske and Freeman. Oct, 2001.

Hunt, Chris, *Dairy Cream Pots*, Bradford, West Yorkshire, England. Chris Hunt, 1978.

Kelly, Henry E., *Scottish Ceramics*, Atglen, Pennsylvania, USA, Schiffer Publishing, Ltd.. 1999.

McNeill, Carol, *Kirkaldy Potteries*, Fife, Scotland, Fife Publicity, 1998, pg 92.

"Where The Price is Right," London, England, *The Sunday Telegraph*, Feb 27, 2000.

Wintersgill, Donald, *Scottish Antiques*, London, England, Johnston and Bacon, 1977.

Chapter Twelve

Silver

This chapter gives the reader a basic understanding of Scotland's silver, its design origins, the various types of objects most specific to Scotland, as well as some guides to identify makers' names, town and date marks, and some price parameters a collector may expect in today's marketplace. The chapter's bibliography provides additional resources. Without reviewing all types of Scottish silver objects, the selection here is intended to present those of distinctive and specific Scottish association.

Scotland's isolation, due to its topography and lack of transport access, caused Scottish silver to be influenced more by Ireland and the Scandinavian countries than by England (See Chapter One). Very little Scottish silver made before the sixteenth century still exists, save for one or two superb Celtic brooches. These brooches however, discussed in Chapter Seven, are quite important design antecedents to Scottish jewellery and other antiques of the seventeenth through twentieth centuries, and the visual similarities are readily apparent.

Despite the lack of specific examples from these early periods, written records testify to the existence of silversmiths throughout Scotland. If anything, the craft was very localized, due again to the geographically-imposed self-sufficiencies of early communities. Accordingly, the gentry turned to local silversmiths for their table and other silver requirements. They were the only ones who had the means to afford silver objects; there was no middle-class, and the poor were just exactly that.

Acts were passed in Edinburgh in the fifteenth century controlling Scottish goldsmiths, establishing standards requiring that objects be assayed (tested) to assure that the standards being set for sterling silver were followed. The assayer's mark, maker's mark, and town mark were required, followed in the seventeenth century by date marks. These regulations were followed with varying degrees of success in various periods and locales.

Wood *mazers*, made and embellished with silver in the Edinburgh area in the sixteenth century, are some of the earliest Scottish silver items still in existence. A *mazer* is a wide, shallow drinking and eating bowl raised on a silver stem. The quality, distinctiveness, and sophistication of these are indicative of the advanced state of the art at that time. A tremendous amount of Scottish silver was melted down during the Reformation, and it really wasn't until the seventeenth and eighteenth centuries that Scottish silver started to have a come back.

Beakers

In Scotland's northeast, a very different Scottish drinking vessel was developed. Called a beaker, it is a tapered silver vessel about 8" high and with considerable adornment, chasing, embossed foliage, strap-work, and the like. Plainer examples were used in churches. Actually, the beaker, later found in horn, pewter and other materials, was introduced to Scotland from Holland. Early in the seventeenth century, exchange students from the University of Leyden attending Aberdeen University brought in this Dutch form. At that time, Aberdeen was one of the principal seaports on the North sea, trading with the Scandinavian countries as well as Holland, Germany, and Russia.

Pair of silver beakers, Edinburgh, 1762-63, maker not identified.
Courtesy of Colonial Williamsburg Foundation

Thistle Cups

Thistle cups are another Scottish form of drinking vessel. Made in the last quarter of the seventeenth century, they resembled nothing so much as what we today would call a baby's silver mug, given as a christening present. About 3" high and originally much larger, they had a side handle, bulging bowl, out-turned rim, and a design just above the foot that resembled floral leaves. Just think thistle shape and you've got it. These are quite impractical as drinking cups because of the rim design, but that doesn't stop collectors from chasing them.

Early thistle cup, silver, by John Luke II, Glasgow, 1709-10.
Courtesy of Colonial Williamsburg Foundation

Quaich

The *quaich* is a small and exquisite drinking vessel, about as quintessentially Scottish as anything. Because of that, and because we like them, we devote an entire short chapter to them; see Chapter Twenty.

Coconut cups

Although sometimes also found in England, silver-mounted coconut cups were more frequently found in Scotland. As her sons of the seventeenth and eighteenth centuries returned from world-wide explorations, they brought home coconuts, apparently a favoured souvenir. These were hollowed out, fitted with a turned wood stem and foot, and embellished with silver rims, shields, floral wreathing, and the like. In the early twentieth century, there was hardly a large house in Scotland that did not have an ancestor's coconut cup proudly displayed on the drawing room's fireplace mantle or dining room's side-board. They had probably been in the exact same spot for better than two hundred years or so.

Tankards

Tankard style cups and mugs appear to have been more of an English than a Scottish form. Having said that, the Scottish ones, while following the English in basic design, tended to be larger with a finial often topping the lid. This same design is frequently found in pewter, see Chapter Eighteen, the ultimate being the "tappit hen."

Teapots

In Chapter Eight we note the extensive consumption of tea in Scotland in the nineteenth and twentieth centuries. Earlier, it was strictly the drink of the aristocracy, the price being well out-of-sight for the common man. Scottish silver teapots, in the first half of the eighteenth century, assumed a unique shape, which persisted into the nineteenth, although in somewhat modified form. Generally, the pot is in the shape of a sphere, with a straight spout (later with curved neck), hinged lid with finial, c-shaped handle (first wood; later silver with insulators), all on a round foot. Decoration was minimal; some scrolling but no rococo embellishments. Ultimately, in the nineteenth century, some Continental influences invaded and the pure form of the teapot became adulterated with more embellishments.

Carved coconut cup on rosewood stand and base with silver rim. 6" h., $750.

Typical Scottish, spherical, silver teapot by Patrick Graeme, Edinburgh, 1728-29. *Courtesy of Colonial Williamsburg Foundation*

The simple teapot could never stand alone, however, and a cream ewer, basin, and sugar bowl followed to provide a tea service. John A. Hyman, in his book *Early Scottish Silver Teawares*, writes:

> The teapot was purchased first, followed by the sugar bowl, and finally the cream boat, as money became available. The cream boat form first appeared about 1740, replacing both baluster and spherical milk jugs. It is possible that the cream boat doubled as a sauceboat, since Scottish cream boats are as large as some English sauceboats.[1]

Monteiths

This large punch-bowl, usually considered to be of Scottish origin (probably because of its Scottish name), most likely was not originally a Scottish form but an English one. Ian Finlay, in his book *Scottish Crafts,* notes:

> Punch, however, must have had a certain acceptance although there is no evidence that it held the important place which it held in English conviviality. It is sometimes remarked that the monteith, that great punch-bowl with scalloped rim which is the centrepiece of so many English collections, was not made in Scotland, in spite of it's name and the story of the name's origin introducing that 'fantastical Scot, Monsieur Monteagh.'[2]

Large silver-crested monteith (punch bowl) by Francis Spillsbury, London, 1733-34. Note the devil face on the figure at the top of the bowl. *Courtesy of Colonial Williamsburg Foundation*

He continues on to point out that the monteith, despite English roots, was often later made by Scottish silversmiths.

Bannock Racks

These very rare and large objects, much like toast racks, held round flat oatmeal cakes.

Fish Slices

Knife-like and with large flat blades, these serving pieces were made in the eighteenth and nineteenth centuries, often with ivory or bone handles and considerable fretting and other decoration to the blade.

Marrow Spoons

These double-ended, narrow scoop utensils are eighteenth century in origin and used to gain access to the marrow at the centres of beef bones. They are quite rare today. In fact, an exceptionally fine marrow spoon, made by George Cooper of Aberdeen in 1740, sold in 2001 for the astronomical sum of £4400 or $6400.

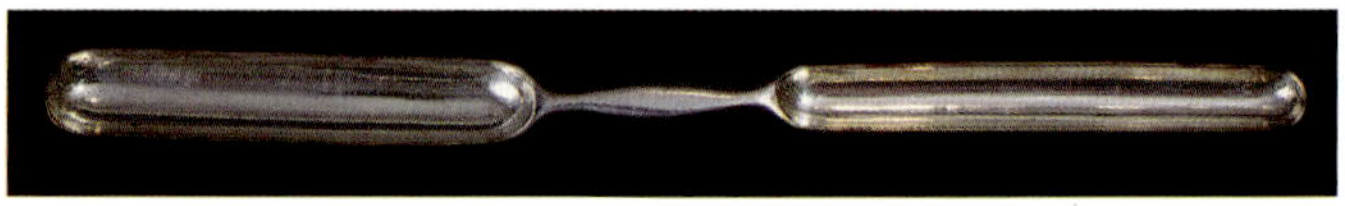

Silver marrow spoon, 8.75" long. $875. *Photo by William B. Bradley*

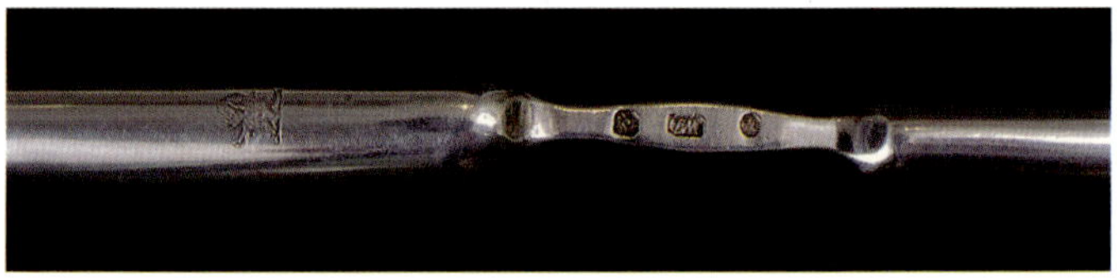

Reverse view of marrow spoon, showing marks for Scotland (thistle), King George III (head) and maker William Davie "W.D.) of Edinburgh, c. 1790. Also, an unusual crest of what appears to be an octopus with tusks over the coronet. *Photo by William B. Bradley*

Spoons

Probably the most often found Scottish silver antique is the ubiquitous spoon. Certainly, one is more likely to find a spoon with provincial Scottish town marks than any other silver article for the simple reason that there were more of them made. Not only can one find the very large basting or hash spoons (12" to 16" long) far larger than their English counter-parts, but smaller teaspoons as well. The smaller spoons were frequently initialled with the husband's and wife's initials as was the Scottish custom. They were numbered sequentially and often the aristocrat's crest of arms were on them. Very early examples of Scottish spoons show the distinctive narrow handle and large bowl. Later examples include a rat-tail extension of the handle on the back of the bowl. Still later, Scottish spoons conformed more to the English and Continental styles as forerunners of today's familiar shapes.

Toddy Ladles

These are smaller versions of English punch ladles, but in a similar shape with the bowl-shaped scoop at the end of a long handle. Toddy ladles are superb examples of the silversmith *cum* artisan changing an object to better fit its changing environment. English punch ladles had a large bowl since punch was basically a weak alcoholic beverage. The Scottish toddy was a far more potent brew, hence a smaller bowl ladle was required. The ladle consisted of a silver bowl with a silver stem attached to a turned wood handle and ended in a silver thistle finial. On occasions, the handle was made of baleen bone, from inside the whale's mouth.

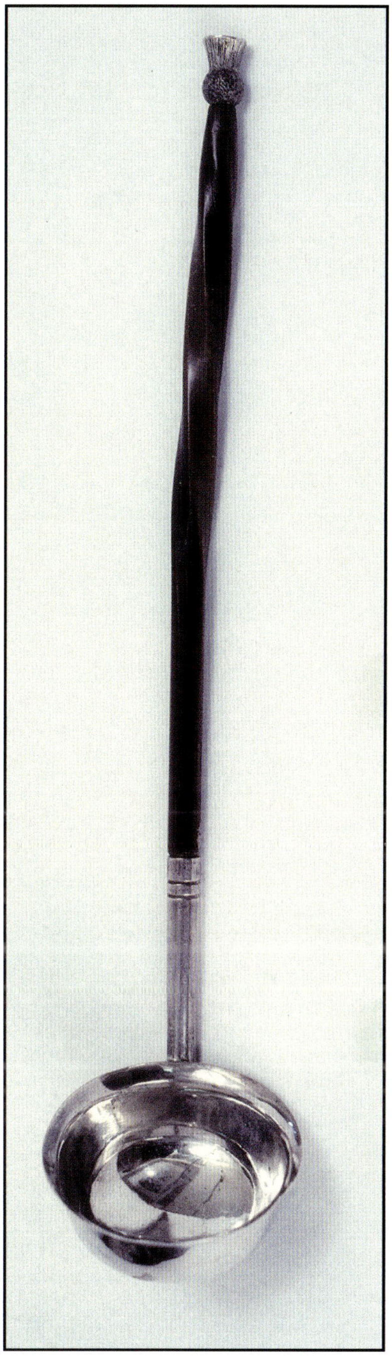

Small, exquisite silver toddy ladle, 7" long, hallmarked Edinburgh, 1900, with twisted baleen handle and silver thistle finial. $350. *Photo by William B. Bradley*

Extremely rare silver toddy ladle in fiddle pattern with oval bowl and shouldered stem, marked for John Mackie of Ellon, c. 1840, $13,000 (in 2000). *Courtesy of Phillips Auctioneers, Edinburgh*

Silverplated condiment set with thistle-shaped containers for salt, pepper and mustard; two with blue liners. c. 1900. $325.

Silver napkin ring with fretted thistle design and claw-set faux amethyst on the side. c. 1900. $175

Pair of salt and pepper cellars of silver plate in thistle configuration. Spoons have thistle finial. $185.

Two small dresser picture frames of agate and silver with easel backs, each 3" h. On left: shield shape with crossed basket-hilt swords behind, hallmarked Birmingham, 1903. $1450. On right: witch's heart, hallmarked Edinburgh, 1904, $1250.

Other silver *objets vertue*. Left: cut glass inkwell with hinged lid of silver and agate. Second from left and far-right: two silver and agate picture frames from the early 20th c. Centre: silver and agate matchbox container. Behind: silver and agate matchsafe or vesta. *Photo by William B. Bradley*

Personal Silver

For lack of a better name, personal silver is the term used here to cover all those silver items used by ladies and gentlemen that do not fall into the jewellery category; many are purely Victorian in origin and use.

Chatelaines

One such item is the *chatelaine.* This was a version of a lady's purse which hung from the belt and could contain whatever was necessary. It could include items such as a silver propelling pencil, small silver case to hold calling cards (an essential part of social etiquette in Victorian days), silver and agate pill box, or vinaigrette containing smelling salts. Similarly, a gentleman would have a silver pen or pencil, penknife, card case, or other necessities in his jacket pockets or attached to his silver or agate watch fob. A proper Scotsman would use his sporran for much of the above. Any one of these articles, in and of itself, can be the cornerstone of a collection, since they were all produced in great quantities and varieties

Hallmarks

The study of Scottish silver hallmarks is a science unto itself and a fascinating topic. An absolute must is a definitive reference book; and none is better than *Jackson's* (See the bibliography at the end of the chapter.) Very simplistically, sterling silver items should have three marks: country of origin (thistle for Scotland), a town mark (three-turreted castle for Edinburgh), and a date mark (a letter). Some pieces will also reflect the maker's mark, which also assists in the dating process. The town's mark frequently used as their symbol an extract from the town's coat-of arms. Some of the more frequently found town marks include those for:

Aberdeen, abbreviation of name to ABD, AB, or ABDN
Dundee, a pot of lilies
Elgin, ELN or ELGIN
Glasgow, a tree, bell, bird, and fish
Inverness, INS or the image of a dromedary (two humped camel)
Perth, a double-headed eagle, later a single-headed eagle
St. Andrews, the St Andrews cross
Tain, the name itself
Wick, the name itself

In the twentieth century, some of what is generally regarded as Scottish silver bears the town-mark for Birmingham, which became the silver and jewellery capital of the United Kingdom. Just one or two examples include a silver and agate standing picture frames in the Scottish fashion, match safes, and the like all bearing the Birmingham town mark of an anchor and date marks for the first quarter of the century. Despite their clear English origin, their appearance is about as Scottish-looking as these forms get. Care must be taken when dating Scottish silver. Two date letters "f" could have a difference of hundreds of years depending on the stamp surround and the correct town identification.

Collecting Scottish Silver

When setting out to collect Scottish silver, there are a number of different routes to follow and attendant costs to be incurred. One could concentrate on specific types, such as toddy ladles, costing today from $250 for a simple nineteenth century example to perhaps $2-3000 for an early hallmarked eighteenth century piece. One collector of our acquaintance is attempting to assemble a collection of small Scottish spoons hallmarked from each town in Scotland where silver was made. This is an expensive proposition, for some little provincial silver spoons go for as much as £500. It may also be an impossible goal, given that the town of Stonehaven is believed to have made only seven spoons in its entire silversmithing history. Another possibility would be to concentrate on collecting a variety of silver objects from one town, for example Dundee. A further route would be to pick a single silversmith and try to build a collection of his production alone. Any of these strategies is more enterprising than going after Scottish silver in general.

---

[1] John A. Hyman. "Early Scottish Silver Teawares," *Antiques Magazine*, June 1997.

[2] Ian Finlay. *Scottish Crafts*, London, George G. Harrap and Co, Ltd, 1948, page 74-5.

Bibliography

Finlay, Ian, *Scottish Crafts*, London, England, George G. Harrap and Co., Ltd, 1948.

Finlay, Ian, *Scottish Gold and Silver Work*, Stevenage, Herts, England, The Strong Oak Press, Revised edition, 1991.

Foster, Gordon, "Silver Lining," Edinburgh, Scotland, *Scottish Field Magazine*, February 1996.

Harper, Jennifer, "Born with a Silver Spoon," Edinburgh, Scotland, *Scottish Field Magazine*, November 2000

Holland, Margaret, "National Pride," Greenwich, London, *Antique Dealer and Collector's Guide*, September 1991

Hyman, John A., *Silver at Williamsburg; Drinking Vessels*, Williamsburg, Virginia, 1994.

Jackson, Sir Charles, *Jackson's Silver and Gold Marks*, Woodbridge, Suffolk, England, The Antique Collector's Club, revised edition, 1989.

Wintersgill, Donald, *Scottish Antiques*, London, England, Johnston and Bacon, 1977.

Chapter Thirteen

Books and Library Items

In a country as ancient as Scotland, the written word has been in place for countless centuries. Starting, as in most civilizations, with handwritten manuscripts on vellum, the advent of the printing press in Scotland in the sixteenth century was the start of Scotland's later publishing industry.

Woodcuts and steel engravings in the eighteenth century were being utilized in bibles and prayer books and late in the century Scottish book-binders were starting to produce quality covers with baroque embellishments on morocco and other leathers. It was the flowering of Scotland in the late eighteenth and early nineteenth centuries, however, that gave the publishing business it's real growth, fed by the prolific works of two Scots who became famous worldwide: Robert Burns and Sir Walter Scott.

Robert Burns, Scotland's Poet Laureate

Probably the best known of the many portraits of Scotland's poet laureate, Robert Burns, this image appears on a tin box. The original painting by Alexander Nasmyth is in the National Portrait Gallery, London.

Robert Burns was born on January 25th, 1759, to a farming couple near Ayr, on Scotland's west coast. Today we would call them subsistence farmers, making barely enough to feed their family. But what they lacked in wordly goods they made up for in strength of character and the way they raised young Robert and his brother, Gilbert. Burns was tutored by an enlightened man by the name of Murdoch and became a voracious reader of anything that became available, when books were few and far between in that countryside. He had an excellent memory and quickly absorbed all the songs and stories that his mother and other women could tell him. By the time he was sixteen he had finished school, but thanks to home-teaching by his father and by Murdoch he learned to read and understand French and Latin. This was no small accomplishment, considering he had a full-time job as a ploughman on the family farm.

Burns established his reputation as a Lothario quite early and continued the pursuit of the fairer sex until his death. He briefly tried to work in the flax business, but came back to the family farm after his father's death in 1784. When the farm's lease expired, the Burns family took up another farm in Mauchline. Here he met black-eyed Jean Armour, by whom he had twins. In 1786, he published his first book *Poems*, which was an immediate success. He quickly became known variously as "the Aryrshire ploughman" or as "the bard from the plough," as he styled himself. Burns was welcomed in literary circles of Edinburgh as a result of his *Poems*, which soon enjoyed a second printing. He was able to travel extensively throughout Scotland, sometimes with not the most savoury of com-

Burns' Cottage. Modest accomodations indeed.

panions. Drink and fleshly pleasures were the order of the day.

This brief review of Burns' life would be incomplete without providing a wee taste of his works. In the opening verse of his poem *To a Mouse, On Turning Her Up In Her Nest, With The Plough, November, 1785,* he wrote:

Wee, sleekit, cowrin, tim'rous beastie
O, what a panic's in thy breastie.
Thou need na start awa sae hasty, wi' bicker ing brattle.
I wad be laith to rin an' chase thee, wi' murd'ring pattle.

In 1787, he returned to farming and married Jean Armour. Burns was not the world's most accomplished farmer and his chosen land was of poor quality, but he was fortunately "bailed out" by being appointed an Exciseman (revenue officer) in Dumfries. While still writing poetry, Burns, who reputedly could not carry a tune to save himself, was approached by a Mr. Thompson to write the lyrics to over sixty traditional Scottish airs, a task to which he turned with great verve. The results have been, according to biographers, "the most beautiful and refined of his works."[1]

But Burns was not a well man. Dissolute living and rheumatic fever brought him down and he died July 18th, 1796, only 37 years old. One of his many biographers wrote:

So Died Robert Burns, the most remarkable person of that age; alike gifted and wretched; the glory and the shame of literature.[2]

A great observer of the commonplace and capable of expressing his observations in the parlance of the common man, Burns was proud yet capable of great rudeness and sarcasm, perhaps what today might be termed "a bit of an oddball." Nevertheless, there are few, if any, other poets whose birth is celebrated worldwide by their fellow countrymen. On January 25th, "Burns' *nicht* (night)" in almost every country around the globe, Scots gather to recite Burns' poetry and sing his songs, over 200 years after his death. Not at all shabby for an Ayrshire ploughman.

Burns' "To a Haggis" (a haggis being a Scottish pudding of minced mutton, suet and oatmeal) is the ode that is emoted by the Master of Ceremonies before serving the dish to the assembly on Burns' Nicht. The first verse follows:

Fair fa' your honest, sonsie face,
Great chieftain o' the pudding-race.
Aboon them a' ye tak your place, painch, tripe or thairm;
Weel are ye wordy o' a grace—as lang's my arm.

Sir Walter Scott, Bart, The Scottish Romantic

Placing Sir Walter Scott second in this chapter is purely a matter of chance; not opinion. It was he who was largely responsible for romanticizing Scotland. Together with Burns, Queen Victoria and Balmorality, he created an image of Scotland that drew tourists from all over the world in the nineteenth, twentieth, and present centuries.

Walter Scott was born in 1771 to an old Borders family, his father being a solicitor (lawyer) in Edinburgh. His family roots drew him to study Border history and poetry. Like Burns, though from a totally different social strata, Scott was a voracious reader of both French and Italian literature and was an excellent student at school in Edinburgh. Lame from infancy, he did not let this hinder him in physical or intellectual pursuits. He studied for the bar and was appointed a sherrif's deputy (local judge) and clerk of sessions (court clerk). Both positions gave him income to support his literary pursuits. He took great delight, every autumn, in vacation rambles over the border countryside.

Sir Walter Scott, Bart., in the library of his beloved Borders home, Abbottsford, on the River Tweed.

Like Burns, his first writing efforts were poetry, the most famous being *The Lay of The Last Minstrel*, published in 1805. His next major effort was *Marmion*, in 1808. These established him as a leader in the field of British poetry.

In 1810 he wrote *The Lady of The Lake*, followed by *Rokeby*. Unfortunately, these involved him in a horrible mistake which plagued him until his death. Unhappy with his London publisher, he formed a business and financial alliance with a Scottish publisher, Ballantyne and Co., in Edinburgh. In 1812, he bought his beloved home Abbottsford, a stately Borders home on the banks of the River Tweed, one of Scotland's best salmon rivers. The setting seemed only to increase his ability to write. In a short period of perhaps ten years, he produced novel after novel: *Waverly*, *Rob Roy*, *The Lord of The Isles*, and *Ivanhoe* among them. In 1820, he was appointed a Baronet. While managing this prodigious literary output, he also held two jobs in addition to acting as bard of Clan Scott, laird of Abbotsford, and editor for a number of books to be published by Ballantyne. Apparently no one was paying attention to the financial side of Ballantyne's business and the company went bankrupt, leaving Scott with a debt of £130,000, a huge sum in those days.

A proud and honourable man, Scott worked the rest of his life to settle the debt. He was reducing it quickly, over the five year period 1825 to 1830, with his usual rapid-fire writing of novels such as *Fair Maid of Perth* and others. But the ignobility of bankruptcy, his wife's death in 1826, and his horrific workload took their toll. He developed apoplexy, had a stroke, and eventually lost his mind. The sole advantage of the latter calamity was that he believed he had paid off the debt and died happy in 1832. His body was buried at nearby Dryburgh Abbey.

Abbottsford.

Favourite Authors

There is far more to Scottish literature than Burns and Scott. Certainly their efforts spurred a number of other authors, William Blake and Robert Louis Stevenson among them. The fine writing tradition in Scotland has continued well into the twentieth century with such authors as James Barrie, John Buchan, Neil Gunn, Neil Munro, and Erik Linklater. Collections of Gaelic poetry, songs, and literature have been assembled, offering a very specialized corner of literary history.

Burns' *Poetical Works*, 1850, privately printed by Redd & Pardon, London, tight spine, some page foxing, $95. *Photo by William B. Bradley*

Biographies of Scott and Burns are legion. It has been said that in the century after Burns' death, every ten years or so at least two new biographies have appeared. Scott also, to a lesser degree, attracted biographical attention. A good, leather covered biography of either can be found relatively inexpensively from specialized book dealers in London or Edinburgh. A Burns biography dating to the second or third quarter of the nineteenth century, profusely illustrated with excellent steel engravings of subject matter from his poems or songs, in tip-top condition, can be found for around $250. A similar one on Scott, dating to the third or fourth quarter, will be about $150 to $200. Early copies of their works, dating to the last quarter of the eighteenth century for Burns and to the first and second quarters of the nineteenth for Scott, can also be found, with a wide range of prices according to condition and rarity. A range of $75 to $500 would be expected today for an early volume in A-1 condition. Plenty of later editions (particularly from the late nineteenth and early twentieth centuries) are findable, with prices from $25 to $100. It would be difficult to assemble a collection of all the output of either Burns or Scott. They were both terrifically prolific writers and the financial burden of such an assemblage would be considerable, not to mention the cost of additional library shelving to house them.

One or two other books merit attention because of their sheer Scottishness. First, Delia Millar's recent book, *The Highlanders of Scotland*, is noted. Kenneth Macleay's watercolours of Queen Victoria's retainers offer a memorable, if somewhat romanticized, view of Victorian Scotland. An earlier publication entitled *The Clans of The Scottish Highlands*, offers 72 hand-coloured prints of watercolour paintings by Robert McIan (1803-57), ARSA. Each print depicts a Scottish man or woman in native attire; some in armour, some full-dress court tartans or other garb. Each clan represented in the picture has a brief history of the clan. Copies are extremely rare; turning up at auction only once or twice a year, and they sell for $10,000 or more. One or two of McIan's clansmen are pictured in Chapter Four.

Another Scottish book worthy of note is John Kelties' *The Scottish Highlands, Highland Clans and Regiments*, published in 1888. On 914 pages in five volumes, it contains colour chromolithographs and steel engravings, as well as 32 clan tartans printed by the same machines that were used to make Tartan Ware (see Chapter Three). A decent set could be found for around $300 to $500.[3]

Gold-stamped cover of Robert McIan's *Clans of the Scottish Highlands* with the Arms of Scotland, targes with crossed basket-hilt swords, thistles, etc.. Two volumes, 72 hand-coloured plates, published by Ackermann's of London, 1845 & 1847. $12,000-15,000. *Photo by William B. Bradley*

One of McIan's hand-coloured engravings, representing "Clan Mac Nachtan."[3]

A McIan clansman, "Clan Macallister." This sad-looking individual is probably depicted awaiting deportation to the Colonies, as part of the clearances. He is shown with all his worldly belongings in the box on which he rests his foot. Original hand-coloured prints can sometimes be found, ready to frame. $325.

Specialized Books

With it's long civilization, Scotland has accumulated a rich infrastructure of specialized books on such topics as church and secular buildings. Scottish architect Robert Billings, in *The Baronial and Ecclesiastical Antiquities of Scotland*, 1901, illustrated many historic buildings. His superb draughtsmanship, combined with his use of light and shadow and beautifully executed steel engravings, make this 4-volume set a worthy addition to any Scottish-lovers bookshelf. The set will run about $350-500, but is difficult to find.

One of Billings' superb depictions of castles and other buildings from his 1901 book.

A Billings drawing of Scottish baronial splendor. Prints such as these, matted and ready to frame, generally are available for $50-75.

One of the more interesting off-shoots of Scottish book publishing appeared at the end of the nineteenth century. David Bryce and Sons of Glasgow, Anderson's of Edinburgh, and Valentine's of London each published a series of miniature books (about 2.5" x 3.25") on a variety of topics: Burns' poems and songs, Scott's novels, Guides to Edinburgh, etc. Anderson's called their book series "The Thistle Library." Bookcovers were in tartan silk fabric, with a variety of tartans employed. Sometimes the name of the tartan is printed inside the back-cover. These tiny books were sold as souvenir items and also were published specifically for businesses to use as Christmas gifts to their employees and customers. Publication dates seem to range from 1875 to about 1910. Similar books are still being published, but are easily recognizable as being"new". Frequently a pencilled gift inscription and date inside the front covers is noted. In spite of the fragility of the tartan fabric covers (often they are ripped or torn), many have survived a century and more in fine condition, selling today for under $50. A collector could concentrate on different titles or different tartans, and be able to fill a short shelf in a year or so.

Other small books by the same publishers have also been observed. These, with very much the same subject matter, are 2.25" x 3.25", occasionally a bit larger, and have a hard board tartan cover. They sell today for around $50 to $100.

Additional miniature books were published by David Bryce and Sons, Glasgow, around the start of the twentieth century. We are aware of two, one a dictionary and the other a Bible. Both complete, they are housed in a side-hinged, tin case, elaborately embossed with a floral design and with a window port in the front containing a magnifying glass. The covers are in gold, tooled leather. The illustrated Bible measures 1.25" x 1.75" and has 676 pages. The dictionary measures 1.25" x 1.25" and has 384 pages. Print can be clearly read with the magnifying glass. They could cost today about $350-400 each, if in perfect condition.

Two miniature books, each in a hinged tin box with magnifying glass. Left: *Dictionary* published by William Bryce, Glasgow, 1900, 384 pages. Back is stamped "Pears." Right: Illustrated miniature Bible, also published by Bryce, 1901, 675 pages. $385 each.

Tartan board covered book in "McBeth" tartan, titled *Church Services*. Red leather, gold-stamped/tooled spine, 375 gold edged pages. Contains prayers, psalms, etc. Published, c.1875 in London, by Eyre & Spottiswoodie. Owner's name in script in front flyleaf. 2.75" x 4" x 1.5". $750.

Tartan board-covered book by Sir Walter Scott, Bart., *Lord of The Isles*. Gold-tooled/stamped black leather spine, gold edged pages. Published by Adam & Charles Black, Edinburgh, 1874. Elaborate gold-embellished edges on tartan covers. 3.75" x 5.5". $850.

Miniature books with tartan silk covers, 1890-1920. $35-50 each.

Book, *Marmion*, by Sir Walter Scott, Bart., published in Edinburgh, 1870, by Adam and Charles Black. Tartan board covers are in very rare and attractive "Malcolm" tartan. Black leather, gold stamped, tooled spine. 317 gold-edged pages. Condition remarkably perfect after 130+ years. 3.5" x 5.5". $950.

Library Items

Books naturally led to book accessories; a few of which are noted here.

Bookracks

Victorians had a penchant for use-specific articles, one of which was the folding, expanding book rack. Usually made of wood, the rack had hinged folding ends, to store flat, and a base that expands according to the number of books you have. The ends are about 9" high; and the rack expands from 12" to 20". The ends were often decorated with thistle or other foliate carving. One Mauchline Ware piece has four separate transfers of Dunkeld. Their value could be about $500 to $750.

Page Cutters and Page Turners

In the early days of book publishing, books were sold with the pages uncut at the edges. Clever Victorians invented a wooden page cutter, which would gently separate the uncut pages without ripping them, cut the edges at the fold, and leave a rather attractive rough edge. Resembling a letter opener, page cutters came in a variety of shapes and materials (See Chapter Nine for a discussion of letter-openers.) Also, to avoid the danger of harming the pages of valuable books with the natural acids on human fingers, the use of wooden page turners was encouraged. Prices for each could be in the $100 to $250 range.

Folding Victorian book holder. Base is oak and the hinged, folding ends are rosewood carved with thistle and foliage. Base 13.5" long expands to 22" long. Ends are 7" h. $600.

Bookends

Stacking books on an open library table did not work well without a set of bookends. Victorian specificity came to bear with the popularity of wooden bookends in the form of your favourite dog, perhaps an Aberdeen Terrier, known as a Scottie in the United States, or a carved wooden thistle. Nice 6" x 9" high bookends could run about $200.

Book and Page Markers

Book and page markers that closely resemble paper clips were used to retain one's place in a book. Often made in Mauchline Ware, wood, ivory, silver, or bone, examples can be found with various decorations. Prices could start at $25 to $50.

If your favourite Scottish author has not been mentioned in this very selective sample, our apologies are offered. Many other worthy Scottish works should be included in a collector's research library.

---

[1]Rev Robert A. Willmott. *The Poetical Works of Robert Burns*, London, George Routledge and Sons, 1869, page xivi.
[2]Rev Robert A. Willmott. ibid, page xlvii.
[3]The reader may have noted the differences in spellings of Scottish surnames. "Mac Nactan," as spelled on the nearby illustration, is today more likely to be "McNaughton." Spellings of names have changed over time, particularly when Scots came to the United States and passed through customs clearance. Many of the people were illiterate and the spellings of their name was determined by the immigration officer's interpretation of the Scots' brogue. We have been led to understand, for example, that there are at least 16 different spellings of the name "MacIntyre."

Bibliography

Billings, Robert William, FRSE, *The Baronial and Ecclesiastical Antiquities of Scotland*. Edinburgh, Oliver and Boyd, 1901.

Kaplan, Wendy, *Scottish Art and Design, 5,000 Years*, New York, Harry N. Abrams, Inc., 1990.

Keltie, John S. (PSA Scot), *The Scottish Highlands, Highland Clans and Regiments*, London and Edinburgh, William Mackenzie, 1888.

Lockhart, J. G., *Life of Robert Burns*, London, John Murray, 1808.

Encyclopaedia Britannica. Chicago, William Benton, Vol 20, 1965.

Logan, James, *Clans of The Scottish Highlands*, London, James Ackermann and Sons, 1845 and 1857.

Shairp, Principal, *Robert Burns*, New York, Harper and Brothers, 1879.

Willmott, Rev. Robert A. *The Poetical Works of Robert Burns*, London, George Routledge and Sons, 1869.

Chapter Fourteen

Advertising, Product Tins, and Pub Ware

Advertising

Many Scottish items with advertising on them are reviewed in other chapters, such as Chapters Eight and Eleven, where information on Scottish stoneware, whisky jugs, cream pots, pot lids, and the like can be found. Some items in domestic use, which carried advertising, can be found in Chapter Eight.

Additionally, there are many advertising items that can be particularly interesting. For example, the odd shopkeeper's sign advertising his type of business. Rulers were favourite stationers' advertising pieces.

Two tobacco tins with lift-off lids, lithographed, 1920s. Left: $165, Right: $115.

Left: Potlid with colour transfer after a painting by Sir Edwin Landseer, R.A., "The Snow Drift," c. 1890, $300. Centre: Shortbread mold of Doulton china, 7.5" dia., $300. Right: Pot lid, for anchovy paste with thistle decoration, c. 1920, $95.

Product Tins

Tin cans were the favourite containers for a multitude of food and work products in the 1850 to 1950 period. Mustard, tea, biscuits, toffee and other sweets and candy, oatcakes, and syrup all were stored and sold in tins. Tobacco tins offered a virtually endless variety of brands of loose tobacco, cigarettes, and cigarette papers for the "roll-your-own" crowd.

Before 1900, most tins were beautifully lithographed with advertising and labels describing the contents. Despite the passage of time, many retain much of the original rich colour to this day. Probably some of the most attractive are large Coleman's Mustard tins, typically measuring 9" x 7" x 6", with the manufacture's logo in gold and inscribed "Manufacturers to Her Majesty The Queen" (Victoria) inside the lid and impressed into the bottom. For added moisture protection, product tins often had an inner and an outer hinged lid. Their most attractive features are the shape of the tin and the colour and designs of lithography. Their vertical sides are often in eight panels, by reason of truncated corners, and scenes of a Scottish castle, highland cattle, or Scottish soldiers. Some early lithographed tins commemorated the Crystal Palace Exposition of 1851 in London and its later counterpart in Edinburgh in 1886. Pre-1900 lithographed, large tins in good condition and with attractive subject matter can run $400 and up. Less resplendant pieces of the same vintage could start at $150.

Product tins made for the biscuit manufacturers Huntley and Palmer of England, and McVitie and Price Co. of Scotland can be found in the shapes of a set of books on a shelf, a soldier's sentry box, and other figural designs. Round, rectangular, trapezoid, hinged lid, and lift lid styles are some of the variations made. In the 20th century, processes other than lithography were developed, including transfer printing and applied paper labels. Some product tins from the 1920s and 1930s offer most attractive Scottish scenes of highland cattle, castles, soldiers, bagpipers, trains such as the famous "Flying Scot," and general Scottish scenery subjects. Their values range from $50 minimum to $200 for rarer and larger pieces.

The famous "Princess Mary" tin was sent to military troops in France during the First World War. While older soldiers received tobacco, younger ones could receive chocolates, complete with a printed note of good wishes. A brass hinged-lid tin of this type, measuring 5" x 3" x 1" today could cost about $100 empty, and with the original contents $300. An earlier and rarer version of a gift of tobacco in a tin from the royals to the troops in the field goes back to the Boer War, c. 1890.

Mustard tin by "J & J Colman," colour lithography. On top is a lion with a scepter and flags of The British Empire. The sides have pictures of various elements of the British armed forces. Hinged lid and inner air-tight lid "Colman mustard manufacturers to The Queen" stamped on bottom. 7" x 7" x 7", c. 1890, $565.

Close-up of scalloped-edge, hinged-lid tin with fine lithography scenes of Scotland, particularly on the lid. $325.

Colourful Scottish historical biscuit tin by "McVitie & Price, Edinburgh." Scalloped sides, lift-off lid. 8" wide. c. 1960. $95.

Colourful paper-covered, lift-off lid biscuit tin from "McVitie & Price, Edinburgh." These biscuit tins were sent full to the troops in France for Christmas in 1914, explaining the name and illustration. It is quite remarkable that so much of the paper has survived over almost 90 years. $175.

Hinged-lid biscuit tin with early lithography scenes of Scotland around the sides including highland cattle, sheep, etc. On the lid are embossed sheep and dogs at rest in fern. 6" h. Stamped on bottom "Carr Biscuit Manufacturers, Carlisle." c. 1880. $325.

Colourful printed tartan shortbread tin, c. 1960, $65.

Early biscuit tin by "Peake Freen & Co" in form of a book. Very colourful lithographed scenes of Mary Queen of Scots. Side clasp to close. 6" x 8", c. 1890. (Reputed to be one of the first tins in book-form). $475.

Group of Scottish shortbread, oatcake and biscuit tins. All printed illustrations, c.1960. $65-95.

Brass, embossed "Mary tin," 1914, showing names of WWI allies. $250.

Unusual lift-off tobacco tin with lithographed lid. This tin was sent to the troops serving in the Boer War in South Africa. Inside was note with printed greetings from "The Scottish Regiments Gift Fund". $225. *Photo by William B. Bradley*

Familiar Black & White™ dogs in form of plastic bar ornament, c. 1960, $185. *Photo by William B. Bradley*

Pub Ware

The Scots are known to have more than just a slight fondness for a "wee dram" (a small drink of whisky) on occasions; any occasion is usually suitable. 'Tis no wonder then, that there are a plethora of Scottish keepsakes and collectables in the pub ware category. Other chapters include beer and ginger beer bottles (chapters Eleven and Fifteen), for example, and pewter measures or tavern mugs (chapter Eighteen). The Scottish pub, for most of the 20th century, was heart and soul of a town's social life. Perhaps that is why there are so many items essential to the pub community.

Pub Figures

The two most familiar pub figures are the Black and White™ whisky (the Scottish spelling of whiskey is without the "e") Scottie dogs and the Dewar's Whisky™ drum major. Early ones were carved wood, later some form of early composition similar to plaster-of-Paris, and still later, molded plastics. One can also find china figures of famous persons associated with a particular drink, like Bonnie Prince Charlie and Drambuie™. These were not made until sometime in the last quarter of the 20th century. The Dewar's drum major comes in at least two sizes, 19" and 9". The Scottie dogs are generally about 8" to 10" high. Prices today are in the $150-250 range.

Ashtrays and Pub Coasters

The second most popular activity in pubs was smoking. Accordingly, marketing types at distilleries and breweries (and there are quite a few such establishments around Scotland) provided promotional advertising ashtrays from the early 1920s until the 1980s. They are difficult to date precisely and come in a vast array of materials and brand identifications. Among the most desirable today are porcelain (Shelly™ for one) and molded metals, including pewter, are also very popular. We won't even attempt to list all the brands of whisky, liqueurs, and beers, but they must number well above fifty. Prices could be in the $25 to $100 range. Pub coasters, generally made from cardboard and dating to the 1950s to1970s period, also offer a variety of collecting opportunities. Prices for them today are in the $15 to $35 range.

Bar ashtray of china with black/gold transfer for "Haig's Glenleven Old Scotch™." 5" dia. x 1.5" h. $95.

Another bar ornament. This is a Scottish Highlander's pipe-band drum major in full "kit", produced by "Dewar's White Label Scotch Whisky"™. 20th. c. Standing 20" high, composition material. $485.

Three bar promotional pieces, Front: small penknife marked "Heather Dew Scotch Whisky"™, $20. Upper left: leather covered dice cup for "Johnnie Walker"™, $45. Front right: Shelly china ashtray for "Black & White"™, $165.

Distillery Measures

Nothing sets off a home bar or country kitchen better than a graduated set of copper or brass distillery whisky measures. Their distinctive shape, with large pouring handle, flared mouth, and bulbous body, is quickly recognizable. These measures were used to mix blended Scotch whisky from the various components of single malts and grain alcohol. There seems to be no rule to the number that constitutes a set. Their sizes range from a diminutive 1/8 gill (3" high) to a gallon (12" high), but a matched graduated set of about five or six makes a super display. A few sets are stamped with the distillery's name, probably dating to the first half of the 20th century. These could cost about $500, since they are now quite rare. On the more reasonable level would be a set of five or so unstamped measures, probably dating from the 1960s to 1980s era, for around $250 to $350. If they have a couple of "dings," they are less likely to be newly minted.

Set of four whisky measures in distinctive bulbous shape. Lead stamps inside rim are verification by inspector that the volumes are correct! $225.

Bar Stuff

In this category are some intriguing items. One is a gorgeous crystal whisky dispenser with the maker's name etched on in gold in a style that is mounted on the wall at the back of the bar. It would be filled with the whisky; then dispensed from the bottom by pressing a drinking glass up and against an inverted plunger, dispensing an exact measure to be poured. It dates to the late 19th or early twentieth century.

Of later vintage, but equally attractive, are manufacturer's measures that are inserted into a whisky bottle, which is inverted into a rack at the back of the bar, and the whisky is measured and viewed through a glass window in the device, in the same fashion as described above. These measures date from about 1920-30 and could cost about $200.

Beer pulls, the handle-like devices that the barmen pull down to draw a pint of beer, are interesting as keepsakes. Old examples with carved wood handles, beer company logos, or china ones are all hard to come by today. Ones in good condition from the 1930s sell today for more than $100. Modern beer pulls, very colourful in ceramic or plastics, could be $50 and up.

Pouring Jugs

Every pub bar-man, or publican in older terminology, would present a measure of whisky in a drinking glass along with a pouring jug of water, with which the patron could then dilute the whisky to his individual taste. (Until the last quarter of the 20th century, ice simply was not available.) The pouring jugs provided another opportunity for the distillers to promote their brands. These contained about a pint of water and measured about 5" high. Early ones were made of china, adorned with the name and logo of the distiller, and suitable advertising messages. Some jugs were manufactured by well-known china manufacturers, such as Shelly, Bell's, or a Staffordshire china producer. Later ones are found in more modern materials, such as plastics. Pouring jugs are quite colourful, come touting a variety of brands, and are generally affordable at $35 to $75; older and rarer ones will run more.

Wall-mounted on wood display plaque is this bar whisky dispenser. Made of cut crystal, with gold lettering and brass mounts, c. 1890. Originally would have had top cover and dispenser spigot at bottom. 13" h.. $975.

Framed advertising plaque for "The Glenlivet Scotch"™, mounted on tartan. 15" x 21", $375.

Chapter Fifteen

Glass

Prior to the 18th century, any wine or drinking glasses found in upper-class Scottish homes had come from the Continent or from England. Because of their high cost, only wealthy people could afford them. Others made do with wooden and horn vessels. In the early part of the 18th century, some glass was being made in the larger Scottish cities of Edinburgh and Glasgow, but it was not until the Industrial Revolution, in the late 18th and early 19th centuries, that Scottish glass made an appearance in any appreciable volume.

Jacobite, or "Amen," Glasses

One of the earliest, and arguably the most spectacular, Scottish wine drinking vessel is a Jacobite, or "Amen," glass. They have a round, footed stem supporting a wine cup and were produced in considerable quantities in the last quarter of the eighteenth century. They are used, along with *quaichs* (as described in Chapter Twenty), to raise a toast in memory of Bonnie Prince Charlie, so sadly defeated at Culloden. They stand about 6" high and are engraved with a variety of Jacobite and Scottish symbols, such as a stylized Jacobite rose, thistles and foliage, and the word "Amen." Frequently there would be an air twist inside the glass stem. Only a comparative few have survived to the present; most remaining ones are in museums or private collections. Only very occasionally will one appear at auctions. The custom had always been that upon toasting "the Prince across the water" (in exile in France), the glasses were thrown into the fireplace and smashed to prevent them from being used for a baser offering than the Prince's toast. They have been reproduced since the 19th century. An authentic one would cost $500 or more.

Wine Glasses and Decanters

We frequently see 19th and early 20th century wine, whisky and liqueur glasses and decanters produced by major glass factories, such as Edinburgh Crystal™. They are still being produced today in some of the same old patterns. Frequently these have acid etched or diamond-etched thistle blossoms and foliage patterns or heavily cut diamond patterns on the sides. Not only have these been made in Scotland, but similar ones were made in the United States in the late 1800s and early 1900s. It is difficult to differentiate one maker, or even one era, from another, since few have a maker's mark. Nevertheless, if they are not chipped or clouded, the etching is crisp, and the overall appearance is Scottish, you can safely pay up to $75 per glass and $250 per decanter. If they date from the 19th or early 20th century, you will have paid just about what you would for a similar new one from a factory store today.

Set of three cut crystal liqueur glasses in shape of thistle blossom, on round foot. Sides have diamond pattern, with thistles acid-etched on glass above. c. 1900, 3.75" high. $375.

Set of five glasses, similiar to those above. $725.

Cut crystal decanter, similar to ship's decanter with large flat bottom. Superbly shaped stopper (thistle) and acid-etching & diamond-cut pattern on thistle motif decanter. 9" h., early 20th c., $485.

Close-up of crystal decanter with diamond cut thistles. 6" h., 20th c., $195.

Silver Overlay Decanters

Another variation of decanters are those covered in filigree silver, or silver overlay. These decanters, sometimes in a distinctive dimpled shape of the Haig and Haig™ whisky bottle, usually have cork stoppers with a silver crown or all-silver plug stoppers. The silver overlay is often in a thistle pattern, and they are most attractive, dating to the 1920s and 1930s. They can cost today about $375, with no chips, interior clouding, or missing silver overlay.

Frosted glass "Haig & Haig"™ "dimple" bottle, with silver overlay of thistle and neck band. 9.5", c. 1920. $325.

Goblets

Goblets, or *rummers*, are sometimes found with commemorative messages etched into the sides. These are basically wide, goblet-shaped glasses, with a short stem and round foot. Often there will be a remembrance to Sir Walter Scott, with his dates, or Robert Burns, sometimes with an etched portrait. Another version is with thistles and "Auld Lang Syne" etched on the side. About 6" high, these could run about $100 and date to the late 19th century.

Glass goblet with round foot, pedestal base. Known in Scotland as a *rummer*, glass sides are heavily etched with bluebells and Burns' *Auld Lang Syne*. 5.25" h., c. 1870. $225. *Photo by William B. Bradley*

Codd Bottles

Just before the end of the 19th century, a Doctor Codd of Dundee, invented a new type of closure for a glass container for a carbonated beverage. Made of green glass and usually about 9" high, the neck of the bottle, about 3" down from the top, was pinched at the factory. Between the pinch and bottle top, a green glass marble was inserted. When fizzy lemonade, for example, was poured into the bottle, the pressure forced the marble up to the top where (with the help of an "o-ring") it sealed the liquid in and the air out. Quite ingenious. Children of the day thought these bottles were great fun and they delighted in smashing the bottles open once they had finished the contents to get the marble. Even when children did not break them, the empty bottles were tossed into the midden (no re-cycling in those days, even in frugal Scotland). Fortunately for bottle collectors, they were embossed at the factory with the name and logo of the distributor of the beverage, and frequently the distributors were chemists and drugstores. Some of the logos are quite distinctive, with swans or horse's heads, for example. Despite the fact that most of the Codd bottles that one can find at antique shops have been dug from the middens, they are often in remarkably good condition. Avoid those that are chipped or rust-stained. At least 25 different Scottish versions exist. Prices are about $35 to $75.

Green Codd bottle showing logo for "Anderson's, Dunoon." $50.

Beer and Ginger Beer Bottles

Prior to the second quarter of the 20th century, frequently beer and ginger-beer bottles were made in stoneware, rather than glass (see Chapter Eleven). Scottish beer bottles in green or brown glass with attractive paper labels, dating from the 1930s or so, can be found at flea markets/shops, etc. for $10 and up.

Whisky Measures

Glass measures for whisky are a much-overlooked, but interesting, keepsake. These heavy glass measures were shaped very similarly to a small wine carafe, and would have a marking to define the quantity. They came in several different sizes: 1/4 gill, 1/2 gill, gill, and 2 gills and are 3" to 7" high, frequently with a verification seal placed on the side or etched onto the glass to confirm the volume. Seals with "VR" (for Victoria Regina) date from 1879 to 1901, those with "ER" (Edward Rex) date from 1901 to 1910; those with "GR" (George Rex) date 1911 and after. These measures were produced for both English and Scottish measurements, which differed. The Scottish ones are about 25% smaller than the English Imperial measures. They were used aboard ships and trains and can be found with the logo of the vendor or publican. Specialist glass dealers in the United Kingdom are good sources; single measures could start at $100 and sets at about $150.

Cut glass crystal sugar shaker. Top is silver-plate, with thistle finial, shaker itself is thistle shaped. 6" h., c. 1920. $150.

Bibliography

Brooks, Brian, *Glass Whisky Measures*, Greenwich, London, England, Antique Dealer and Collector's Guide, February 1996.

Collins, Verite Reily, *Whisky Galore*, Birmingham, England, Antiques Magazine, March 22, 2002.

Chapter Sixteen

Horn

Being a people of frugal persuasion, the Scots tended to make use of everything possible that was close at hand. Previously noted was the use of cut-down swords to make some of the early dirks. A by-product of the raising of cattle and sheep for food were their horns. Ram's heads and horns made the regimental snuff-mulls noted in Chapter Ten. Both ram's horns and highland cattle horns were utilized for pocket snuffs and table snuff mulls, respectively. Once the horners (again, see Chapter Ten) came on the scene, the art of heating the horn in hot water and shaping it for an intended use opened a vast array of possibilities. There were many other imaginative uses of horn, mostly in the area of the kitchen.

Napkin Rings

Napkin rings of horn can be found in a range of styles, as many as 20 or so variations exist dating from the mid-1800s to the present. A favourite was a ring with silver thistle affixed with pins through the horn ring. The Cross of Saint Andrew or initials in silver were also used. Another style often encountered has a ring with a small, silver-mounted cut cairngorm on the side. These are affordable today starting at $35.

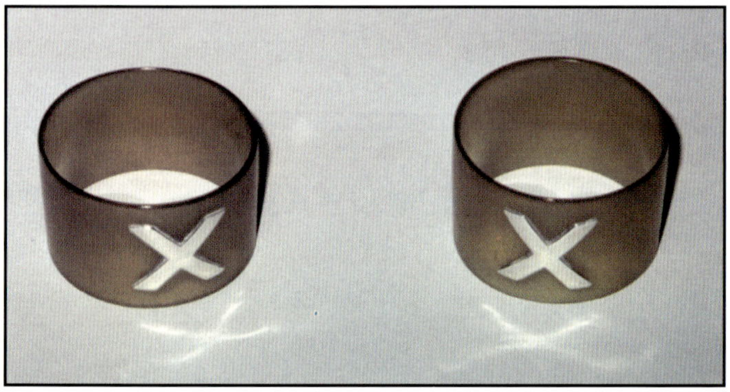

Pair of horn napkin rings with silver St Andrew's Cross affixed, 20th. century, 2" dia. $185 pair.

Assortment of 20th century horn articles. Front, left to right: Horn napkin ring with silver-mounted cairngorm, $185. Ring with affixed silver thistle, $75. Ring with silver-mounted cairngorm, $185.. Back, left to right: Horn stirrup cup with silver band on rim, c. 1840, 3.5" h., $365. Dark horn beaker, $65. Stud box with silver-mounted cairngorm, $265. *Photo by William B. Bradley*

Spoons

Jam spoons, soup spoons, serving spoons, porridge spoons, and tea spoons were made in large quantities, judging by the number one can still find. Probably a cottage industry, these spoons were made in different shapes and sizes. Popular were spoons whose handle terminated in carved thistles or those with a silver-mounted cairngorm on the handle. Colours range from almost black to highly translucent pale yellow, with variations between. A small jam spoon, measuring perhaps 4" long, can be found for under $35. A large, handsomely crafted serving spoon, measuring 12" long, with the handle carved in the traditional fiddle pattern, could run $75 or so. Horn spoons stamped with a souvenir event, such as "National Exhibition, Glasgow, 1938" occur. One of the neatest items is a child's porridge spoon, about 6" long, with a whistle built into the handle so the child can summon Mama for "more porridge, please." These can be about $100 to $125.

Three horn spoons, $50 each.
Photo by William B. Bradley

From left: Two silver and stone ornamented spoons, $85 each. Horn sugar spoon with carved thistle end, $50. Horn flour scoop, $40. Horn spoon with silver fittings, $125. Dark horn-shaped handle spoon, $85.

Beakers

These attractive horn cups have no handles and are found in sizes ranging from 3" to 12" in height. Sometimes they are crafted from a single horn but more frequently with the flat bottom inset into rounded sides. On occasion, the bottom is clear glass or a plastic. Older beakers are still findable with silver rims attached and with a silver shield on the sides bearing the original owner's initials inscribed. These are frequently hallmarked and most date from the 1890 to 1925 period. Beakers could also be decorated with silver thistles or silver-mounted cairngorms. Horn beakers were often included in Victorian picnic baskets. Queen Victoria and Prince Albert loved to picnic and the tradition continues in Scotland today. A small plain horn beaker can run about $35, a silver-mounted larger one, hallmarked c. 1890, will cost about $225. Presentation pieces will generally command a premium, especially if a famous name appears.

Horn presentation beaker with silver rim and silver shield escutcheon, 6" h., $265.

Three horn beakers. Two smaller ones, $40/each; larger one, $85.

Mugs

Horn mugs are usually found with a single handle attached with pins to the side of the mug. It can be plain or with silver rims and a silver round foot, and sometimes with a shield for the owner's initials. These obviously lend themselves today for use as a christening present for a new baby. Some have two or three opposing handles. Other additions could include silver-mounted cairngorms or amethysts. Prices today range from $50 to $250.

Sugar and Flour Scoops

Small scoops crafted out of horn were used in homes to measure flour and sugar for cooking. They measure about 6" long with a wide, flat bowl and a short handle, frequently carved into a thistle shape. They run today about $35, when you can find one.

Powder Horns and Drinking Vessels

The large horns found on Scottish highland cattle lent themselves to practical and decorative use as powder horns and as drinking vessels. Powder horns inscribed with maps, decorative scenes, and so forth can be found from specialist antiques dealers. (Beware of old horns with more recent scribing.) They can appear both in their original horn configuration and flattened out, frequently decorated with silver fittings, cairngorms, etc. Horns in all sorts of shapes and styles were used as snuff boxes (see Chapter Ten). An unusual application of horn, open at the wide end and with silver fittings on a six-foot-long chain was used to scoop water from a stream while mounted on horseback. A mounted man who dismounted to slake his thirst from a highland *burn* (stream) was vulnerable to attack. This clever use of a horn probably saved a few lives over the eons.

Pair of horn tapered condiment pots with silver fittings, early 20th century, $185.

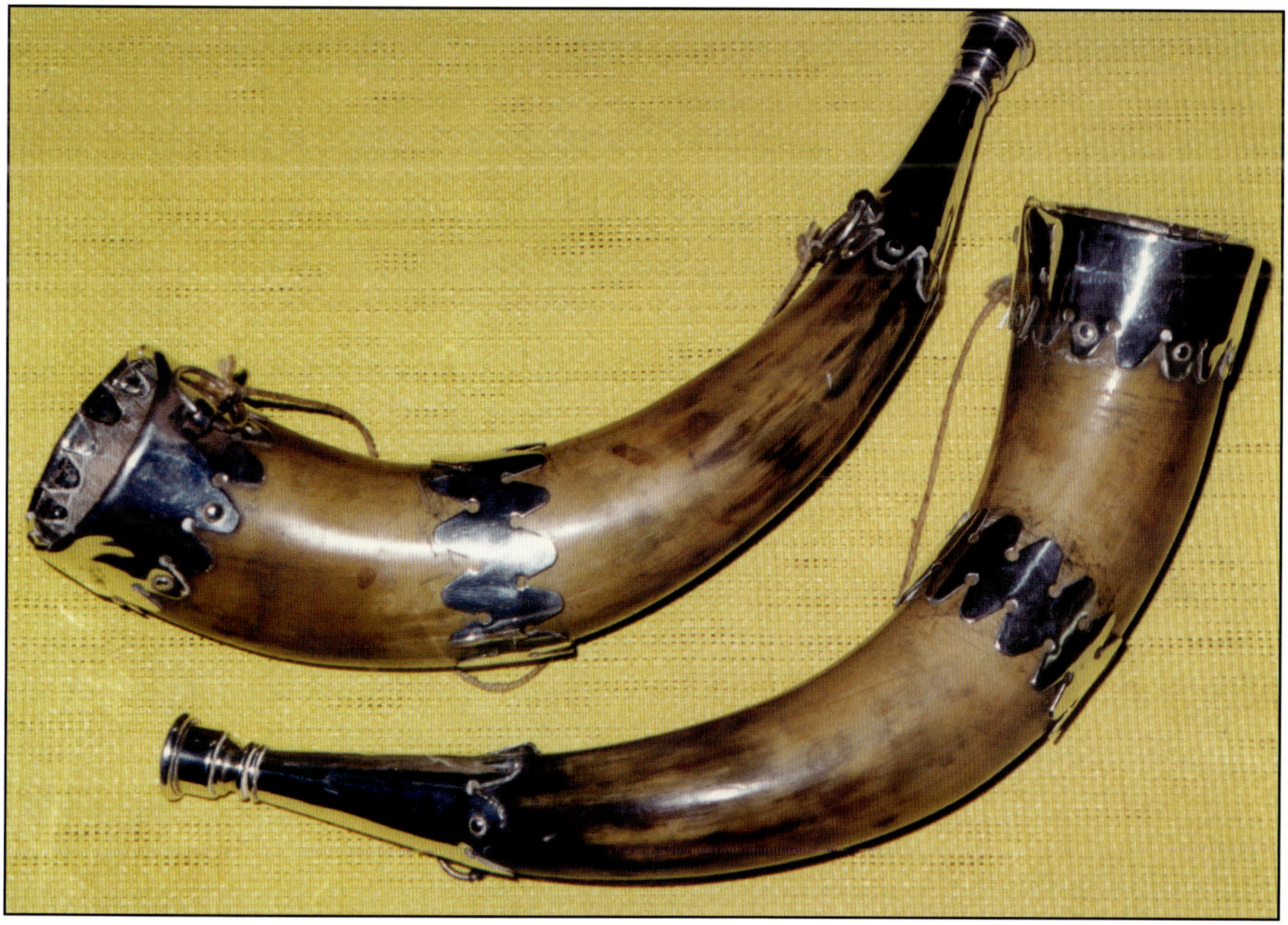

Matched pair of working hunting horns with silver-nickel fittings, 17" long, mid-19th century, $775

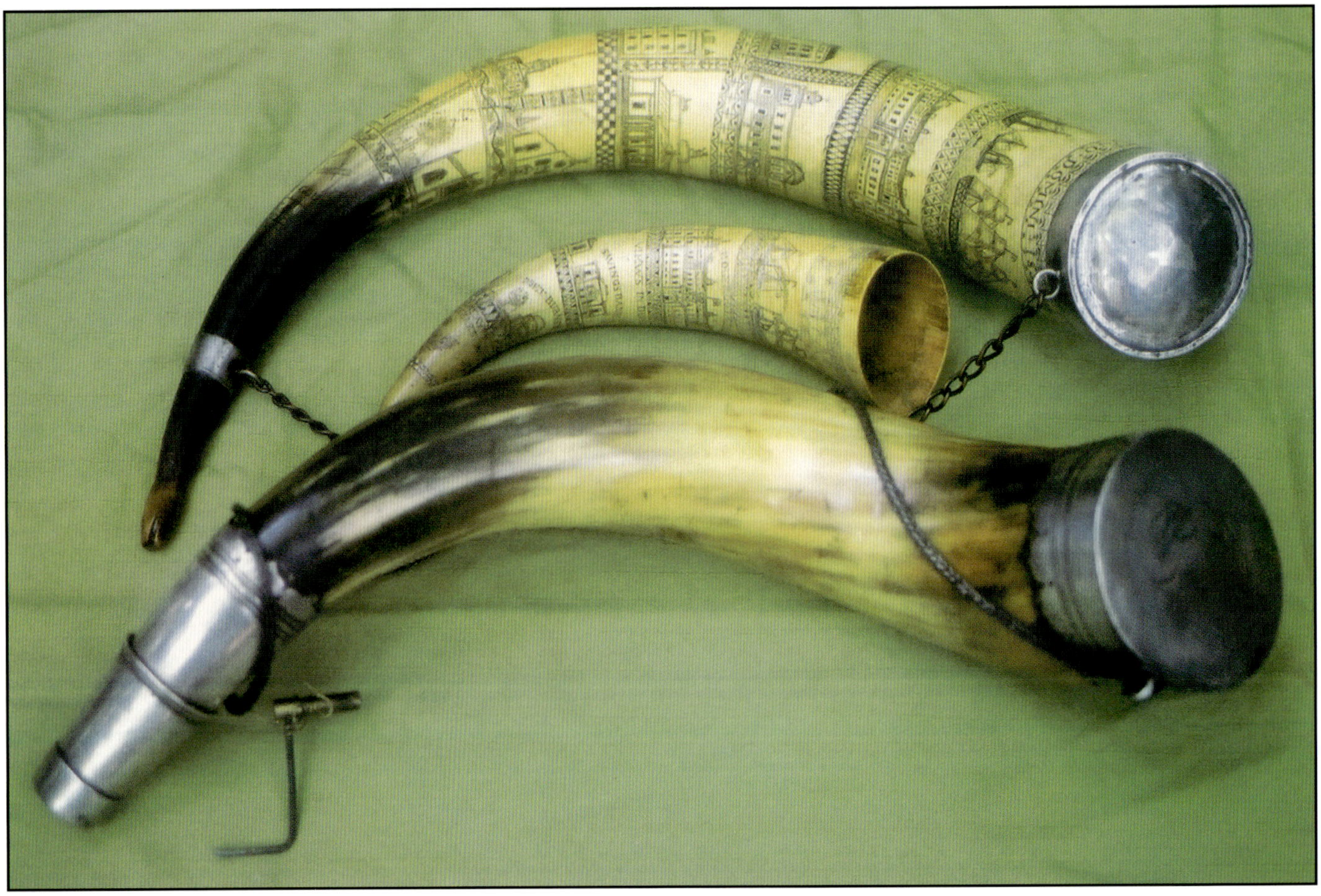

Top: Pair of horns with inscribed scenes of Glasgow and Edinburgh; larger of two is 15" long, $3000 pair. Bottom: Large drinking horn, 17" long, presented to a Cameron Highlander for service in the Napoleonic campaigns, 1802, $2500. *Courtesy of James D. Forman*

Examples of three pressed horns. From left: Large powder horn, 18" long, dated 1696, with Arms of Irvine of Drum, silver mounts, $5000. Victorian horn with large cairngorm at top, thistle finial at bottom, silver fittings, c. 1880, $875. Small early powder horn, decorated, $1100. *Courtesy of James D. Forman*

Nice old powder horn, probably late 18th century with brass fittings. Royal Coat of Arms sScribed probably at later date. 6.5" long, $1000.

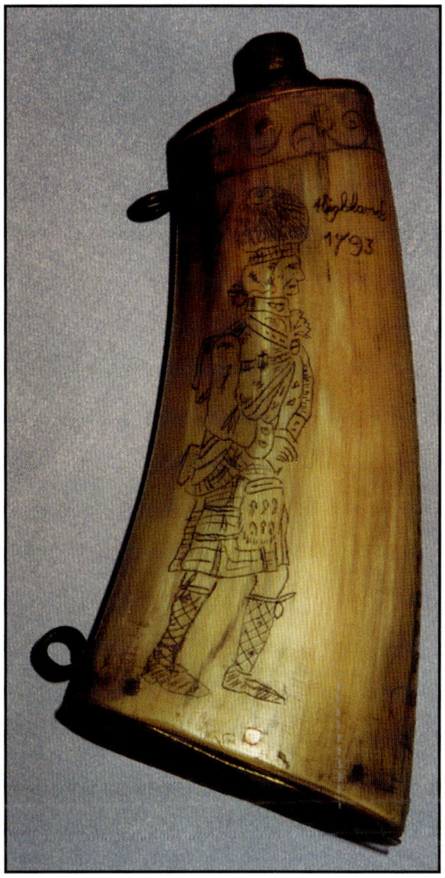

Reverse side of powder horn showing 78th Highlander in excellent detail.

Stud Boxes

Stud boxes have been referred to as stamp boxes and even as snuff boxes, but the configuration lends itself better to being kept on a dresser for shirt studs and cufflinks. Generally oval in shape and, about 3" to 4" at the widest point, and with lift lid, stud boxes almost always are set with a silver-mounted cut cairngorm or pale blue amethyst. Prices today could be $150 to $275.

Bibliography

Hardwick, Paula, *Discovering Horn*, Guilford, Surrey, England, Lutterworth Press, 1981.

Chapter Seventeen

Sports Antiques

Scots are very sports-minded, but only some of the sports yield items of interest to the antiques market. In Scotland and the entire United Kingdom, prices paid at auction for such things as football (soccer) jerseys, cricket caps, cricket bats, etc. that have been worn by champion players can run into the thousands of pounds, just as a Babe Ruth autographed baseball does (in dollars) in the United States. Scottish golf, fishing, hunting, and curling keepsakes also are avidly collected.

Golf

Saint Andrews, the "holy of holies", is the home of golf. The Royal and Ancient course in the Kingdom of Fife on Scotland's east coast has attracted more die-hard golfers than any other course in the world. It was here that golf was born, some say in the 17th century. The Golf Museum here is well worth a look-in after a once-in-a-lifetime, expensive, and probably damp round, after the obligatory refresher at the well-patronized "19th hole." Not solely at Saint Andrews, but at antiques marts, shows, and auctions, pieces of golf memorabilia can be found. Old golf balls include "featheries" (the inside filled with feathers) and gutta-percha (a rubber composition). Prices are in the thousands of pounds for the most rare and oldest items, but old balls in the $100 range can be found today.

Old golf clubs offer a bit more of an opportunity for the golf collector today. Wooden-shafted clubs dating back to the turn of the century are found, but greater quantities in the 1920s to1940s era are available. It is important that they not be recently re-gripped, over-cleaned, and be in generally decent condition. These clubs have a variety of different shapes and brand names to differentiate them. Just as today's golfer is constantly in search of the club to solve his scoring problem, so was the golfer of seventy-five years ago. Most interesting is the wide variety of logos stamped on golf clubs, and a large number of Scottish maker's are represented, even some manufactured in Scotland but stamped for sale with an American department store logo. Some of the golf club designations sound foreign to our ears today: cleeks, niblicks, and mid-irons, for example. Clubs from the 1920s would cost today about $50 and they can range well into the hundreds for the old and rare. Other golf memorabilia that can be found include scoring pencils, scorecards, matchbooks, ashtrays, marked tees, and so forth.

Fishing

Trout and salmon fishing have been a part of Scottish country life for eons, and the equipment to indulge in these pastimes is quite specific, attractive, and collectible.

Fishing Rods

Old wood or bamboo fishing rods, are beautifully made and still usable after a hundred or so years of use by man and boy. The price for an old rod can easily run into several hundred dollars.

Lures and Flies

Less expensive and most interesting are old lures and flies. Old hand-tied flies are real works of art, and obviously the variety is endless. A shadow-box collection of old flies hanging on the wall is a source of fascination, especially if it has the original bone labels with the fly name printed thereon. A relatively nice selection of old flies can be found today for a few pounds each, say $3 to $5.

Reels

Fishing reels come in a very specific size and type for each different kind of fishing. At auctions, older salmon reels in particular can command prices in the thousands of both pounds and dollars.

Woodcut "Salmon-fishing in the Highlands." From a Drawing by M. S. Morgan. c. 1860, depicting a salmon being landed by the kilted fisherman. Behind him is a junior *ghillie* (game-keeper) at the ready with a net. Below is the senior *ghillie*, also kilted, with a creel on his back and a long gaff in hand to land the beast. 14" x 9.5", $195.

Log Books

Old log books, recording the daily catch on a specific river or estate, can give a fascinating glimpse into the sporting past. They can run $100 and up but are rare.

Gaffs

Gaffs were used to grab the fish once the angler brought it close to land. Today a collection of gaffs can make an interesting wall display. They can run to $100 and up. A nice find for a collection would be a salmon gaff, preferably by the English maker Hardy™, which is considered "the best of the best," with a Royal Appointment, no less.

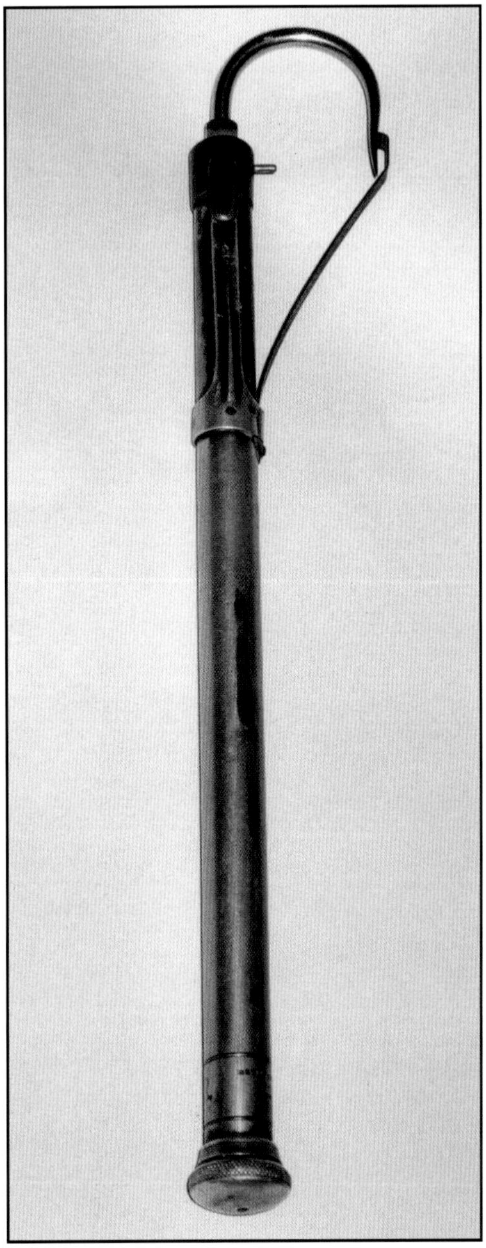

Telescoping salmon gaff, 15" long extending to 40" long, aluminum and brass. The knob at end acts as a "priest." Stamped on bottom by famed fishing supplier Hardy Bros, The makers, Alwnick, England. Also has Royal appointment designation, c. 1920. $325.

Creels

Another part of a fisherperson's equipment is a creel, used to take your catch home. This is a hinged-lid basket, with sides of woven willow, suspended from the shoulder with a leather or canvas strap. They come in all shapes and sizes. Often they are used today as a wall hanging. Fisherwomen sometimes use old creels as a handbag.

Priests

One of the more unusual pieces of fishing equipment is a nasty-looking little miniature truncheon or billy with leather wrist band, which in Scotland is called, somewhat irreverently, a "priest". Once a salmon is hooked, played, gaffed, and landed in the boat or loch-side, the beast (in Scotland, it's not called a fish, it's a beast) is dispatched with a sharp blow to the head from the priest. If you see a nice old priest today for $100 or even a bit more, buy it and dazzle your fishing buddies with the story.

Hunting

Hunting as a sport has its own divisions. You could hunt fox, more English than Scottish, perhaps. You could shoot game birds, such as pheasant, partridge, or grouse. You could stalk deer.

Deer-stalking

In Scotland, deer stalking is as much a ritual as a sport and has provided articles which are much sought after. The stalker's shooting stick is one.

A variation of the shepherd's crook is the shooting stick. A single straight piece of blackthorn is topped with a deer horn fitting in the shape of a short "V", and about 4.5-5' high. This enables the deer-hunter to steady the rifle for a "sure-shot". A handy walking support, even if you're not after "the Monarch of the Glen", and it should set you back about $100. Still another variant is the shooter's stick/seat, which is illustrated nearby, a handy device for a breather on a long day on the moors.

Another deer-stalking item is the spotting telescope, used to find the elusive red deer stag. Spotting scopes are the traditional telescoping kind (think Admiral Nelson), and if you ever find one it could cost around $300 to $500. Usually contained in a brown leather case with shoulder strap, they measure about 12" long non-extended and almost 3 feet long extended.

Walking stick with folding seat (very handy on the moors while on a long stalk). Bamboo with woven cane seat. 30" h., c 1920, $575.
Photo by William B. Bradley

Cartridge or shell bags are canvas and leather with a shoulder strap, often stamped with the Scottish manufacturer's name or vendor's logo. Those from the 1930s can be found today for about $75. They make a nice wall-hanging, and there are women who will covet one as a handbag.

Rifles used for stalking and shotguns for shooting game birds comprise a field of collectibles all to themselves.

Old estate game books, sometimes dating back to the 1800s, come up at auction on the rare occasion. They can detail the names of the people in a shooting party and the specific number of birds shot. For hunting enthusiasts, they make a fascinating gift.

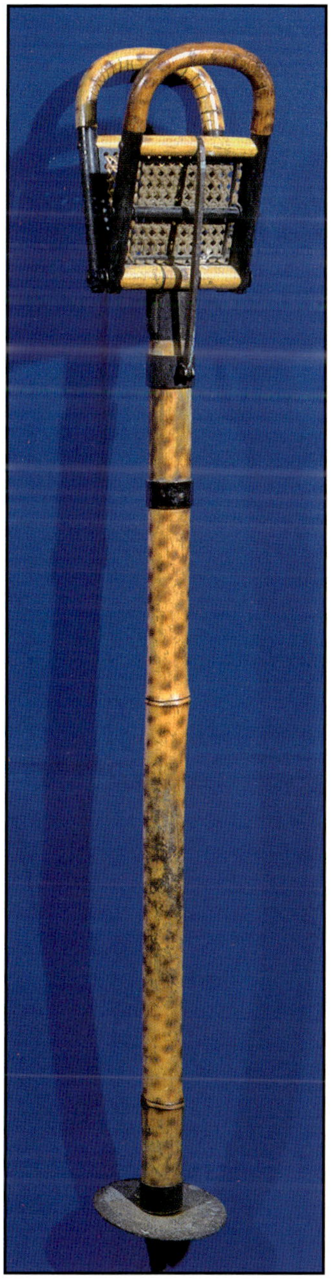

Same walking stick showing the handles and ski-pole style base.
Photo by William B. Bradley

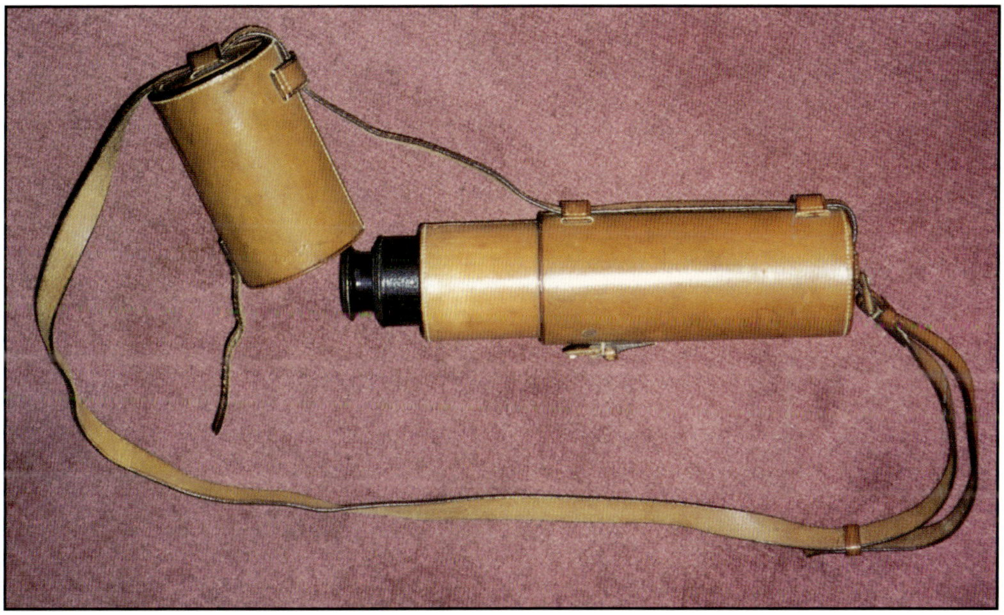

Spotting scope for the hills and "a'chasing the deer." Leather case with carry strap, 12" long, $475.

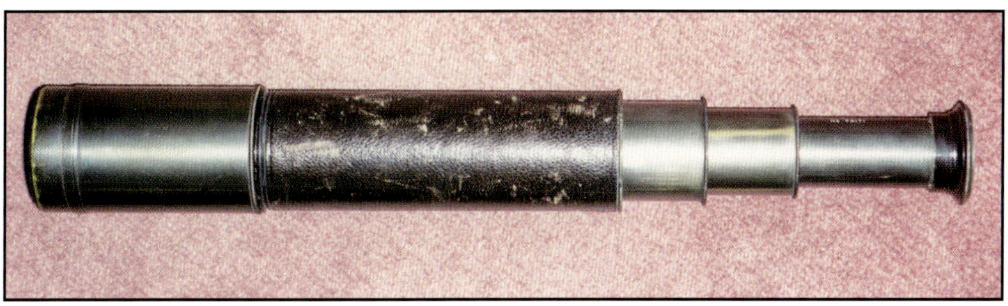

Spotting scope, partially extended. Fully extended it measures almost 3' long, c 1900.

Well-used game bag, c. 1920. Leather and canvas, stamped inside "J. Graham & Son, Inverness." 10" x 10", $75.

Perhaps one of the more important "sporting accoutrements," a pocket flask from "Bullouch Lade & Co, Ltd." Leather top with pull-off bottom of Brittania metal provides a cup. Flask itself is glass. (Note the peep hole in leather to show the remaining volume of "highland dew.") 8" h., $285.

Curling

Curling is a uniquely Scottish sport, although in recent times it has emigrated to Canada by Scottish-Canadians. Two teams at opposite ends of an ice rink push a curling stone towards the bulls-eye target, aided by sweepers from the same team who vigorously broom the ice to increase friction and help guide the stone close to the target. This explanation has none of the nuances, but you can get the idea. A pair of curling stones made from granite with handle, c.1880, weight approximately 20 pounds each. They could be attractive displayed in a family's trophy room and could cost today about $400 and up. A miniature curling stone may make a good keepsake (and is certainly more "transportable"). Silver- and brass-mounted granite inkwells in the shape of a curling stone can be found dating to the early 1900s. They can cost under $300.

Two curling stones in minutia form. Left: Paper-weight curling-stone with silver handle, pink Peterborough granite, 1.75" dia., $95. Right: c.1890 inkwell curling stone, gray Aberdeen granite, brass lid and well, 1.5" h., $285. *Photo by William B. Bradley*

Trophies

A Scottish keepsake field worth a look is the broad area of sports trophies. Any stellar achievement in sports usually is commemorated in some fashion, and trophies are found for fishing, stalking, shooting, golf, whatever. Stuffed birds, stag heads, and mounted fish are trophies you can find today, some for under $500. The stories you could spin might be worth it.

The ubiquitous two-handled trophy on a square wood base, suitably engraved and dated, can be found in materials ranging from hallmarked silver to silver plate and pewter, starting today at about $50. Magnificent silver pieces from the 19th century can be in the $250 and up price range. Other awards might consist of brass plaques on wood wall-hanging shields, engraved and dated, starting today at around $50. There are cigarette cases, ashtrays, silver drink cups, glasses, *quaichs*, and punch bowls all possible as trophies.

One fascinating area consists of pins relating to each sport and engraved with the recipient's name and achievement. For example, a stag-head pin, a pheasant pin, a pin in the shape of a golf club, or a curling stone with crossed brooms, the list could go on. A nice little silver pin of these types could be available at $35 and up.

Information, pricing, and other particulars on almost any equipment for Scottish sporting activities can be obtained from an auction catalogue for the preceding August sale at Gleneagles, Scotland, run by Sotheby's™. It offers needed parameters to be well informed about recent market values.

Bibliography

Sotheby's, August Gleneagles Sale, Catalogue, Sotheby's, 112 George Street, Edinburgh, Scotland.

Chapter Eighteen

Pewter

Jelly mold of pewter, with fruit and vegetable assortment at top. Bottom unscrews to allow jelly, aspic, or ice cream to be decanted and stand upright. 6" h. Stamped with British Patent Office Mark for 1868 and "Pint + 1/2", $385.

Pewter is an alloy of which the principal ingredient is tin. Since tin alone is too soft a metal for domestic use, hardening agents are added: copper, bismuth, antimony, and lead. Without a doubt, pewter was the principal material used for all sorts of domestic and church purposes in Britain over the centuries. Records kept since the fifteenth century by The Worshipful Company of Pewterers in London reveal the extent of the use of this alloy, as reported by Charles Hull, in his book *Pewter*:

> The range of artifacts that have been made in pewter since the fifteenth century is impressive. Domestic items include chargers (up to 33" or 84 cm. in diameter), plates, flagons, tankards, jugs, candlesticks, porringers, saucers, dishes, bowls, basins, soup tureens, vegetable dishes, straining dishes and bowls, carving plates heated by hot water, punchbowls, loving-cups, caudle cups, wine goblets, beakers, babies' bottles and feeding spoons, pepper pots, sugar casters, salts, spoons, teapots, tea caddies, coffee pots, salvers, biscuit barrels, tobacco jars, cigarette boxes, snuffboxes, sandwich boxes, wine funnels, barber's bowls, inkpots and standishes, jelly and confectionary moulds, hot-water bed-warming pans, chamber pots and measures in all capacities up to one gallon. Pieces for church use include wine flagons, chalices, patens, cruets, as well as organ pipes. Surgical items such as syringes and bleeding bowls were made of pewter and so were pilgrim badges, money, tokens, toys, whistles, buttons, chimney ornaments, candle moulds, and a host of other everyday utensils.[1]

Scotland's pewterware manufacture was entirely separate from that of England, although they appear to have followed parallel paths. The "Incorporation of Hammermen" was the Scottish equivalent of the English "Worshipful Company of Pewterers." Hammermen included such allied crafts as blacksmiths, cutlers and armourers. Because Scotland was a much poorer country than England, in the sixteenth and seventeenth centuries the Scottish pewter industry never produced the variety of goods noted above, demand just wasn't there. As a result, Scottish pewter is much more rare than English.

Left: A pepper pot in typical bulbous form, very nice old patina, with knob finial, 5" high, c. 1830, $185. Right: jelly mold with a different top design, 5.5" high, $385.

A further reason that Scottish pewter today is found less often is because a lot of the pieces when damaged were melted down to make new pieces, tin, the principal ingredient in the alloy being in short supply in Scotland. However, the pewter that has survived is often of superior quality to it's English or continental counterpart. While Scottish pewterers supposedly were required to strike their wares with a maker's mark, enforcement was lax. As a result, much of Scotland's surviving pewter is hard to identify.

The use of pewter in general, in all countries, Scotland included, started to decline roughly at the start of the eighteenth century. It was at this time that Sheffield plate, copper with silver exterior, and Brittania metal, a tin and antimony alloy, appeared. Both of these, as well as white iron, iron and tin, gave better results than pewter, so the phase-out was begun. At the same time, pottery and porcelain became cheaper to produce. Pewter manufacturing went into a deep sleep, not really to be aroused until the twentieth century. Some resurgence occurred in the Art Nouveau period and again starting in the 1950s, for model figures, jewellery, and as replacements for some silver objects when silver prices soared to astronomical levels.

Best-known of the Scottish pewter pieces are measures, tankards, tavern pots, and ecclesiastical pieces. Today, despite the bountiful array of objects noted above, the only pieces we associate with pewter for collectors are tankards and spirit flasks.

One of the most attractive specifically Scottish forms of pewter is the strangely-named *tappit hen*. This is a

Left: Small half-gill measure, 2.5", c. 1869, $85. Right: Half-pint measure with Queen's Crown, "VR 86" (1886), 4.5", $185.

Uniquely shaped Scottish tappit hen. Side inscribed, "Presented to Sgt B. Innes, by WOs, & Sgts Mess, 1 King's, August 78." 10" high, $650.

graceful, large liquid measure with a tapered top and bottom section and a concave centre section. The dome-shaped lid had a thumb-piece to open it, and sometimes a finial top. There is conjecture that this finial vaguely resembled a rooster's crest, hence the name "tappit hen." Another theory is that the name came from the drinker's jiggling the thumbpiece when he was ready for a refill, creating a tapping noise to attract the publican's attention.

Scots liked to be independent of the English in as many ways as possible, or that they could get away with. Accordingly, Scotland had it's own set of liquid measures. A Scottish pint, which was the capacity of most tappit hens, was the equivalent of three English Imperial pints. Other Scottish measures in the same format as the tappit hen included the *chopin* (1.5 Imperial pints) and the *mutchkin* (.75 Imperial pints). Because the English government was unable to bring the recalcitrant Scots into compliance until 1855, it is said that the tappit hen "can be found in 19 different sizes."[2]

Occasionally, a pewter plate, reputed to be of Scottish origin will come to light, but with the prevalent absence of marks, one can never be sure. A fine discovery is a delightful bachelor's teapot made of pewter with a wooden handle. We assume the name came from the fact that it held only one cup. Scottish pewter pot-bellied measures, vaguely resembling a pear, come in a variety of sizes: 1/2 gill, gill, 1/2 pint, and pint. They show nineteenth century maker's marks, as well as a town stamp and sometimes an inspector's seal to certify the correctness of the measure. Glasgow and Edinburgh town marks appear to be the most prevalent.

---

[1] Charles Hull, *Pewter,* Princes Risborough, Bucks, England, Shire Publications, Ltd, Shire Album # 280, 1992, page 5.
[2] Donald Wintersgill, *Scottish Antiques*, London England, Johnston and Bacon, 1977, page 29

A bachelor's teapot, so-called because it contained only one cup of tea. Beautiful patina on pewter, dark ebonized wood handle, and top finger-lift. Stamped on bottom "I Vickers, 619," c. 1860, 5" h., $485.

Pair of rare pewter candle-sticks (possibly altar pieces). Finely-made and shaped on round foot. No identifying marks, but believed to be Scottish, c. last Q. 18th century. 7.25" h. x 4.25" base dia. $850.

Bibliography

Hull, Charles. *Pewter,* Princes Risborough, Bucks, England, Shire Publications, Ltd, Shire Album # 280, 1992.

Wintersgill, Donald. *Scottish Antiques*, London England, Johnston and Bacon, 1977.

Chapter Nineteen

Art Works

There are many fine examples of pictures, paintings, and engravings that were done in Scotland, on Scottish subjects, but not necessarily by native Scots. This sampling cannot possibly include the entirety of the subject, but will concentrate on the Victorian era.

Painters

Prior to the seventeenth century, there really were no Scottish painters other than those who painted coats of arms, castle interiors, and the like. Portrait painters came from overseas. In the nineteenth century Scottish subjects started to be memorialized. Scottish painters seized on the literary works of Robert Burns and Sir Walter Scott and started to illustrate the rich images that their poetry and writings provided. As noted by Wendy Kaplan in *Scottish Art and Design, 5000 years*:

> National pride undoubtedly played a part in the artistic utilization of Scott's work. His treatment of Scottish history and daily life would have given his following of artists confidence in the intrinsic value of such subjects, whilst the wide circulation of his poems and novels meant the illustrations to these would be readily understood by the general public.[1]

Arguably one of the foremost portrait painters of the early nineteenth century was Sir Henry Raeburn (1756-1823). Perhaps best remembered for his heroic tartaned and weaponed portrait of Colonel Alistair Macdonnell of Glengarry, Raeburn was a master of character portrayal, and provided a valuable historical account in pictures of a half-century of Scottish life. Raeburn led the way, but he was quickly followed by the likes of William Allen, Thomas Duncan, and David Scott, who tended to paint historical subjects, and David Wilkie, John Philip, and John and Thomas Faed, who focussed on character study.

One of the more striking paintings of Scottish chieftains, "Colonel Alistair Macdonnell of Glengarry," by Sir Henry Raeburn, 1812, here in a hand-coloured mezzotint engraving dated 1922 and signed by H. Macbeth Raeburn (engraver) in pencil, lower left. 16" x 26" in custom wood frame, $1350.

Other artists followed the dual underpinnings of Scottish nineteenth century art, namely national history and national character. Sir Edwin Landseer (1802-1873) is a prime example. Born an Englishman, he discovered Scotland on a visit in 1824, and quickly became a regular visitor at many of the stately homes of the aristocracy of the nineteenth century. He became a confidant of Scott, and was appointed Animal Painter to Her Majesty for Scotland. His specialities were oil paintings of animals, Scottish vistas, and narrative subjects. He was a leading illustrator of Scott's works. Some of his most memorable works include "Monarch of the Glen" and "Death of The Stag in Glen Tilt." A contemporary of Landseer was Horatio MacCulloch (1805-1867), who was probably a more influential force on Scottish landscape painting and painters than any other of his day. A native Scot, he was a great contributor to the popular Victorian image of the highlands of Scotland. His 1864 heroic landscape "Glencoe" is about as Victorian and Scottish as it gets.

Steel engraving, c. 1890, "The Chieftain's Friends," after the original painting by Sir Edwin Landseer, RA, 9.25" x 8". $85.

Steel engraving, c. 1890, "The Young Chief's First Ride." Note the expression on the child's face. Charming Victorian Scottish scene after original painting by E. Tayler, 7.5" x 5", $105.

Oil on canvas painting in original stretcher and frame. Very fine bucolic scene, signed by Horatio McCulloch (1805-1867), RSA, 24" x 15.5. Framed to 32" x 24", $7500. *Photo by William B. Bradley*

Another painter of the same era was Kenneth MacLeay (1802-1878). Born a highlander (Macdonald of Keppoch), MacLeay specialized in miniature portraiture. He received a commission to do a miniature of Prince Albert, Queen Victoria's eldest son, and later posthumous portraits of The Prince Consort. The Queen then commissioned him to paint a series of her retainers at Balmoral along with other clansmen. These thirty-four watercolours were completed and published in 1870 in book form as *The Highlanders of Scotland*, with hand-coloured lithographs. Many later versions have been published, and the bibliography at this chapter's end details one of them. Individual copies of the figures from the 1870 and other nineteenth century versions can be found on occasion for around $500. The original watercolours are in the collection of Her Majesty Queen Elizabeth II, in Buckingham Palace.

In Chapter Thirteen, details are provided on a book published in 1845, with hand-coloured illustrations of original watercolours by the painter Robert McIan (1803-1856). He started his career as an actor, turning to painting in his thirties, with some quite creditable results. His *Clans of The Scottish Highlands* contained a remarkable series of seventy-two watercolours depicting Scottish men and women of various clans in their native costumes. A study of these provides a very interesting overview of Scottish dress from the 1500s to the mid-nineteenth century. Being both an actor and an artist, McIan took liberties from both fields. Some of the poses are quite theatrical and some of the costumes are a bit outlandish. Nevertheless, these representations of the Scottish clans are colourful. Two or three, nicely matted and framed, can work wonders on an otherwise plain wall. Ready to frame, these original hand-coloured prints, not reproduction lithographs. are available today for $250 to $350 each.

A member of "Clan Mac Millan" (sic) at work, as depicted by Robert McIan, 1847. Original print, 10.25" x 14.25", $325.

A McIan clansman depicted for "Clan Grant."

Exquisite detail on architect R. W. Billings' steel engraving of "Glammis Castle," now spelled with only one "m", 1901, 10" x 7", $65.

One doesn't think necessarily of architects as being artists, but there is one good Scottish exception. Robert Billings' book *The Baronial and Ecclesiastical Antiquities of Scotland* is referenced in Chapter Thirteen. Not only are his pencil drawings of various Scottish structures a good architectural reference and of pure historic value, many of the structures being no longer with us, but as straightforward artistic efforts they can stand on their own. These 1901 steel engravings, matted and ready to frame, can be found today for about $50.

The modern antiquer of modest means is probably not in the position to acquire an original Landseer or MacCulloch painting. Further, the best of these seldom come to market. However, the faithful reproductions of these and many other works of art in contemporary steel engravings or woodcuts offer an opportunity that should not be dismissed out-of-hand. For a relatively small amount of money, under $100 each and sometimes for as little as $25, a nice collection of nineteenth century Scottish subject steel engravings can be assembled for a wall or album display. When one considers that the image is the same on the Landseer steel engraving as the million-pound original in Buckingham Palace, one should be well satisfied with the differential in-pocket.

Animal Art

Rural Scotland of the nineteenth century was an artist's paradise if one's favourite subject was animals. Native and non-native Scots alike turned out masses of paintings of all types of animals, among the favourites were the picturesque highland cattle, Scottish blackface sheep and dogs, not to mention domestic animals such as race horses, prize cattle, and pigs. Several artists are worthy of mention. Alfred deBreanski, Sr., active from 1869-1925, specialized in scenes of Scottish landscapes, particularly with highland cattle and sometimes sheep. His work will sell for $10,000 and up. His brother Gustave and son Alfred, Jr. also painted similar subjects. Archibald Thorburn (1860-1935) specialized in watercolour illustrations of deer and other highland animals, but his favourites were birds. His illustrations of pheasant, partridge and ptarmigan (in field), are among the best of their kind. Original Thorburn's can still be found for under $5000. Another painter who specialized in *cooes* (highland cattle) was a Derbyshire man, Louis Bosworth Hurt (1856-1929). Hurt's work, almost always in oils, frequently featured the cattle in the foreground, looming clouds and hills in the background with a touch of colourful highland loch thrown in for good measure. Hurt's better paintings generally sell at fairly good prices; very occasionally for under $15,000, more often $20,000 and up today. Oddly, in the late twentieth century, Hurt and deBreanski developed quite a following in the Far East, and their prices soared. Following the collapse of the Japanese economy, things have returned a bit closer to normal.

Typical of the genre, this oil on canvas painting by A. DeBreanski, Jnr, (Fonteville) (1877-1945). Back label on canvas shows it was in a sale in 1910 at Marshall Fields department store in Chicago. Original frame, 24" x 36", $6500.

An example of Fonteville deBreanski's work, "Evening on a Perthshire River," oil on canvas, signed and dated 1910, 30" x 20", $8500.

A typical example of the work of Louis B. Hurt (1856-1929), with highland cows and swirling mists, 36" x 23", $25,000.

Highland cows and sheep on the Scottish moors by Charles Jones, a British painter, c. 1890. Monogram "CJ" in red at lower right, 24" x 18", $15,000.

Very fine oil on canvas painting, depicting red deer stag on the alert in the highlands, signed and dated W. Watson, 1867. Watson of Leith, Edinburgh, exhibited actively in the 1870-80 period. 18" x 24", $7500.

One of a pair of oil on canvas paintings by Daniel Sherrin (1868-1940), a British artist who specialized in the Scottish genre, 39" x 28", $6500 pair.

The Glasgow Boys

Around the end of the nineteenth century, a new artistic movement came to be. Centered around the eminent furniture designer Charles Rennie Mackintosh of Glasgow, the so-called Glasgow Boys were in vogue during the thirty or so year period before World War I. Their style, whether you cared to characterize it as impressionistic, natural, or rustic realism, was the antithesis of the Victorian's sentimentalism. Two of the leading lights of this new movement were John Lavery and James Guthrie, who managed to capture some of the new middle-class activities such as tennis, as well as bucolic farm scenes. The Arts and Crafts period in Scotland coincided with the Glasgow Boys; both were short-lived. Glasgow alone offered insufficient support to sustain them, but they were influential in Europe and around the Western world.

Scottish art since World War I has not seemed to have the cohesiveness present in the Victorian days and later at the high point of the "GlasgowBoys." A short period of Victorian "renaissance" style art followed; close on its heels a period in the twentieth century of Scottish modernism ensued. To an "art-outsider" (your writer), it appears that during the twentieth century, Scottish artists were searching for a new way of expressing their Scottish characters, without "copying" the styles of the past. The world opinion as to the success of this quest remains to be seen.

---

[1]Wendy Kaplan, *Scottish Art and Design, 5,000 Years*, New York, Harry N. Abrams, Inc., 1990, page 121.

Bibliography

Harris, Paul and Halsby, Julian, *The Dictionary of Scottish Painters, 1600-1960*, Edinburgh, Canongate Publishing, 1990.

Kaplan, Wendy. *Scottish Art and Design, 5,000 Years*, New York, Harry N. Abrams, Inc., 1990.

McEwan, Peter J. M., *Dictionary of Scottish Art and Architecture*, Woodbridge, Suffolk, England, The Antique Collector's Club, 1994.

Miller, Delia and Amelia Murray MacGregor, *The Highlanders of Scotland*, London, Haggerston Press, 1986.

Chapter Twenty

Quaichs

A *quaich* is a drinking and toasting vessel and a unique and ancient part of Scottish society and folklore. The name is derived from the Gaeleic word *cuach*, which simply means "a cup." It probably began as a wooden or horn drinking cup, eons before silversmiths started to make quaichs in the second half of the seventeenth century. It is the earliest of Scottish secular vessels to emerge from the gold and silversmiths of the country. There is no doubt but that this vessel, or one similar to it, was the basic drinking and eating container for the Scottish masses. While there are many variations, which we will comment on shortly, a *quaich* is best envisioned as a shallow bowl with two opposing handles, called *lugs* (Scots' for ears), jutting horizontally from the lip. Another vessel with a somewhat similar configuration (and perhaps more familiar), might be described as a wine-taster.

Two 17th c. turned and carved sycamore quaichs. Nice examples of the simple, everyday drinking vessels from which the legacy of the Scottish quaich is derived. Larger ale bowl measures 4.75" dia. x 7.5" across the lugs (handles). Smaller sprit bowl measures 3" dia. x 5" across the lugs. $2500 pair. *Courtesy of Davidson Collection*

If the reader's memory is revving at full speed, he/she may recall in Chapter Eight the description of the construction of the *luggie*. Early wooden *quaichs* were constructed in the same "coopering" fashion. Alternating staves of light and dark wood were joined together most skillfully, as described by Ian Finlay in his excellent book, *Scottish Gold and Silver Work*:

> In all but the plainest and most workaday examples, it was usual for the alternating wooden staves to be of different colours or even different materials. The woods employed are most often plane-tree, contrasting with the darker laburnum, mahogany or walnut. Coopered quaichs of ivory and ebony are known. Staves are beautifully "feathered" to each other and call for much skill in construction. In nearly all such stave-constructed quaichs, the handles conform closely to a pattern, for they are each part of the stave from which they project and have to be accommodated to the width and nature of it. They are therefore narrow in plan and deep in elevation and tend to fall away toward the ground with a marked droop.[1]

Gradually, wooden *quaichs* started to be become augmented by silver embellishments. These included rims, round feet, plates fitted to the tops of the lugs, and the like. The bottom of the inside of the *quaich* was often found with a silver "boss", insert or medallion. These were inscribed with a religious motif ("Amen") or later expressions of loyalty to Bonnie Prince Charlie ("God Bless the Prince Steurt of Scotland"), or the Gaelic *squab ase*, the literal meaning of which is "sweep it up." Some of the *quaichs* that had scalloped silver plates on the lugs would have the husband's initials on one lug, his wife's on the opposing one. These *quaichs* varied in size from 2" to 3" in diameter, all the way up to 7" to 8". Some *quaichs* found their way into churches where they were used for communion services.

Very rare provincial silver quaich engraved with simulated staves and flowers (thistle, rose, and tulips). Shaped lugs are engraved and initialed. Maker's mark "HR" (co-joined) for Hugh Ross of Tain, c. 1730. 2.63" dia,. 4.63" across lugs. $5000. *Courtesy of Davidson Collection*

Oak quaich with applied silver foot-ring, rim, and lug supports. c. 1800. 2.75" dia. x 3.5" across lugs. $1000. *Courtesy of Davidson Collection*

Impressive silver-mounted oak quaich with maple lugs. Silver rim is inscribed, "the oak of which this cup is made was part of Alloway Kirk," along with further verses from Robert Burns' epic poem *Tam O' Shanter*. Underside of lugs are inscribed "To D. Aird, Esq., Jamaica from Hew Aiken, Air." Maker's mark "PA", for Peter Aitken, Glasgow, c. 1820, 2.38" dia. x 3.38" across lugs, $3500. *Courtesy of Davidson Collection*

Ian Finley comments on the *quaich*'s social significance as follows:

> The number of quaichs associated with historic personages, such as those linked with the name of Prince Charles Edward or the quaich made from the Wallace oak at Torwood, Stirlingshire, made it obvious that this type of vessel was held in particular regard and had a special significance in Scottish social ritual. In the seventeenth and eighteenth centuries men no doubt carried small quaichs in their pockets as they carried knives, spoons and snuff-boxes.[2]

The earliest all-silver *quaichs* rather faithfully copied their wood-stave predecessors, even to the extent of copying in the silver the lines delineating the stavejoints. These were starting to appear in the second half of the seventeenth century, hall-marked by Scottish provincial silversmiths in, among other towns, Inverness, Aberdeen and Perth. Other motifs also started to show up, including the Tudor rose and the Dutch tulip (see Chapter One, references to Mary of Orange), probably a shrewd piece of early political diplomacy. The thistle, now the undisputed Scottish "emblem" really didn't start to flower until later, in the eighteenth century.

Group of interesting quaichs. Top left: Tartan Ware quaich in "McPherson " tartan, cut to replicate stave construction. c. 1860, 2.63" dia., 3.83" across lugs. $850. Lower left: Quaich of Mauchline Ware with laminated strips of sycamore and laburnum. Transfer printed legend "From the Athole Plantations, Dunkeld, McLean & Son, Publishers," c. 1870, 2.5" dia. x 3.5" across lugs. $485. Centre, top & bottom: Pair of bellmetal quaichs, bowl of each inset with silver 4-d coin dated 1838. Base of each vessel is inscribed: "John Moore" and "James Moore," probably sons born shortly after the start of Queen Victoria's reign. 2.38" dia., 3.63" across lugs. $1250 pair. Upper right: Horn quaich with shaped lugs and silver mounts, inscribed "AC" and "1855." 2.75" dia. x 4.13" across lugs. $750. Lower right: Silver-mounted and laburnum wood quaich carved with woven Celtic roping on bowl and lugs. Silver rims to bowl and foot have Tuscan key design. Bowl base has silver insert with image of young Queen Victoria dated 1837. 2.75" dia. x 4.75" across lugs. $1500. *Courtesy of Davidson Collection*

Carved oak quaich with silver rim, foot, and bowl insert. Insert inscribed, "Squab ase"(literally "sweep it up" in Gaelic). Inverness hallmarks, maker's mark "F & McB" (Ferguson & McBean), date obscure, c 1840. 2.25" dia. x 3.25" across lugs inscribed with serpent heads. $950.

Silver-mounted wooden quaich with intricately cut and joined sections of sycamore and laburnum. Silver rim and foot, and fret-engraved silver lugs, c 1840. 2.13" dia. x 3.75" across lugs. $750.

Quaichs are not only found in wood, silver-embellished wood and all-silver, but also in marble, horn, stone, pewter, bell-metal (an alloy of copper and tin), brass, gold, and ivory. The majority of *quaichs* have the traditional two handles, or "*lugs*," but it is not unusual to find an occasional one with three or four *lugs*. Sometimes the *lugs* contain silver-mounted cairngorms or amethysts. The shape of a *quaich* gradually changed over time, the early shallow bowl became deeper and deeper, until *quaichs* made in the eighteenth and nineteenth centuries became more like a dish than a bowl. Modern versions have generally continued this pattern. For a time the *quaich* seemed to have partially dropped from popularity, but appeared to have a renewal in the mid-nineteenth century with the impetus of Balmorality, Sir Walter Scott's novels, et al.

When and how are *quaichs* traditionally used? As pointed out, the early ones were simply drinking vessels. The silver-embellished *quaichs* and the later all-silver *quaichs* had several uses with more being invented as we speak; see chapter end. For example:

Christening presents. A silver *quaich*, suitably inscribed from the donor to the "wee" donee, is a treasured memento. (I still have mine, presented by my Godfather.)

Pair of unusual quaichs. Left: Silver and agate mounted. Lugs are inlaid with agates (jasper and bloodstone) in the form of a Maltese Cross with intricate chasing. Hallmarked Birmingham, 1906, 1.88" dia. x 3.5" across lugs. $750. Right: Unusual horn quaich with three lugs, each fitted with silver-mounted pale amethyst, c. 1890, 2.38" dia. x 4" across lugs.$525. *Photo by William B. Bradley*

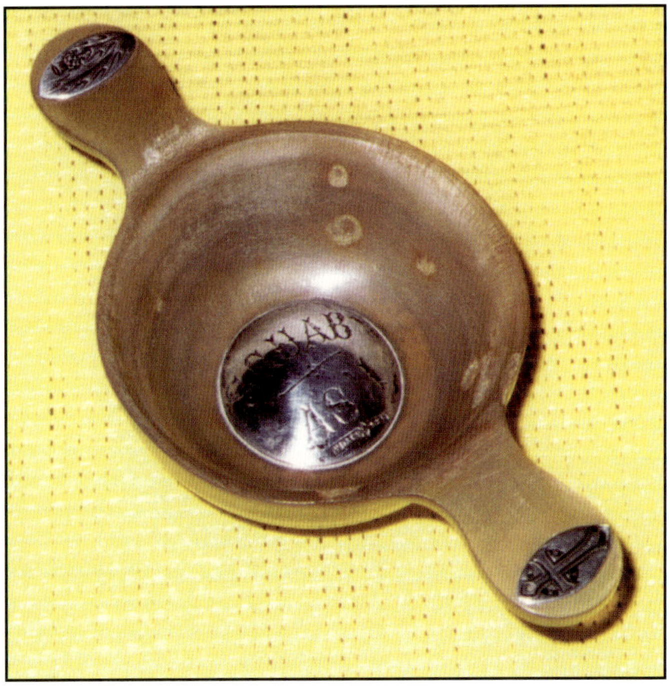

Silver-mounted and shaped horn quaich. Silver medallions on lugs engraved with Celtic cross and thistle. Silver bowl insert inscribed, "Squab ase" and maker's mark "W D & Co.", c 1870. 2.38" dia. x 4.63" across lugs. $750.

Presentation present. As a retirement gift, a graduation present, a sporting event prize or similar occasion, an inscribed silver *quaich* is most welcome.

An honorarium. When money might be out-of-line or crass, a *quaich*, suitably engraved makes a superb "thank-you" to a guest speaker.

Toast to the haggis. As part of the traditional haggis ceremony at a formal Scottish dinner, after emoting Rabbie Burns' ode "To a Haggis," the master of ceremonies takes the *quaich*, takes a sip of the "dew of Scotland," toasting the entire assemblage and then offers the *quaich* to the bagpiper who piped in the haggis party. The piper drains the *quaich* of it's remaining liquid, turns it upside down facing the audience, kisses the bottom, and—holding it in his right hand—elevates it to the sky with a flourish. The piper has offered the traditional "kiss to the Prince across the water" (see Chapter One) and the master of ceremonies has "paid the piper."

Small silver quaich with pierced lugs. 1.88" dia., 3" across lugs, $525.

Close-up of foot of quaich showing hallmarks for Edinburgh, 1900, and maker's mark "H&I" for Hamilton & Inches. *Photo by William B. Bradley*

Wedding present. We recommended to a best-man-to-be that he purchase an antique *quaich*, use it at the wedding-dinner to toast the bride and groom in lieu of a champagne flute. Following the toast, he then presented the *quaich* to the bride and groom as his wedding gift to them. We were told it was a huge success.

Other than adorning a mantlepiece or a shelf for all to see, are their any practical uses for a *quaich*? Although not recommended with silver, I know one man who uses his wooden one for peanuts, another for paperclips. I personally prefer mine to savour a "wee dram," it somehow tastes far better than in an ordinary glass.

A large, 5" diameter, all-silver quaich with three lugs in finger-hold form. Hallmarked 1901, Edinburgh, by Hamilton & Inches, $950.

Where to see nice old *quaichs*? There is a fine collection of them (and other Scottish artifacts as well) in a collection housed at the Colonial Williamsburg Foundation in Williamsburg, Virginia. When you're on your visit to Scotland, the City Museums of Inverness, Dundee, and Perth all have examples from silversmiths in their area. And, of course, there's the old stalwart, The Royal Museum of Scotland in Edinburgh.

As to prices, most difficult. Anything with a Bonnie Prince Charlie connection has long rested in a museum or a family home, probably for over two centuries. Periodically, an old *quaich* will appear at an auction resulting from a house close-down. If you're sure of the provenance, you could pay up to $5000 for a fine example of an early *quaich* dating to the seventeenth or eighteenth century. More likely you'll run into more modern late nineteenth century versions. If they have good form and character, pay up to $1000. Silver *quaichs* dating to the first quarter of the twentieth century could command a price in the region of $500-750. One should not consider this steep, when you compare it to a new *quaich* from a quality shop such as Hamilton and Inches in Edinburgh, which will set you back £250, or roughly $400.

Check the hallmarks. *Jackson's* silver reference book is an essential part of your antiquing briefcase, especially when it comes to evaluating a *quaich*'s value. If by sheer chance you run across a date mark pre-1900 made by any of the provincial Scottish silversmiths in Inverness, Tain, Dundee, Aberdeen, Perth, etc., it's probably worth at least two to three times the same article with an Edinburgh or Glasgow mark. Why? Simple. Fewer were made and even fewer survive.

[1] Ian Finlay, *Scottish Gold and Silver Work*, Stevenage, Herts, England, The Strong Oak Press, Revised edition, 1991, Pg. 118.
[2] Ibid., Pg. 120.

Bibliography

Finlay, Ian, *Scottish Gold and Silver Work*, Stevenage, Herts, England, The Strong Oak Press, Revised edition, 1991.

Foster, Gordon, "Silver Lining," *Scottish Field Magazine*, Edinburgh, Scotland, February 1996.

Hyman, John A., "Scottish Drinking Vessel," *Antiques Magazine*, June 1997.

Jackson, Sir Charles, *Jackson's Silver and Gold Marks*, Woodbridge, Suffolk, England, The Antique Collector's Club, revised edition, 1989.

Wintersgill, Donald, *Scottish Antiques*, London, England, Johnston and Bacon, 1977.

Chapter Twenty One

Small Collectibles

Communion Tokens

The taking of communion in Scotland, in the seventeenth to nineteenth centuries, was quite a different affair than it is today in churches that follow the practice. And it was not to be taken lightly. Before being admitted to communion, one had to demonstrate one's sincere readiness and depth of knowledge to partake in the sacrament. Those who were able to do so to the minister's satisfaction, were given a token, which admitted them to the church on the day of communion, sometimes given only every seven or nine years. These tokens, small discs, about 1.5" in diameter, were usually made of lead; sometimes of brass, tin, copper or whatever. Shapes ranged from squares, oblongs, triangular or round; you name it.

Each token was distinctly marked with an identifying symbol, parish name, church image or other device to assure that no imposters got to the communion table. Frequently found symbols included the sun, a fish, a communion cup, a heart, a vine and so on. Often they were crudely made by the local blacksmith, plumber or pewterer, utilizing a punch or die. Most are dated (very handy for collectors), and the range is extensive, tokens being issued by The Church of Scotland and others as well. The practice of the use of tokens was carried by Scottish immigrants in the eighteenth century to The United States, where the use of tokens was widespread in Scottish communities. In Scotland, this old tradition started to die out in the early part of the twentieth century when printed cards came into use.

As is the case with many antique collectibles, the interest in communion tokens comes and goes. In the first quarter of the twentieth century, there was a great interest in them. Then, for the next fifty years, very little. Some revival in interest has been noted in more recent years. Older is usually rarer, and therefore more valuable. But you should be able to find interesting examples dating to the mid-nineteenth century for prices ranging from $10-30.

Coins

After the 1707 Treaty of Union, Scotland no longer made its own coinage. Thus ended a long history of coinage, since the first Scottish coin was struck in 1136, in the reign of King David I. Scotland's mint produced coins until 1870, but they were the "English" versions. There are coins produced in the twentieth century with Scottish symbols (thistle, lion, crown and Cross of St Andrew), but they are not, strictly speaking, Scottish coins. Any collector desiring to start a collection of true Scottish coins, therefore, must look to coins minted in the eighteenth century and earlier. This writer will not attempt even to "skim" this very specialized collecting area; even the names of coins are totally different, century-to-century, from 1200 forwards. Some of the names have a fascinating ring to them, *bawbee, bodle, pistole, merk, ducat* and *noble,* among others. The suggestion is made to anyone interested in Scottish coins, that they should start with a specialized reference source, two of which are listed in the bibliography at the end of this chapter.

Canes

Also called walking sticks by the English and Scots, there are several canes which are quite specific to Scotland. The first that comes to mind in the shepherd's crook. About 5 feet high, and usually made out of Scottish blackthorn or hawthorne, the top of the stick is mounted with a carved ram's-horn handle, terminating in a reverse thistle. Essentially a craft product, each stick is differ-

Handle of a shepherd's crook carved from a ram's horn. Stick is blackthorn; 57" from top of handle to rubber tip. Note thistle carved at bottom of handle, c. 1920-30. $250. *Photo by William B. Bradley*

ent, because of the different colours in the horn itself, ranging all the way from almost translucent to almost solid black. The nicest ones are honey coloured with striations of black. Smaller versions of the shepherd's crook measure about 3.5', and because of their size are more properly called walking sticks.

Another form of Scottish walking stick is the carved serpentine. Made out of one piece of wood, the 3.5'+/- stick is hand-carved with perhaps a Celtic pattern of sea monsters and Celtic roping or thistles and foliage. One unusual example was carved with the United Kingdom's flowers, the rose for England, the thistle for Scotland, the shamrock for Ireland, and the leek for Wales. Be prepared to pay in the range of $100-250 for a horn-handled shepherd's crook. Carved sticks would start at about $100. Examples you might run across would date to 1880-1950.

Carved oak walking stick, 37" long, with thistle finial carved at top. Below are entwined carved thistles, roses, shamrocks, and leeks, the national flowers for Scotland, England, Ireland and Wales, c1860, $275.

For more formal occasions, a gentleman's walking-stick would be used, frequently ornamented with a carved handle-top, sometimes out of ivory or other fine material. A dog's head was a favourite subject. Round silver knobs on both gentlemen's and ladies canes can also be found, sometimes with a presentation message engraved thereon.

Gadget or system canes became quite popular in the nineteenth century. A cane with a flask built into the stick and one with a spotting scope (read telescope) built-in, both useful for deer-stalking, have been seen, as well as a cane whose top unscrewed and became a pipe. These gadget canes, if you can find one, would cost anywhere from $400 and up.

Doorstops and Boot-scrapers

Cast metal doorstops, c.1850-1930, can be found and they come in a range of designs with Scottish motifs. Whether they were all actually made in Scotland is probably a matter of doubtful conjecture; nevertheless they certainly have a Scottish association. There are at least

Painted metal doorstop of a highland officer in full kit and with his foot on unexploded shell. 14" h., c. 1900, $650.

four different versions of kilted Highland soldier doorstops that have been seen, and there are more. Brass or painted cast metal, they are about 10" high and heavy. A Scottish plowman, with his wooden plow being pulled by a massive Clydesdale horse, complete with a verse from Rabbie Burns, is another theme. Scotties or Aberdeen terrier dogs come in a variety of versions: mother and pups, single dogs; I would think that the diligent collector could uncover similar doorstops and boot-scrapers in other Scottish dog breeds: deerhounds, shelties, Skye terriers, as well as other Scottish animal breeds such as Aberdeen Angus bulls and red deer. Costs could be in the $75-200 range.

Doorstop of highland officer in bronze,. 12" h., c. 1900, $650.

Combination doorstop and boot scraper of cast metal. A familiar theme of the plowman and his horse and a verse from Burns' poem *To a Wee Mousie* (see Chapter Thirteen). 12" w. x 6" h., c. 1930, $175.

Cast brass Scottie dog (more properly called an Aberdeen terrier) doorstop, 20th c., 6" h., $175.

Pokerwork or Pyrography

A popular form of decoration in the Arts and Crafts period, roughly 1870 to 1920, was what the Scots called poker work, known in the United States as pyrography. Any wooden object that could be beautified by this form of decoration can be found. The use of a hot poker to burn in a design, sometimes augmented by chisel-scooping, was the technique employed.

In Scotland, the design was frequently one of foliage and thistle blossoms. Examples include a hand mirror with wooden back beautifully worked in an intricate foliate design, several trinket, Bible, and other boxes with poker work, and a small conservatory garden spade. A most spectacular specimen seen is a large, 2' x 3.5' pokerwork image of Robert Burns, done on two joined boards of Scottish pine. It is an artful copy of the famous Nasmyth portrait of Burns, and was brought to the United States by a Scottish grandmother about 1890.

Poker work does not appear ever to have been a particularly popular collectible, and accordingly prices are about what one would expect for the object itself, without a poker work premium. Nevertheless, the pokerwork adds a most attractive addition to what would otherwise be an ordinary object. Pokerwork was another of the Victorian's pastimes.

Children's Banks

Children's banks (money boxes) are becoming a fascinating collecting area. They come in a huge variety of shapes, sizes, and materials and some can be found in Mauchline ware and Tartan ware. There are also a number of children's banks in cast metal dating back into the early nineteenth century. These come in literally hundreds of designs of buildings, mechanical banks, and so on. The Scottish reputation for thriftiness or frugality lends itself to saving money, a habit that Scottish Victorians were anxious to instill in their offspring. Money boxes in the shape of the familiar British post office red letterbox were a favourite form. Puzzle banks were also a frequent format. These could only be opened if one knew the secret, often in moving the lid in an exact sequence to access the money. Glass banks with the image of a Scot can be opened by breaking the glass. Some of the rarer mechanical banks can run into the hundreds of dollars, if not thousands, but a nice collection of banks with a Scottish theme can be started with examples today starting for $25-50.

Maps and Charts

The first atlas of Scotland, with a map by Timothy Pont, was published in Holland in 1654. However, perhaps the most famous early map of Scotland was by John Speed in 1611. According to author Bob Weir:

> Because of it's detailed figures, this picturesque example is easily the most sought after map of the country and that is reflected in the price. A cool £3000.[1]

However, he advises that colourful maps of Scotland dating to the 18th and 19th centuries can be found today for sums of £60 and up ($100). There are old maps that have survived and are available for surprisingly modest prices. One could do worse than to find a colourful 200-year-old map of Scotland to bring home, provide it with a complementary mat and frame and hang it on the living-room wall.

Horse Brasses

Scottish horse brasses dating to the last half of the nineteenth and first half of the twentieth century are quite attractive and reasonably priced collectibles. These are brass medallions, about 2" to 3" in diameter, attached either singly or in a multiple sequence to bridles and other horse harness as decorations. Found on both pleasure and working horses, particularly the plowmen's magnificent Clydesdales, there are several Scottish themes that can be found. First and foremost is the thistle, in a variety of shapes and sizes, some with foliage wreath surrounds and some alone. A close second is the image of Rabbie Burns, also in several different variations. Red deer heads, images of Balmoral, with and without Queen Victoria, the Cross of Saint Andrew, and the Lion Rampant of Scotland are others that were made. Prices could be in the $20 to $75 range. The early pieces were cast in sand and their backs show a rough texture as a result. Modern ones are shiny, light, bright, and cheap.

Two typical horse brasses. Left: The ubiquitous thistle. Right: The Queen's crown, each 2.5" dia. $35 each.

Boxes

One can find a variety of boxes for different uses with Scottish themes. Document boxes are often decorated with carved thistles or other Scottish emblems, or perhaps with silver accouterments with *repoussé* thistles. Letter boxes, desk boxes and salt boxes are discussed in other chapters. The tea caddy needed air-tight protection to preserve the fragile tea's quality. Tea caddies came in a variety of shapes and sizes, not to mention materials. Silver mounted boxes may have handsome bun feet with two in-set, silver, removable, canisters flanking a glass mixing bowl. Such a caddy, embellished with the owner's crest or coat of arms, is a magnificent example of the genre.

Another favourite is a similarly configured caddy in tortoiseshell, with silver initials and crests pinned to the lid top. A particularly Scottish example is sheathed in *shagreen* (sharkskin), which is green with mottled white dots. Any tea caddy worth its sugar is going to command a price well into four or even five figures.

Head-mugs

The Royal Doulton™ company has head-mugs with a Scottish figure "Auld Mac," popularized in a song by the 1920s music hall character Sir Harry Lauder. They come in three sizes, went out of production in the 1960s, and can be found today for $75 to $200.

A selection of wooden boxes. Front: A wall-hanging letter box in oak with intricate Celtic geometric carvings, c. 1880, 10.5" wide. $375. Back left: Hinged-lid document or Bible box with detailed geometric circular wood-chip carving. On lid are initials "T.W" (for owner Tina White of Kirkcubright), 11" x 6" x 6", c. 1860, $350. Back right: Stained pine wall-hanging salt box with brass hinges, 10" x 10" x 6", $250.

Most unusual tea caddy of oak. Hand carving around entire box of thistles, leaves, the head of Bruce (front center of box). Metal escutcheons are engraved, "Scots, wham Bruce has aften led, Carved from oak of old abbey, Dunfermline, Not so sour as I thought," "Tea Caddy." (the latter on lock face above Bruce's head). 8" x 5" x6", $950.

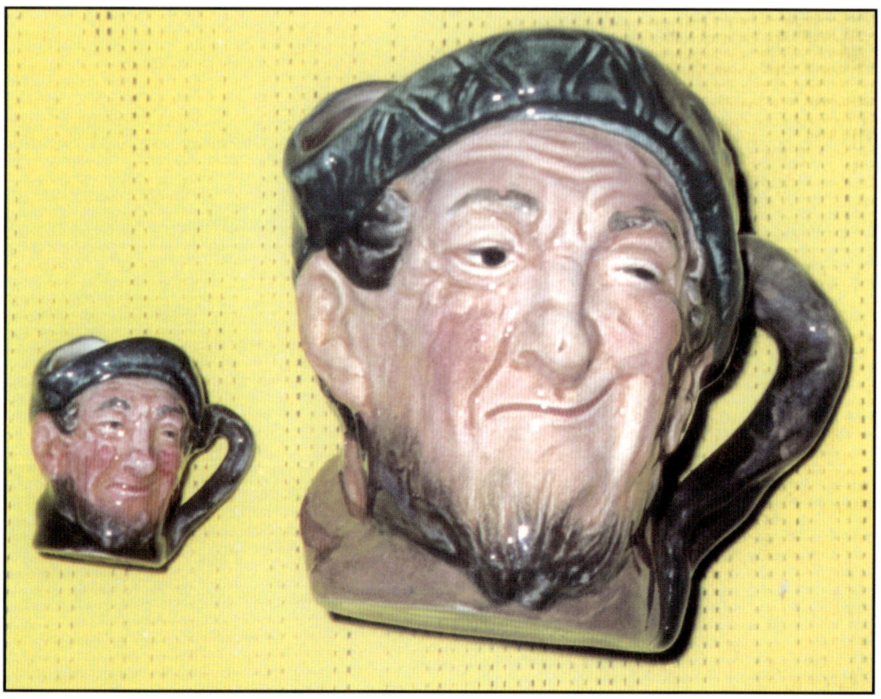

Royal Doulton head mugs of the character Auld Mac, popularized by Scottish music-hall comedian Sir Harry Lauder in the 1920s. This character was discontinued in 1960s. Left: Rare miniature size, 2.25" h., $225. Right: Large size, 6", $200.

Britains Toy Soldiers

Several Scottish Regiments received the Britains™ treatment, and boxed sets of these cast metal toy figures can be found. Those dating back into the 1930s are quite expensive, but late twentieth century examples can be found for $100 and up, depending on the number of figures, condition, and rarity.

Tartan Pen Knives

Produced with Sheffield™ blades, these folding pen-knives (with one, two or more blades) and with printed tartan metal sides are often available at street markets. Dating as early as the 1920s, with a lot more made in the 1950s and later, they can be found in a variety of sizes and tartans. Prices start around $20.

Printed, tartan-covered penknife with maker's logo and name "Richard's." Blade of Sheffield steel, 4" overall, 20th century, $45. *Photo by William B. Bradley*

Victorian Policemen's Truncheons

These are full-sized policemen's truncheons, complete with carry wrist-strap, measuring around 17" long and frequently made of a hard wood such as *lignum vitae*. They are painted with such varied designs as the Royal cipher, a crown, an owner's initials, or a branch of the military force. The skill of the design can be quite high. If the paint looks too new, it probably is. Prices today are in the $350 plus range.

Close-up of policeman's truncheon, hand-painted with compass rose, thistles, and Queen's crown. Made of hard wood, probably *lignum vitae*, 17" long overall, c. 1880, $450.

Corkscrews

Old iron, steel, and brass corkscrews can be found with a variety of Scottish associations. Most pertinent is an iron style with a handle formed in the shape of a thistle, with two finger-pulls to provide leverage to extract the cork. Other's can be found with drink manufacturers' logos. Prices today can be from $10 or $15 and up.

Miscellaneous

Many other Scottish antiques can be cherished keepsakes. A nice barometer reflects the Scots habit of always keeping an eye on the weather and talking about it, endlessly. A collection of old single-malt whisky glasses might be another. A distilleries map would be a good place to start and get enjoyably educated at the same time. All you have to do is keep both eyes open, have on a sturdy pair of shoes, ask questions, and enjoy.

---

[1]Weir, Bob, "Charting Success," *Scottish Field*, Edinburgh, Scotland, December 2001.

A complete child's dress outfit from the late 19th century displayed on a doll from the 1950s. The outfit came with a cabinet photo of the proud owner. 36" h., $750.

A wall-hanging barometer with thermometer and carved wood with finials and drops. Edwardian, probably c. 1910, Ivory-backed thermometer with Centigrade and Fahrenheit scales. Nicely detailed barometer face, 18.5" overall. $475.

Close-up of *papier-maché* tray made by Jennings & Bettridge, London. Elaborate, gold-painted, oriental-style borders. In centre is hand-painted copy of the painting "Return of the Chieftains". British Patent Office mark for 1869. 17" x 13", $1750.

Bibliography

Barteson, Donald. *Scottish Coins*, Princes Riseborough, Aylesbury, Bucks, England, Shire Publications, Ltd. (Album # 189), 1987.

Finlay, Ian. *Scottish Gold and Silver Work*, Stevenage, Herts, England, The Strong Oak Press, Revised edition, 1991

Purvey, P. Frank. *Coins and Tokens of Scotland,* London, B. A. Seaby, 1972.

Rau, William. "Collecting Antique Walking Sticks," *Antiques Journal*, May 1996.

Wintersgill, Donald. *Scottish Antiques*, London, England, Johnston and Bacon, 1977.

Epilogue

And so, dear reader, the time has come to part. I do hope you've enjoyed your Scotia journey, as much as I have enjoyed writing it for you. More importantly, I hope you've managed to absorb a bit of Scottish history, an understanding of her people and their idiosyncrasies, both positive and negative, as well as an appreciation for and better understanding of her antiques. If so, we've both done our respective jobs. And now, I bid you a very Scottish farewell. *Safe hame, and haste ye back.*

Appendix

A wide variety of gold and silver goods in Scottish styles, including the St. Andrew's Cross, Maltese Cross, arrow, shield, endless knot, and anchor, appeared on goods in the catalog of Joseph Cook & Sons, Ltd., of Birmingham, in the 1880s.

ESTABLISHED 1846.

JOSEPH COOK & SONS, LTD.

Manufacturers of

INLAID GOLD AND SILVER GOODS

In Granite, Scotch Pebbles (all kinds),

Iona Stone and Connemara Marble.

TOPAZ AND AMETHYST GOODS A SPECIALITY.

This Trade Mark is a | J. C. & S. | Guarantee of Excellence.

TERMS OF BUSINESS.

5% 1 month. 2½% 3 months. Afterwards Nett.

All Accounts under £1 nett.

NEW ACCOUNTS.

Ledger Accounts will be opened with any member of the Trade on receipt of satisfactory trade references.

All communications to be addressed—
HIBERNIAN WORKS,
LIVERY STREET,
BIRMINGHAM.

Telegrams:
"HIBERNIAN, BIRMINGHAM.

Telephone:
1553 CENTRAL

HIBERNIAN WORKS,

LIVERY STREET,

BIRMINGHAM.

TO THE TRADE.

WE have pleasure in placing before you this copy of our new Catalogue.

In compiling this Catalogue we have endeavoured to illustrate as far as possible our different classes of goods, but owing to the immense variety, we are unable to show all our designs. We shall be pleased at any time to quote for and submit designs to any requirements.

We beg to draw attention to the fact that all goods shown are our own productions.

It is very difficult for retailers to differentiate as to who are manufacturers, as factors in a small way get goods made up for them, and have them stamped with their own initials, and thereby pose as manufacturers.

A visit to Birmingham at any time, and a call at our works, will be greatly appreciated, and, we venture to say, will afford the majority some pleasure in seeing the goods produced.

In conclusion, we would draw attention to the fact that for 40 years all our business was done with the wholesale houses, but during the last 15 years we have gone direct to the retailers. The tendency is growing stronger for the retailer to buy from the manufacturer, and our actions of the last 15 years have proved to our entire satisfaction that it is beneficial to both parties to save the middle-man's profit.

J. COOK & SONS, LTD.

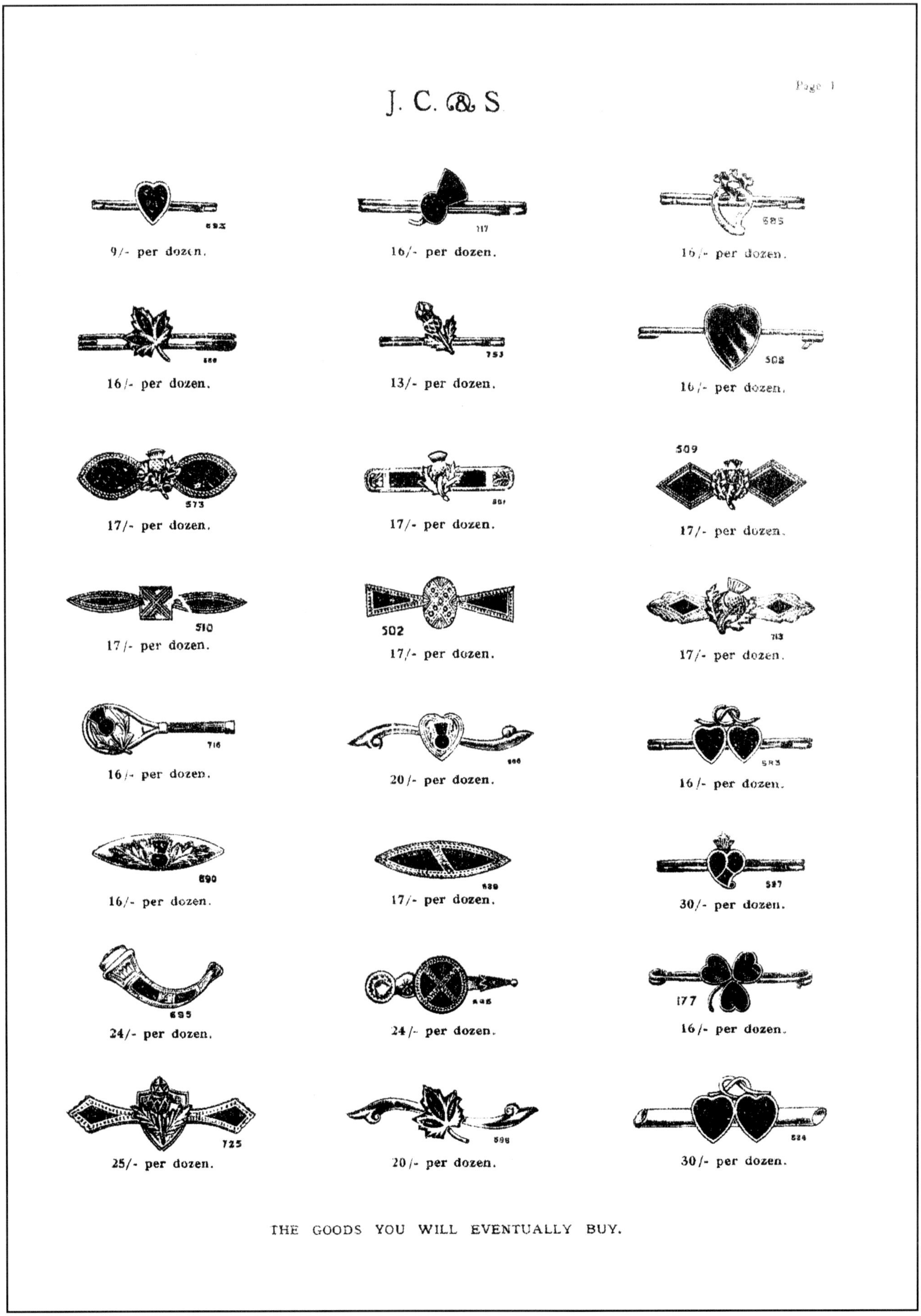

J. C. & S.

Page 1

9/- per dozen.	117 — 16/- per dozen.	685 — 16/- per dozen.
16/- per dozen.	753 — 13/- per dozen.	508 — 16/- per dozen.
573 — 17/- per dozen.	17/- per dozen.	509 — 17/- per dozen.
510 — 17/- per dozen.	502 — 17/- per dozen.	713 — 17/- per dozen.
716 — 16/- per dozen.	20/- per dozen.	583 — 16/- per dozen.
690 — 16/- per dozen.	17/- per dozen.	587 — 30/- per dozen.
695 — 24/- per dozen.	24/- per dozen.	177 — 16/- per dozen.
725 — 25/- per dozen.	20/- per dozen.	30/- per dozen.

THE GOODS YOU WILL EVENTUALLY BUY.

J. C. & S.

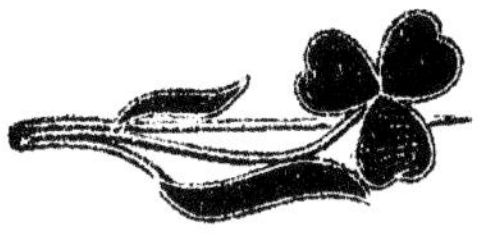
520
48/- per dozen.

536
54/- per dozen.

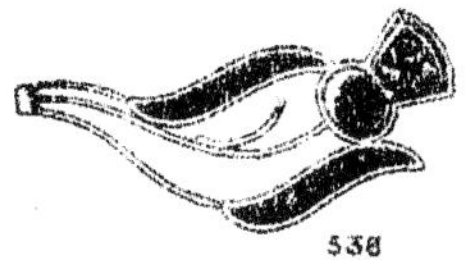
538
48/- per dozen.

515
21/- per dozen.

522
30/- per dozen.

692
30/- per dozen.

512
26/- per dozen.

587
24/- per dozen.

718
24/- per dozen.

504
24/- per dozen.

729
42/- per dozen.

916
24/- per dozen.

569
30/- per dozen.

726
24/- per dozen.

523
16/- per dozen.

505
30/- per dozen.

68
20/- per dozen.

69
16/- per dozen.

199
28/- per dozen.

207
32/- per dozen.

67
24/- per dozen.

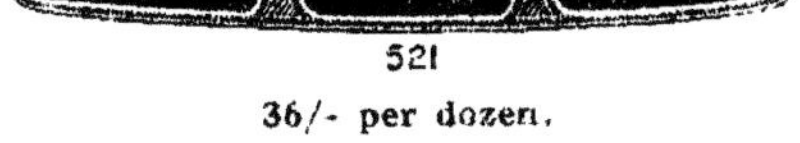
521
36/- per dozen.

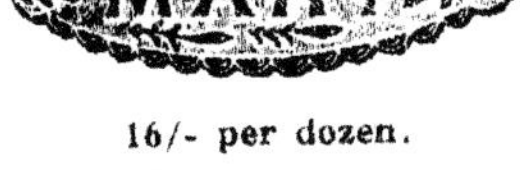

16/- per dozen.

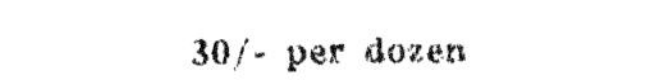
575
30/- per dozen

OFTEN IMITATED BUT NEVER EQUALLED.

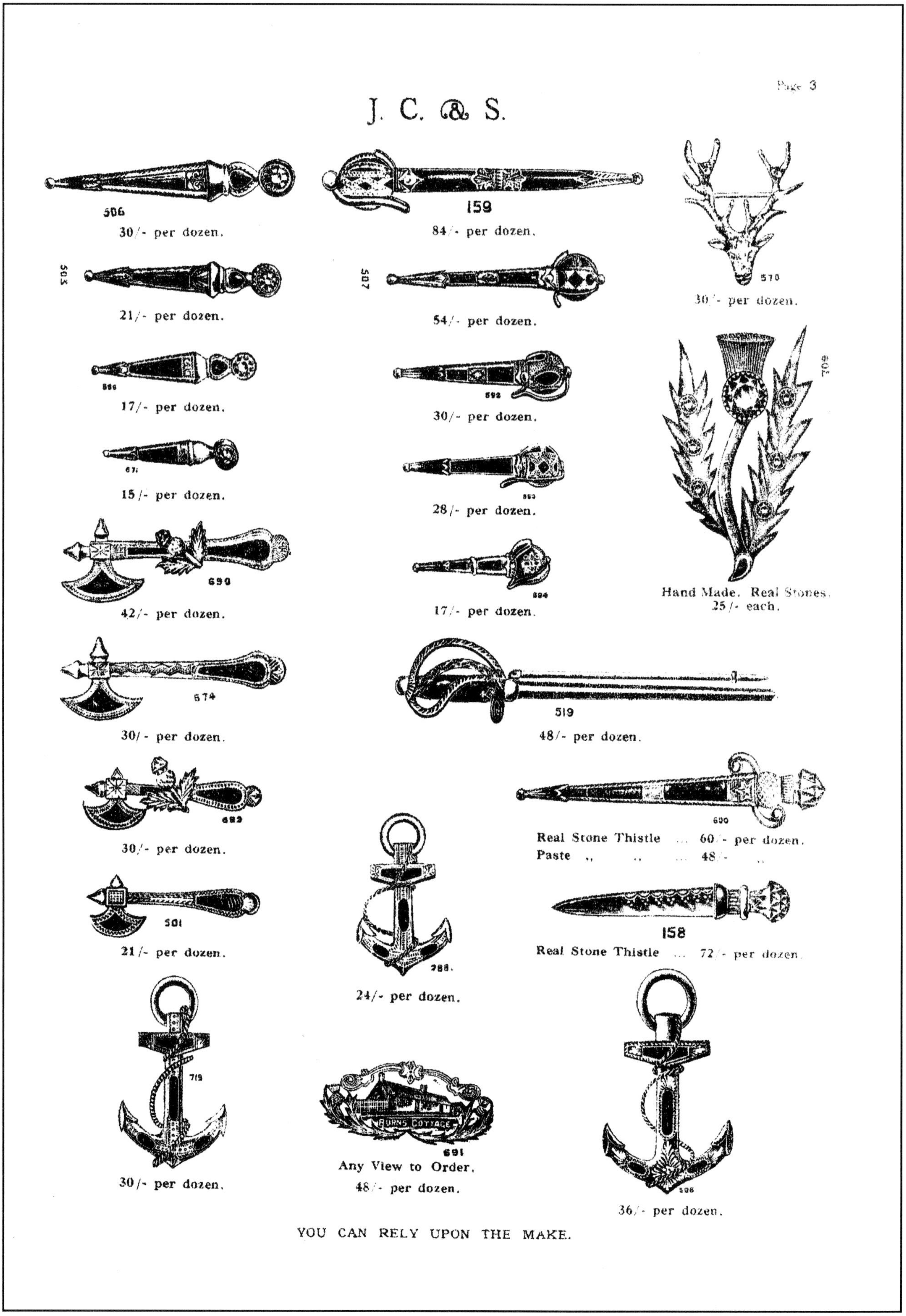

Page 3

J. C. & S.

506
30/- per dozen.

159
84/- per dozen.

570
30/- per dozen.

503
21/- per dozen.

507
54/- per dozen.

709
Hand Made. Real Stones.
25/- each.

17/- per dozen.

592
30/- per dozen.

671
15/- per dozen.

28/- per dozen.

690
42/- per dozen.

17/- per dozen.

574
30/- per dozen.

519
48/- per dozen.

682
30/- per dozen.

600
Real Stone Thistle ... 60/- per dozen.
Paste ,, ,, ... 48/- ,,

501
21/- per dozen.

288.
24/- per dozen.

158
Real Stone Thistle ... 72/- per dozen.

719
30/- per dozen.

BURNS COTTAGE
691
Any View to Order.
48/- per dozen.

36/- per dozen.

YOU CAN RELY UPON THE MAKE.

J. C. & S.

515

26/- per dozen.

571

28/- per dozen.

514

28/- per dozen.

511

28/- per dozen.

535

60/- per dozen.

500

28/- per dozen.

517

42/- per dozen.

572

32/- per dozen.

534

84/- per dozen.

547

48/- per dozen.

532

48/- per dozen.

560

48/- per dozen.

162

132/- per dozen.

531

48/- per dozen.

546

48/- per dozen.

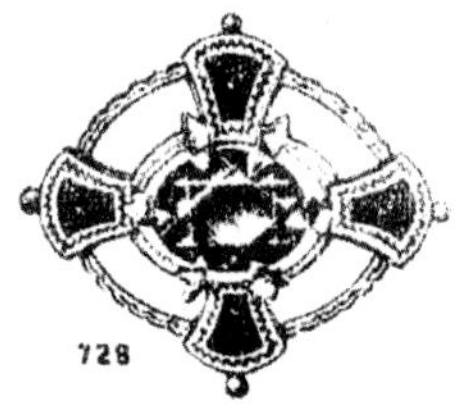

728

30/- per dozen.

330

84/- per dozen.

548

72/- per dozen.

724

30/- per dozen.

Any design of Brooch can be done as Hatpin at the same price.

ALL MANUFACTURED AT OUR OWN WORKS.

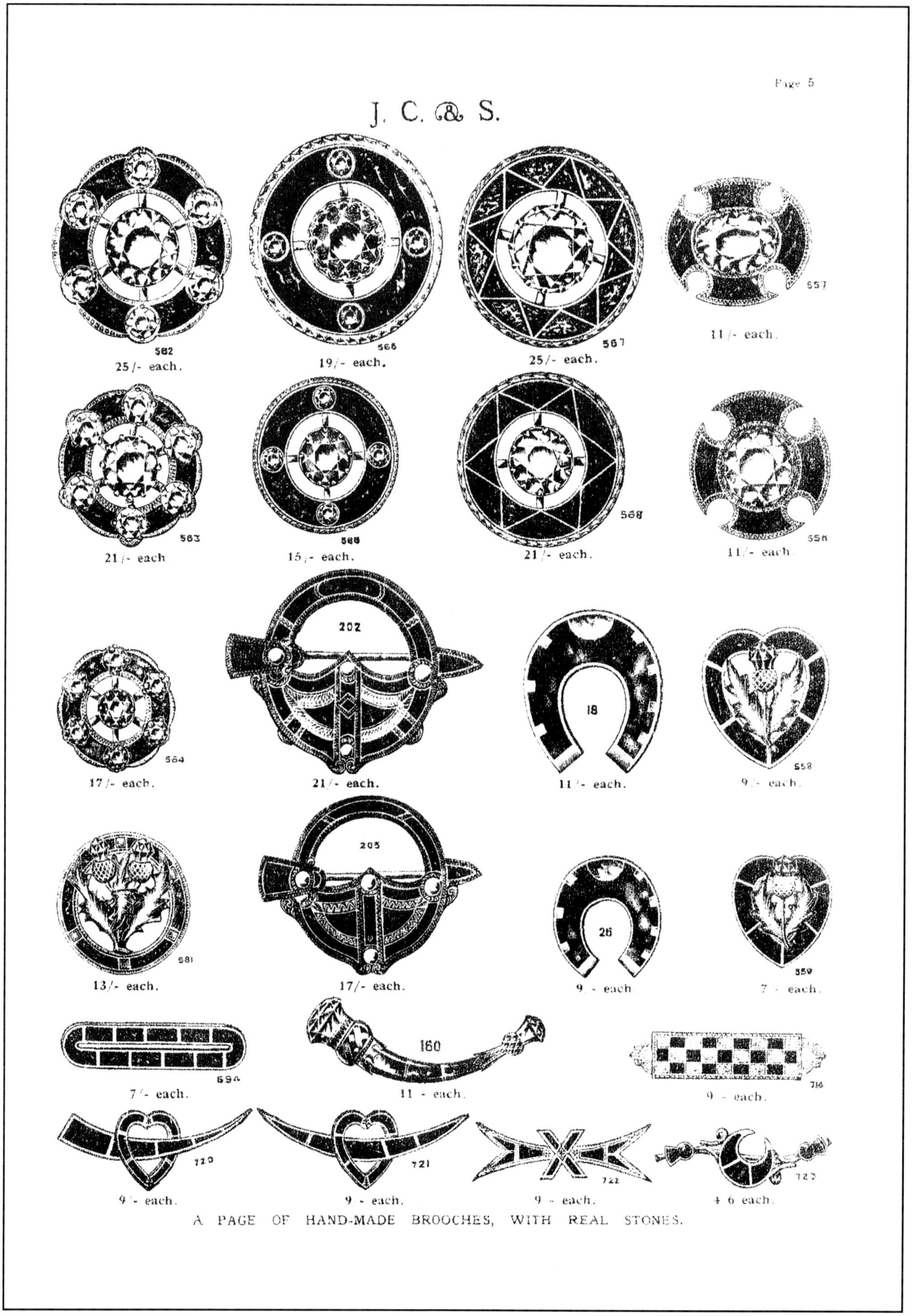
Page 5
J. C. & S.
582
25/- each.
566
19/- each.
567
25/- each.
557
11/- each.
563
21/- each
565
15/- each.
568
21/- each.
556
11/- each.
564
17/- each.
202
21/- each.
18
11/- each.
558
9/- each.
581
13/- each.
205
17/- each.
26
9/- each.
559
7/- each.
594
7/- each.
160
11/- each.
714
9/- each.
720
9/- each.
721
9/- each.
722
9/- each.
723
4/6 each.
A PAGE OF HAND-MADE BROOCHES, WITH REAL STONES.

J. C. & S.

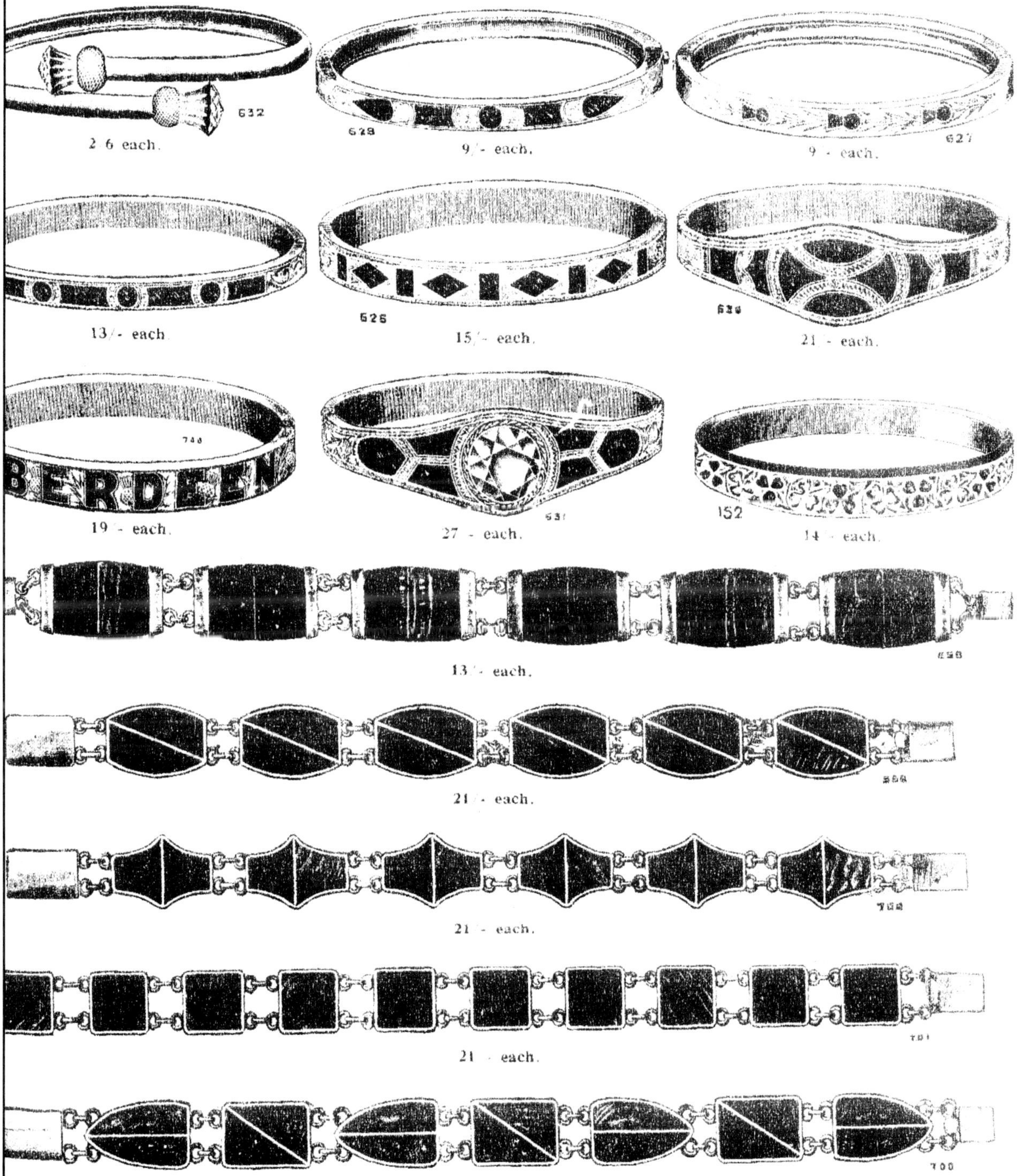

WE HOLD THE LARGEST STOCK OF INLAID BANGLES ON THE ROAD.

J. C. & S.

Page 10

TRY US FOR AN APPRO.
PARCEL OF INLAID
GOODS.

679
E.P.N.S. ... 3 - each.

751
Silver ... 11 - each.

752
Silver ... 11 - each.

613
E.P.N.S. ... 2 6 each
Silver ... 7 - ..

612
E.P.N.S. ... 5/6 each.
Silver ... 15/- ..

611
Silver ... 15 - each.

754
E.P.N.S. ... 5 6 each.
Silver ... 15 - ..

612
E.P.N.S. ... 5 6 each
Silver ... 15 - ..

618
Any Town or Motto.
Enamelled Silver, 15 - each.

675
E.P.N.S. ... 6 - each.
Silver ... 15 - ..

616
E.P.N.S. ... 5 6 each.
Silver ... 15 - ..

614
E.P.N.S. ... 5 6 each.
Silver ... 15 - ..

678
Any View.
Silver ... 9/- each.

619
Certain Coat of Arms.
E.P.N.S., 3/6; Silver, 7/6 each.

676
Any Coat of Arms.
Silver ... 9/- each.

677
Any View.
Silver ... 9 - each.

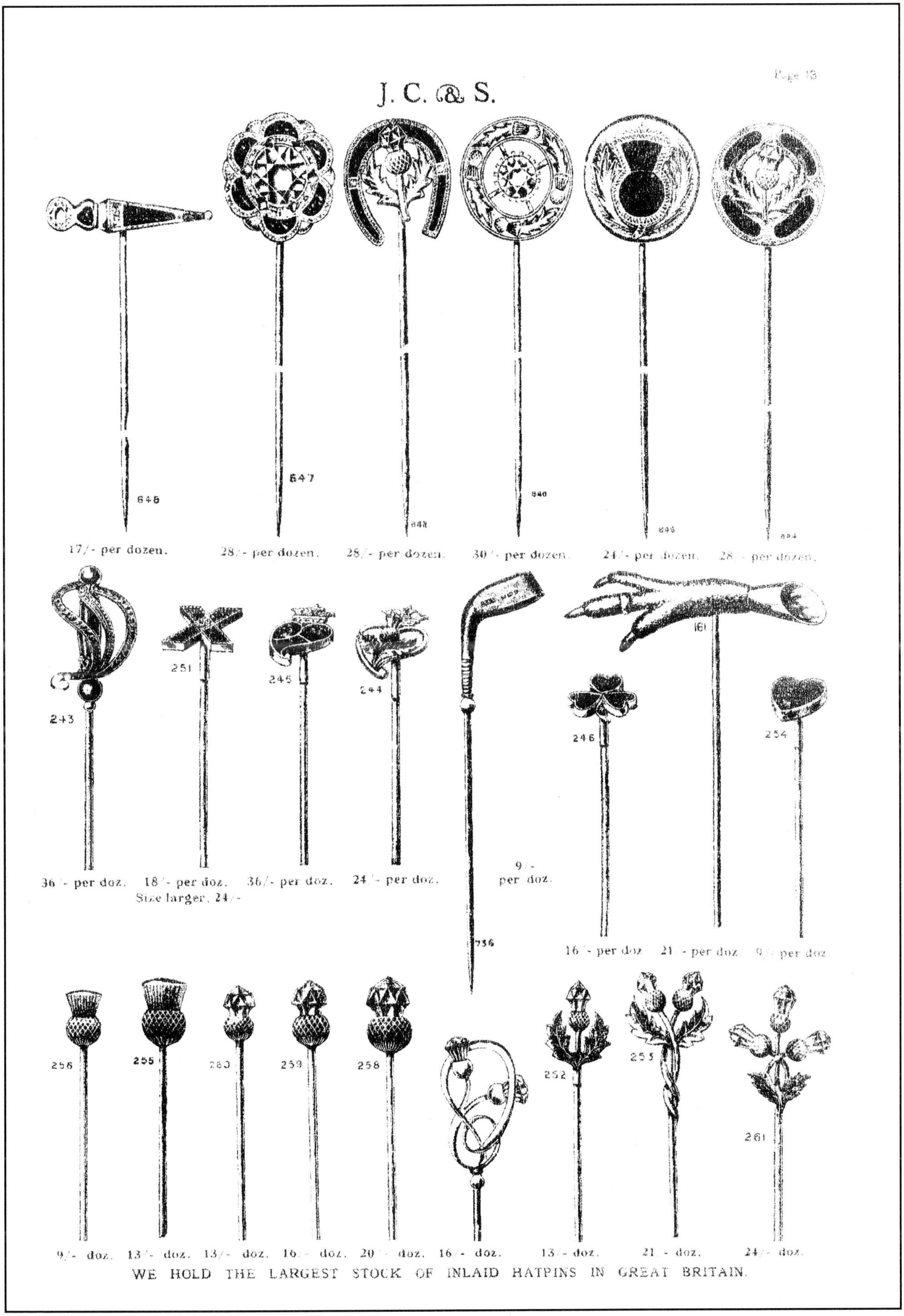
Page 13
J. C. & S.
648
647
17/- per dozen.
28/- per dozen.
28/- per dozen.
30/- per dozen.
24/- per dozen.
28/- per dozen.
243
251
245
244
161
246
254
736
36/- per doz.
18/- per doz.
Size larger, 24/-
36/- per doz.
24/- per doz.
9/- per doz.
16/- per doz.
21/- per doz.
9/- per doz.
256
255
260
259
258
252
253
261
9/- doz.
13/- doz.
13/- doz.
16/- doz.
20/- doz.
16/- doz.
13/- doz.
21/- doz.
24/- doz.
WE HOLD THE LARGEST STOCK OF INLAID HATPINS IN GREAT BRITAIN.

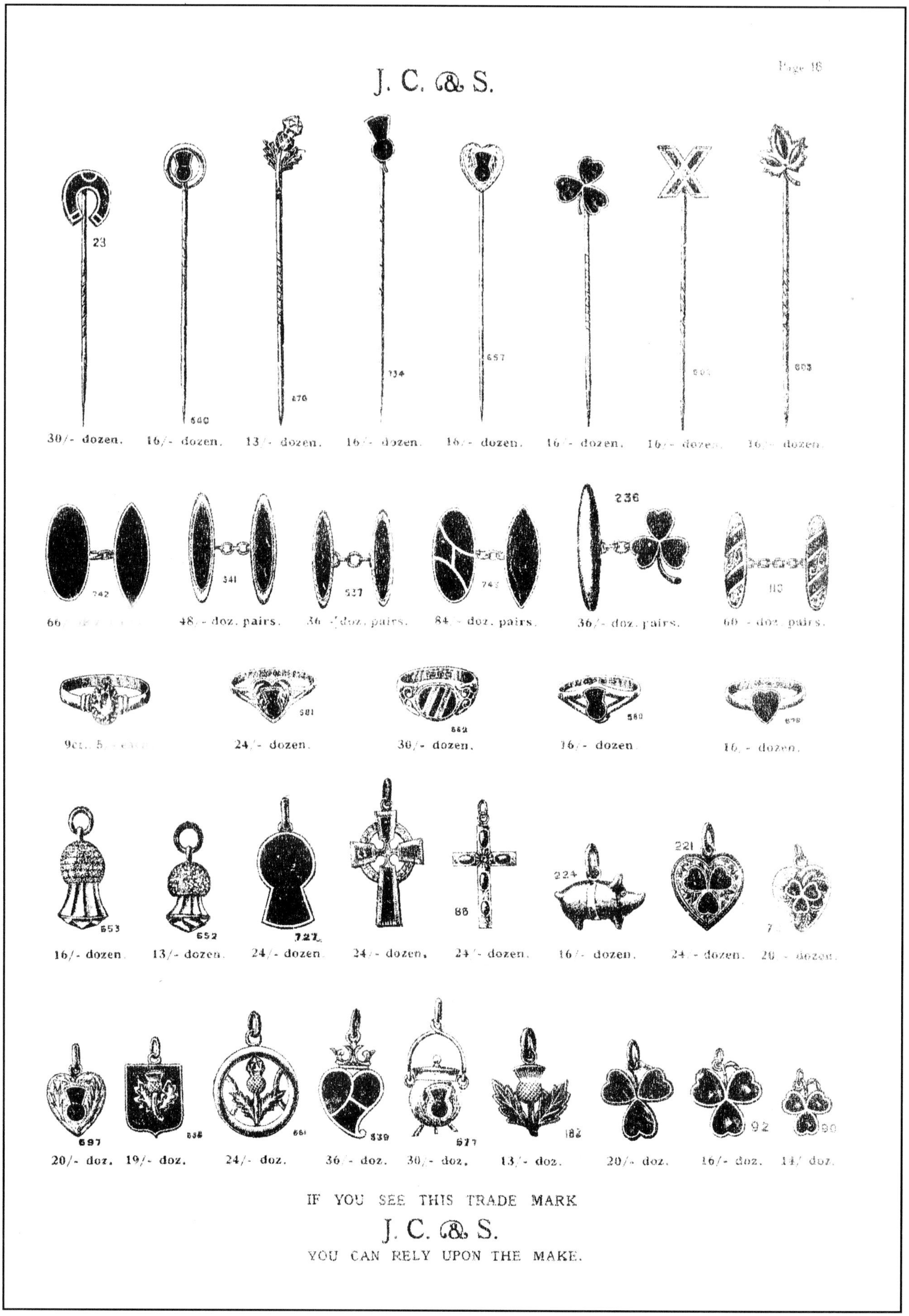
J. C. & S.
Page 18
23
640
734
657
603
30/- dozen.
16/- dozen.
13/- dozen.
16/- dozen.
16/- dozen.
16/- dozen.
236
242
341
537
110
48/- doz. pairs.
84/- doz. pairs.
36/- doz. pairs.
60/- doz. pairs.
581
582
580
24/- dozen.
30/- dozen.
16/- dozen
16/- dozen.
653
652
727
86
224
221
16/- dozen.
13/- dozen.
24/- dozen.
24/- dozen.
24/- dozen.
16/- dozen.
24/- dozen.
697
677
182
92
90
20/- doz.
19/- doz.
24/- doz.
36/- doz.
30/- doz.
13/- doz.
20/- doz.
16/- doz.
14/ doz.
IF YOU SEE THIS TRADE MARK
J. C. & S.
YOU CAN RELY UPON THE MAKE.

Glossary

Agate: one of the many varieties of quartz. Scottish agates were termed by the local populace "pebbles," hence the old description of Scottish agate jewellery as pebble jewellery. For details, see Chapter Seven.

Ancient tartan: reputedly the tartan that had come "down through the ages". Usually somewhat muted in colour.

Ashet: Scottish meat-platter. A "Scotized" pronunciation/ spelling of the French *assiette*.

Assayed: the process of confiming the contents of a precious metal object.

Balleen: The small bone-like "strainers" in a whale's mouth to separate food. Used in Scottish toddy ladle handles.

Ballock: a knife used in skinning and field-dressing game.

Balmoral: Queen Victoria's beloved Scottish highland home. Also, a type of Scottish bonnet.

Bannock: a Scottish baked delicacy, similar to a "pancake".

Baronet: a hereditary title, below the Peerage.

Basket-hilt sword: a sword peculiar to the Scottish Regiments. See Chapter Five.

Barrel bracelet: a bracelet with cut rounds of agate with metal end-caps joined together to form a bracelet. See Chapter Seven.

Beaker: a small drinking vessel without a handle.

Birlinn: Scots name for the Viking sailing vessels.

Blamange: a French dessert of custard-like consistency, much favoured by the Scots.

Bonnet: a flat-topped hat, worn by both Scottish military and civilian men.

Breachan: old name for a plaid. See Chapter One.

Burn: Scottish for a small stream.

Cairngorm: Scottish quartz mined in the Cairngorm Mountains, much used in jewellery.

Cantle: The top part of a sporran, usually metal and rounded, with purse below.

Cedar Ware: one of many varieties of Mauchline Ware. See Chapter Two.

Chatelaine: a Victorian era lady's belt, from which could be hung various personal objects, such as a small purse, glasses, etc.

Chemist: a pharmacist. Also describes the Scottish version of a US drugstore.

Chopin: name for a pewter measure.

Citrine: a form of quartz, usually pale yellow; much used in jewellery.

Clan: the Scottish name for an "extended-family"; those with the same name or having loyalty to a particular individual who would be recognized as the Clan Chief or Chieftain.

Claymore: a large, heavy sword; distinct from the later, smaller and lighter basket-hilt.

Clearances: the 18th c. process whereby thousands of Scots were forced from their lands and shipped to the US, Canada and elsewhere. See Chapter One.

Cones: a part of the sporran, which held the tassels in place.

Crofters: the term used to describe Scottish highland tenant farmers.

Curling: a competitive sport involving gliding stones down an ice rink.

Devolution: the political process whereby Scotland was given back some of it's "self-rule" at the conclusion of the 20th c.

Dirk: the bayonet-like scabarded knife worn on the hip by members of Scottish Regiments, as well as civilians in formal dress.

Dress tartan: generally the brighter version of the several different tartans which each clan traditionally wears.

Dram: a measure, usually of whisky; as in a wee dram.

Featheries: early golfballs, filled with feathers.

Fern Ware: type of Mauchline Ware with fern design

'Fifteen: refers to the attempt in 1715 by James VIII (the "old" Pretender), to take back the Scottish throne.

'Fourty-five: refers to the attempt in 1745 by Bonnie Prince Charlie (the "young" Pretender) to take back the Scottish throne.

Flashes: Coloured garters to hold up stockings worn with kilt; cloth ends hang below top of stockings.

Fuller: vertical depression in sword blade; also called blood gutter.

Garter and buckle: honorary decoration awarded by royalty; form also used in Scottish jewellery.

Ghillie: game-keeper or fishing guide.

Girdle: flat round metal cooking surface, used to bake bread over open fire.

Haggis: Scottish delicacy of spiced meats in sheep's stomach lining, featured at Scottish banquets. Addressed by MC with Burns' *To a Haggis*.

Hame: Scots for home.

Highland lock: firing mechanism on a Scottish flintlock pistol.

Horse brass: small round brass medallion hung on horse's harness; frequently with thistle design.

Hunting tartan: tartan with subdued colours so as to be less visible "in the field".

Interlace: Celtic design used on jewellery; from old designs used on tombstones and other artifacts.

Jacobites: supporters of the old and young Pretenders.

Kettle: iron or brass vessel to heat water for tea.

Kilt: the essential Scottish clothing. Tartan fabric, pleated in the rear, with a plain front apron. Different clans wore different tartan kilts.

Kirk: Scots for church.

Leek: vegetable, also national symbol for Wales.
Luckenbooth pins: pins, often with entwined hearts, given by man to his fiancée. Name derives from the locked booths used by jewellers on Royal Mile, near St Gile's Church in Edinburgh.
Lug: Scots for ear; also refers to the handles on a quaich.
Luggie: drinking/dipping wooden bowl with vertical handle; sometimes in US called a piggin.
Match safe: air-tight container to hold early matches; before invention of safety matches.
Mary pin: version of Luckenbooth pin, with double M design.
Mauchline: town in southwest Scotland; principal source of 19th c. wooden souvenir items called Mauchline Ware.
Mazer: wide, shallow drinking and eating vessel on raised stem.
Midden: Scots for garbage dump.
Miracle: brand name for 20th c. copies of old Scottish agate jewellery,
Monteith: large punch bowl, inaccurately attributed to Scottish origin.
Munro's: Scottish mountains over 3000 ft high; mapped by, and named for, Sir Hugh Munro, 4th Baronet of Lindertis; (the author's grandfather).
Mutchkin: Scottish pewter measure.
Muted tartan: tartan with muted, or softer colours.
Nicht: Scots for night.
Niello: amalgam of metals used to decorate silver jewellery; frequently blue or black.
Pagenator: page-turner, often wood, Mauchline Ware, similar to letter-opener.
Pebble jewellery: Scots for early agate jewellery, silver or gold.
Penanular pin: Round pin with break in circle to facilitate attaching the pin to cloth.
Pig: Scots for stoneware foot-warmer.
Plaid: the tartan length thrown over the left shoulder and pinned to the jacket with a plaid pin. Originally, this was the ends of the tartan cloth used to wrap around oneself for a kilt.
Plane wood: Scots for the wood called sycamore in US, used in Mauchline Ware.
Poker-work: Scots for wooden objects decorated by means of burning in a design with a hot poker. Known in US as pyrography.
Pretender: The "old" Pretender (1715) and the "young" Pretender (1745) tried to regain the Scottish throne.
Priest: Scots for small billy-club, used to knock the freshly caught salmon on the head.
Pub: Scots (and English) for a bar.
Publican: The owner of a pub.
Quaich: small drinking vessel; generally round, shallow on round foot: used to make toasts.
Restrikes: modern reproductions of bonnet badges.
Ricasso: upper end of sword-blade, immediately below the hilt.
Rose: the national symbol for England. Also used by Jacobites as a symbol, called Jacobite rose.
Saltire: name for the Scottish flag of white cross on blue background.
Salt-box: usually wall-hanging box next to cooking fire, containg salt.
Scones: Scots for baked round biscuit-like confection.
Setts: different pattern in tartan; i.e., broad sett, vs. narrow sett.
Sgian dubh: Scottish knife worn in stocking while wearing kilt. Sgian is Gaelic for knife, dubh is Gaelic for black. (black knife, as in concealed weapon).
Sgian achlais: ancient Scottish knife, concealed under armpit. Possibly precursor of sgian dubh.
Shako: helmet, often worn by cavalry units. Has front peak and often plume on top.
Shamrock: the national symbol for Ireland.
Shagreen: cured sharkskin, used to decorate boxes, cigarette cases, etc.
Shortbread: Scottish confection of butter, sugar and flour.
Shepheard's crook: staff used by shepheards, with horn handle.
Silicon Glen: high-tech area between Glasgow and Edinburgh, similar to California's Silicon Valley.
Signet ring: man's ring with recessed crest or initials; used to seal letters with sealing wax to identify sender and to discourage letter-tampering.
Snaphance: form of firing mechanism on early guns and pistols.
Snuff: ground tobacco leaf stems; sniffed into nostrils. Also called sneesh in Scotland.
Solicitor: Scots for lawyer.
Sporran: worn with kilt. Purse-like object, hanging from waist at front of kilt.
Spurtle: Scots for wooden porridge stirrer.
Squab ase: Gaelic for "sweep it up", meaning to finish the drink. Often found inscribed inside bottom of a quaich.
Sweetheart pin: small replica of military bonnet badge, given by man to wife or sweetheart.
Targe: Scottish shield; usually wood, hide and spikes to deflect blows from enemy.
Tappit hen: Scots for large pewter measure with hinged lid.
Tartan Ware: Mauchline Ware objects covered with different tartan paper.
Thistle: the national symbol for Scotland.
Tinkers: itinerant gypsies who travelled in caravans and repaired pots and pans.
Toasting fork: metal fork with trident-type end and long handle, to hold bread to open fire, thereby avoiding toasted fingers.
Toddy: a mixture of alcoholic beverages of the owner's choice (often whisky or rum); sometimes heated.
Tourie: the pom-pom (usually red) on the top of the flat balmoral bonnet.
Treen: generic name for small wooden objects.
Trivet: small metal stand on feet to keep hot object (such as teapot) from scorching the surface below.
Vesta: small box-like container; often associated with matches.
Victorian era: the reign of Queen Victoria, 1838-1901).
Vinaigrette: a container to hold smelling-salts or perfume; specifically to overcome the disagreeable smells of city streets, pre-modern sewage disposal.
Wally dugs: Scots for small models of dogs kept on the fireplace mantle as decoration.
Wemyss: a particular form of Scottish china. Highly decorative, from east coast village of Kirkaldy.
Usquabae: Gaelic for whisky

Index

The "Old" Counties.